INSIDE
THE FIRM

INSIDE
THE FIRM

INSIDE THE FIRM

THE UNTOLD STORY OF THE KRAYS' REIGN OF TERROR

TONY LAMBRIANOU
WITH CAROL CLERK

JOHN BLAKE

Published by John Blake Publishing Ltd,
3 Bramber Court, 2 Bramber Road,
London W14 9PB, England

www.johnblakepublishing.co.uk

www.facebook.com/johnblakebooks ▉
twitter.com/jbbooks ▉

First published in Great Britain in 1991 by Smith Gryphon Ltd
Published in 1992 by Pan Books Ltd,
a division of Pan Macmillan Publishers Ltd
This paperback edition published 2009 by John Blake Publishing

ISBN: 978 1 85782 609 8

British Library Cataloguing-in-Publication Data:

A catalogue record for this book is available from the British Library.

Design by www.envydesign.co.uk

Printed in Great Britain by CPI Group (UK) Ltd

3 5 7 9 10 8 6 4 2

Papers used by John Blake Publishing are natural, recyclable products made from
wood grown in sustainable forests. The manufacturing processes conform to the
environmental regulations of the country of origin.

Every attempt has been made to contact the relevant copyright-holders, but some
were unobtainable. We would be grateful if the appropriate people could contact us.

This book is dedicated to Mum and Dad,
Chris, Leon, Jimmy, Nicky and David Lambrianou,
Wendy Mason-Lambrianou, and Prince.

TONY LAMBRIANOU was born in Bethnal Green, at the heart of London's East End, in 1942. His Greek Cypriot father was a restaurateur. His mother, a Geordie, came from Irish stock and brought Tony and his four brothers up as strict Catholics. A trusted member of 'The Firm', he was imprisoned until 1983 for his part in the murder of Jack 'The Hat' McVitie. He died in 2004.

CAROL CLERK is the former hews editor of *Melody Maker*, winning *The Publisher* Award for Best Feature in 1985. She has had books published about The Pogues, Madonna and The New York Dolls, and has also written with Reggie Kray. She continues to write for various music publications.

ACKNOWLEDGEMENTS

I would like to thank the following people for their help and inspiration in the writing of this book: Carol Clerk for her dedication; Robert Smith for the opportunity, and his continuing encouragement; Wendy Mason-Lambrianou for putting up with me; Bryn, Lorenza and Leonard Thomas for their friendship; Matt Smith and Allan Jones of *Melody Maker* for their kindness to Carol; the management and staff of the Harrison Arms; and the Kray brothers, Reg, Ron and Charlie, for being the men they were.

CONTENTS

FOREWORD

I'll only ever tell this story once, and when it's done I'm going to walk away from it for the rest of my life. I don't want to dwell in the past any more, but to be free of it I must confess it.

I once made a promise to a remarkable woman, my probation officer Mrs Jean Heath, that I would some day write of my experiences as a professional criminal and a member of the Kray twins' notorious firm. Mrs Heath has since died, and I owe it to her, my loved ones and myself to offer this true account of a career which grew out of violence, flourished on fear, culminated in murder and ended in prison.

So much has been said and written about the Kray gang that we have now become the stuff of legend. But at the heart of that legend there are real live people, and if I hope to achieve anything, it's to present them through the facts and not the fantasy of the way we lived.

Up until the time that Reggie Kray admitted his part in the murder of Jack The Hat McVitie, every loyal one of us held our silence over the events of a unique era in British crime. Now perhaps it's time for a member of the firm to have a say. For years we've been hearing what everybody else has had to say about us, in courtrooms, books and newspapers, and the twins have taken their chance to reply in print.

I intend, with this book, to set the record straight for all of us who stood together in the dock and went to prison for our crimes.

THE FACTS

On Wednesday, 5 March 1969 my brother Chris and I were sentenced to life imprisonment for the murder of a villain called Jack The Hat McVitie. The Old Bailey judge, Mr Justice Melford Stevenson, recommended that we each serve at least fifteen years. Eight other men received prison sentences in what was one of the most famous trials of the century.

Ronnie Kray was given life imprisonment, with a recommendation that he should serve thirty years, for the murders of McVitie and another villain, George Cornell. Reggie Kray received the same sentence and recommendation as his twin brother for the McVitie murder. He was also sentenced to ten years, to run concurrently, for being an accessory to the Cornell killing.

Ronnie Bender and Ian Barrie were each sentenced to life imprisonment with a twenty-year recommendation, Ronnie for the murder of McVitie and Ian for the murder of Cornell. Charlie Kray and Freddie Foreman, charged as accessories to the McVitie murder, were sent to prison for ten years each. Connie Whitehead received seven years for the same offence and Albert Donaghue, the only man to plead guilty, went to prison for two years, another accessory to the murder of Jack The Hat.

CHAPTER ONE

DYING BY
THE SWORD

'Ronnie, you're wanted.'

Ronnie Kray turned round to face the screw, a principal officer, who had just walked in behind us. Only a minute earlier, we had been escorted out to the toilet from the cell at the Old Bailey where we were waiting to be called up for sentence.

He was in the prime of his life, Ronnie, a striking figure with his jet-black hair and usual immaculate dress: a blue suit, crisp white shirt, blue tie and black shoes. He took a drag on his fag, always a Player, threw it on the floor, stamped on it and said, 'Here I go, Tony. The first man ever to get a forty-year recommendation.'

As I looked back, he was walking away, out of the toilet. His feet were clipping the floor as though he was marching. I went back to the cell and told the others, 'They've just taken Ron up.' It was beginning.

If Reggie Kray was on edge, he was trying not to show it. He said, 'Sit down, Tony, I'll give you a massage.' It's an old boxing trick. To have your neck and shoulders massaged helps to ease tension.

I remember Charlie Kray lighting a cigarette while my brother Chris stood quietly in thought and Ronnie Bender, the joker of the pack, just smiled. Even under pressure like this, he did his best to keep everyone's spirits up.

I was thinking, 'Well, look, I'm twenty-six, I'm the youngest. If anyone's going to survive, I'm going to be the one. At least I've got half a chance.' I thought of my daughter, and wondered how old she would be when I got out. How old would my son be? Could my marriage survive? Would I ever see my father again in freedom?

In the back of my mind I kept hoping for the best, but I knew in my heart what we were up against. During the trial itself, in reply to questions from our QCs, the judge had frequently said, 'No doubt these men will be taken to a higher court where the matter can be dealt with.' What he meant was, 'In my eyes you're already convicted, so the Court of Appeal can sort this out.' I knew I was going down.

We heard Ronnie marching back and Ian Barrie's name being called out. Ian, a big, thick-set Scotsman with short, fair hair, punched his fist into his hand and walked out of the cell door as Ronnie walked in.

For a moment no one uttered a word. Then Reggie and Charlie said together: 'Well, what did you get?'

'Oh, only a thirty,' Ronnie replied. 'I'm glad all that's over.' And he carried on smoking a fag as if nothing had happened. Ian Barrie came back as Reggie's name was called. Ian leaned stiffly against a wall and closed his eyes: 'Twenty recommendation.'

Back came Reggie, who seemed more concerned about his concurrent sentence than the main term. I thought, 'God almighty, he's got thirty years and he's worrying about the ten.' By now I was a bit edgy because Chris had gone up and his sentence would probably indicate what I could expect.

When he returned, he said, 'Life and a fifteen rec.' He added: 'You're going to get a twenty here, Tony, watch it.'

I said, 'Thanks . . . thanks for that.' With his words ringing in my ears, I was called into court and went up the stairs to the dock. It was like walking down a V-shaped funnel with a chair at the end, and eight screws on either side of it who absolutely dwarfed me. I was told to sit in the chair. There was dead silence.

I was trying to look around the court but at the same time appear inconspicuous. 'It's nothing to do with me. . . .'

The room was crowded: it was like being in the middle of a circus. There were celebrities and high-ranking coppers and politicians galore. Nipper Read, John du Rose, Frank Cater and Harry Mooney, the officers in charge of the investigation leading to our arrests, were sitting in the well of the court beside the prosecuting counsel, listening to the judge but looking at me. Sir George Younger, the Assistant Chief Commissioner for Crime at Scotland Yard, was there too. Glancing to my right, I saw my brother Jimmy, my father, my wife and old Charlie Kray, the twins' dad, leaning over. I saw Micky Duff, the boxing promoter, who smiled slightly, actors Charlton Heston and Richard Greene, and a lot of people who looked as though they were titled. On my left, the press area was jam-packed. I remember my eyes resting on John Pearson, who later wrote *A Profession of Violence*, the best-selling book about the Kray gang. A couple of people were drawing.

My QC, James Ross, jumped up and tried to urge the judge not to give me a recommendation because of the ages of my kids and my father. He said, 'This man has a wife and two children, one of whom was born on remand. . . .'

The judge snapped, 'I don't think there's any need to go into this. We've heard all we want to hear, Mr Ross. You can sit down.'

Then, turning to me, he said: 'The decision against you, in my view, was the right finding of guilt. You'll go to prison for a very long spell indeed, for life, and I recommend that you be detained for a period of not less than fifteen years.'

Everybody was staring at me, to see how I'd take it. The police were waiting for a reaction from the dock. I went to say something, but thought better of it. All I did was look up to where my family was sitting, and wink. Back in the cell I told the others what had happened, and I felt a relief it was all over.

Next one up was Ronnie Bender, who came back bitterly complaining about his 'life and recommended twenty', which he didn't deserve in a million years. He had been given the blame for a lot of things he didn't do. But before long he was back in full control, looking for the light at the end of the tunnel as he had been throughout the trial. A tall, broad man with fair hair in a college-boy cut, he had been described by one newspaper as having 'the looks of a pop star', which tickled him.

Charlie went out and got a ten. Earlier, he'd seemed happy enough. I think he'd been looking at four years, maybe even an acquittal. Now he was going away for a long time for helping to dispose of a body he'd never even seen. This, combined with the fact that we'd all been lifed off, certainly quietened him down. Ronnie looked at him as though nothing had happened.

Fred Foreman came back after also getting a ten. He said: 'They took a fucking right liberty.' But apart from an initial look of disbelief, he showed no emotion and said no more about it. Fred has been accused of more things he never did than any other man in British criminal history, probably because of his reputation and his association with and loyalty to known criminals. Yet I've always found him a very good friend, a gentle man, a man with a heart, very well liked and respected. Poor Freddie got ten years for nothing, same as Charlie.

The last one to be sentenced was Connie Whitehead, who received seven years over McVitie. A fairly small man with thinning hair and pointy features, he'd been jumpy before he went out there, although he was a nervous character anyway. When he came back, he looked very uncomfortable indeed.

Reggie said to me: 'If he starts complaining, I'm going to fucking hit him on the chin.'

And Ronnie told Whitehead, 'I don't want none of your fucking lip, shut your mouth. *Seven years. . .*'

Feelings were running high against Connie Whitehead. The twins hated him. His name came up regularly throughout the evidence in the Cornell case, yet he wasn't charged with any offence. He was, however, convicted as an accessory to the McVitie murder.

He kept saying to us, 'I don't know what you mean, they didn't question me about it.' We're talking about a murder!

I remember Reggie saying, 'He's definitely done us up.' And all the way through our period on remand, Connie had dreaded ever being put in a cell with Ronnie Kray. Ronnie knew that, and he used to shout, 'You're with me tonight, Whitehead!'

The tenth sentence handed out that day was to Albert Donaghue, who didn't appear in the dock with us. He was of Irish descent, a very big, very quiet man, who had been around the twins for several years. Of all the people in the firm, Donaghue was the last person I would have expected to go against us. I could not believe it when he went the other way. He was held and sentenced separately from the rest of us, like various other ex-associates who had decided to give evidence against us to the police.

As we sat in that cell, the nine of us, I thought about the sentences and about something which had happened six weeks earlier. I was having a shower one Saturday morning in the maximum security block in Brixton, where we were being kept on remand. Freddie Foreman was with me. He said: 'I'm going to show you something.' He handed me a slip of paper, and written on it were two thirties, two twenties, two fifteens and two tens. Had anybody else given me that piece of paper I would have thrown it away, but because it was Fred I had to take seriously what was being suggested to me. Was it just coincidence that those were exactly the sentences we got? I believe he got that information from a very good source and that our sentences were handed down from somewhere other, higher, than the court.

After sentencing we were taken away from the Old Bailey in a police coach, and the crowds outside had grown even bigger than they had been when we arrived. It was sheer chaos. News of the sentences was being flashed on television, everybody was waving and the security was incredible. We had a massive police presence. There were plain clothes detectives with radios, armed police, dog handlers, motorbikes and patrol vans.

The coach was driving Chris, Ian, Ronnie Bender, Connie Whitehead and myself to Wandsworth to begin our sentences, and taking Reggie, Ronnie, Charlie and Freddie Foreman back to Brixton to be further remanded pending the Frank The Mad Axeman Mitchell murder trial. On the way my brother started singing. I was saying, 'What are you singing about?', and there's Ronnie Bender going, 'We've got to start somewhere.'

Wandsworth Prison is called the Hate Factory. It's a hard prison. We should drop a bomb on it and wipe it from the face of the earth, only it would leave a very ugly scar.

Chris and Ronnie Bender had been on remand there while the rest of us were in Brixton. The Governor of Wandsworth at that time was Mr Beastie, who was known as The Beast. One day Chris walked past a strongbox, a high-security cell, and saw a geezer hanging in it. He said to the Governor, 'I think somebody's been murdered.'

The Beast said, 'Listen here, Mr Lambrianou, you'd better thank your lucky stars it's not you. Now get out of here. I don't want to see you again.'

When we arrived at Wandsworth, I could not believe my eyes. We drove in the gates and there were no cons to be seen, only screws. About three hundred of them. They were everywhere. It would have been nothing to be ashamed of to say we were frightened, five of us standing in the yard with that number waiting for us. They wanted to kill you in that nick, but on this occasion they didn't try.

As soon as you enter a prison, there are three things you have to do. You sign for your property, you see the Governor and you see a doctor, who is supposed to give you a medical check but is usually reading *The Sporting Life*.

We were Category A prisoners, so we had to wear prison uniforms, complete with a yellow patch, which meant you were an escape risk and could be quickly spotted at all times. I was taken to a cell in E Wing, right opposite the topping shed, the only gallows in existence today. Chris was put on D Wing, with Ian Barrie and Connie Whitehead, and Ronnie Bender was taken to the prison hospital, which was on my wing, for observation – not an unusual occurrence for a lifer.

My cell was next to the office of the PO, the Principal Officer. A screw was placed on full alert outside my cell twenty-four hours a day. My clothes were taken off me before I was locked in the cell for the night – banged up, we called it – and kept on a chair outside. A red light was glowing, and it would be kept on all day and night from then on.

At seven-thirty that evening, the door opened. Standing in front of me was the canteen screw with the canteen orderly. I was given half an ounce of tobacco, papers and matches, and informed that the cost would be taken back from me the week before I was released, which I found highly amusing. I signed the paper and wrote something like 'the year 2000' on it.

I lay on that bed and didn't know what to think. How do you start a life sentence? It's a very hard thing to accept. You can't visualise doing it. You cannot see an end.

Then I thought about Chris and what he must be going through. He was now doing life and a fifteen-year recommendation for absolutely nothing. How would he cope with that? I had to live with the thought that my brother went down for something he never did. To this day, he has never complained about it. I stood accused and I admit my part. I never murdered anyone, but I was there, and I played a leading role afterwards. I'm not proud of it. I deserved to be punished because a man lost his life and nothing can ever bring that back. But I had watched my brother, who was innocent, take it on the chin. The police, the prison authorities, the Home Office, MPs, lawyers and other criminals all knew from the beginning that Chris had nothing to do with it.

The whole case against Chris and me was based on one question: did we know that Jack The Hat was going to be killed? The case against Chris was that I had told him. But I had said nothing to Chris. All I did was invite him to a party. For my part, I thought that Jack was going to get a beating, which he deserved. I didn't know he was going to be murdered; I don't think Reggie Kray knew he was going to be murdered.

I stayed awake through my first night in Wandsworth and I thought back to the McVitie murder, how Reggie had stabbed him to death, how I had wound up in this position. I thought of Jack The Hat, because if he had somehow known what happened afterwards he would have been the first person to jump up and say, 'They shouldn't be doing that for me.' He would have turned over in his grave. He couldn't stand police, prison officers, anyone in authority – just like the rest of us. They were the enemy.

I didn't blame the twins for my predicament, because the choice was mine. My attitude to life was always this: if you live by the sword, you have to be prepared to die by the sword. If Jack The Hat had wanted to go out of this world, that's the way he would have chosen to do it.

It was, nevertheless, a ghastly thing to happen to anybody. It was horrifying. It will live with me for the rest of my life.

It happened on Saturday, 28 October 1967, a day when Chris and I had arranged to meet two brothers called Alan and Ray Mills to introduce them to the twins. The Mills brothers were from a respected family in west London. We had friends all over the city and because of our rivalry with the Richardson gang, who were running a major operation south of the river, it was nice to have allies.

Ray Mills was very friendly with one of the hardest men in London, Pretty Boy Roy Shaw. He was a handful. Frank Warren, who went on to become a well-known boxing promoter, originally made his name through promoting fights with Shawey. At this time Roy was in a maximum-security mental hospital. He and three other men had got fifteen years each for armed robbery on a security van. Roy Shaw did the three guards on his own. A couple of years after being sentenced, he was found insane and sent to Broadmoor. Now Shawey wanted the twins to send something to him there, so he had contacted Ray Mills, who in turn had got in touch with Chris.

We met the Mills brothers at seven o'clock in a pub called the White Bear in Aldgate. I made a phone call to find out where the twins were, and we then went on to the Carpenters Arms, the Krays' own pub in Bethnal Green.

We arrived to find Ronnie and Reggie with their Mum and Dad, Violet and old man Charlie. There was young Charlie and his wife Dolly, Ronnie Bender, Albert Donaghue, Connie Whitehead, Scotch Jack Dickson, Sammy Lederman, Harry Jew Boy and Ronnie Hart, a cousin of the twins. A few girls were there too – Blonde Vicky, who eventually married Ronnie Hart, Reggie's girlfriend Carol Thompson, and Bubbles, who was the girlfriend of Frankie Shea, Reggie's brother-in-law, but who went out with Ronnie Bender in the end.

Everyone was on good form. Ronnie shook hands with the Mills brothers and then, as usual, left Reggie to do the talking. Ronnie was quite happy standing to one side, looking smart with a gold chain on his waistcoat. The men always wore a three-piece. Everyone was drinking, everyone was happy and Reggie was chattery. Lovely. Come eleven o'clock, Reg said, 'We're going for a meal, me and Carol.' As far as I knew, Ronnie was going home.

Chris and I took the Mills brothers to the Regency Club in Stoke Newington, a place they had heard of and wanted to see. It was run by the Barry brothers, Johnny and Tony, who were paying protection money. The Regency had three clubs in one – the top part, the middle part and our private club downstairs. We stayed in the main, middle bar until midnight and then went for a private drink.

And who was at the bar downstairs? Jack The Hat. He made a beeline for us. He knew Ray Mills from the Moor, for they had both done time at Dartmoor. We all had a drink together, although we knew there was bad feeling between Jack and the twins. It had got to the stage where he was going to get a hiding, but the twins weren't about that night and there was nothing really to concern me. My brother Nicky was there with a girl, and there must have been about another fifty people.

All of a sudden, there was a tap on my shoulder. It was Tony Barry. He said, 'Have you got a minute?'

I followed him out into the office and there were Reggie Kray and Ronnie Hart. I had a feeling something wasn't right here. Hart said, 'Is Jack down there?'

I said he was.

He asked, 'How many people are down there?'

Reggie wanted to know if there were any women down there. He was biting his lip, and he'd obviously had a few to drink. This wasn't the Reggie I had left an hour ago.

He said, 'Bring Jack round to Blonde Carol's.' I'd never been to

Blonde Carol's; I didn't even know her. Chris knew her; Jack The Hat knew her. She was an old girlfriend of his. She was a club girl, out for a drink, and she didn't care who it was with. She lived in Evering Road, not far from the Regency.

I went back downstairs and I said to Chris, 'They're having a party at Blonde Carol's.'

Jack broke in, 'Party, what party? Come on, let's all go.' He was loving it. He didn't know what was waiting there.

Neither did I. I knew there was a chance of him copping a right-hander, but little did I know that Tony Barry had taken a gun round there. . .

Jack was driving a cream and blue Mark II Zodiac. He was wearing a checked suit, a brown trilby hat with a brown band around it and black shoes. He was drunk on Bacardi and Coke. Chris was in the passenger seat and I was in the back with the Mills brothers, who thought it was going to be a normal party.

Jack The Hat was the first one down the stairs into the basement flat. I was directly behind him. Chris followed me, and then came the Mills brothers. In the room were Ronnie Kray and two boys called Terry and Trevor, who were friends of his, one dark and the other fair. Reggie and Ronnie Hart were there, and I saw Ronnie Bender in the kitchen.

I was very surprised to see Ronnie Kray there because I had thought he was going home. He came over to me, pushed past me and did Jack right underneath the eye with a sherry glass. There was a two-inch cut, and his hat was knocked off.

Ron said, 'I've had enough of you, you fucking cunt. Keep your mouth shut. Now fuck off.'

That's all Ron said and, having said it, he turned back and walked over to where the record player was.

Jack walked back towards the door, slamming his fist into his palm, saying, 'Who the fucking hell do they think they are?' And he punched a window. It was later said that he broke a window trying to dive through it to escape. That's not true. He just punched the pane out.

Next thing, Reggie was on him. This was the first time I'd seen the gun. He tried to shoot him in the back of the head, and I jumped back expecting an explosion – which didn't come. The gun wouldn't work. The Mills brothers were standing there in total shock.

As soon as Reggie pulled the gun, I realised it had gone too far. It put us in a very dangerous position. Unwittingly, Chris had helped me to set Jack up by taking him to Blonde Carol's, so now it was our row too. And the moment we got involved like that, there was no way out of it. Jack would come back at us. He was more than capable of doing to us what we ended up doing to him. He'd threatened Reggie more than once, and he was known to be a man who carried, and used, a gun. Whatever way, Jack The Hat was going that night.

When the gun failed to go off, I said to Chris, 'Go and get one of ours.' At that point, I knew we might have to do him ourselves.

Chris went home to our father's house, about half a mile away, to get a Smith & Wesson .38 police special.

By now Reggie had let go of Jack, who was sitting on the sofa and saying: 'What's all this? What have I done?'

Reggie said, 'You know what you've fucking done.' The gun came out again. Again it just clicked. 'They gave me a fucking duff 'un,' said Reg.

The two boys, Terry and Trevor, jumped on Jack and started punching into him. Ronnie Hart was thumping him. The next thing I saw was Reggie with a knife. It was happening so fast. There was a carving knife and it was held in Reggie's hand, Ronnie Hart was getting Jack in a bear hug round his neck, and Hart was shouting, 'Do him, Reg, go on, Reg, do him,' words which Ronnie Kray has been falsely accused of yelling.

It has also been stated that Ronnie Kray shouted at Reggie, 'I've done mine, you do yours.' Ronnie said no such thing. He took no part in it, and never said a word.

Jack The Hat showed no fear throughout. Contrary to other reports he wasn't dripping with cold sweat, and he never uttered the alleged famous last words: 'I'll be a man but I don't want to die like one.' That's a load of crap. Jack said nothing. I doubt if he even saw it coming.

I saw the first one go and I turned away then. I walked out of the room. I don't think I believed it was really happening. He got it three times with the knife, but he must have been dead with the first one.

The scene went quiet. I walked back into the room. I didn't want to look, but I had to. I saw the blood. I saw Reggie pointing the knife into his neck as if he was trying to find his jugular vein. The knife was arched. And then it went straight through. His neck opened up from ear to ear. I could see right in there. All I remember is him sliding down. Reggie didn't pin him to the floor with the knife, as other people have claimed. The ones in the belly had taken the blood out of him. It was absolutely everywhere, soaking all over the place. It was like someone got a bucket of red paint and threw it over the floor. There was a gurgling sound from Jack, and all of a sudden more blood came out of his mouth and ran all down him.

I've seen some bad things in my time – I've seen men badly stabbed, near death – but this was worse, like nothing I'd ever seen. If you were going to describe a gangland killing, that's how you'd describe it. It looked like what it was. And I'll never forget the smell. Death smells like something singeing, like hair and blood burning, but with some different, heavy odour about it, a terrible, terrible smell that never leaves you.

I'm convinced to this day that Reggie didn't realise what he'd done. That wasn't the Reggie Kray I'd known for all those years. He was like a different person. When it was over, he stood there looking, for a second. The knife was twisted to bits. The gun, a brand-new Mauser .32 automatic, was lying there useless.

Jack was on the floor in the middle of the room. His hat was about a foot away from him, all crumpled up. I'll never forget his eyes. They were staring up at the ceiling. Strangely enough, he looked peaceful lying there. He wasn't in any shock, from what I saw.

Chris wandered back in towards the end of all this, with the gun that we no longer needed. The deed was done. And then, suddenly, everybody seemed to snap out of it.

Ronnie Bender came in. 'What's happened, what's happened?'

Someone said, 'Look on the floor and you'll see what's happened.'

The two boys and the Mills brothers were running out of the room. Reggie Kray was wiping his hands. He'd cut himself. He turned to me and said, 'Get rid of that, Tony,' and with that he, his brother and Ronnie Hart were gone.

I was left in the flat with Chris, Ronnie Bender and Connie Whitehead, who'd just appeared on the scene. We've got a body on our hands, we've got a flat covered in blood, it's about one o'clock on a Sunday morning and everything's got to be taken care of. Where do you begin? We were up to our necks in it now. We went out for a drink and we wound up with this.

We got an eiderdown out of the bedroom and laid it on the floor. As we tried to move Jack, we had to be careful. We were worried about his head falling off because of the huge cut across his neck. We rolled him gently over. Everything was hanging out of his stomach. His liver fell out, and we scooped it up with a little shovel and burned it on the fire which was going in the grate.

We emptied his pockets. He had about £40 on him, all covered in blood, and a few papers, which we burned along with his watch. The bits of carpet where the heavy blood was were burnt immediately. We took his keys, three of them on a ring.

Finally we got him wrapped up in this eiderdown, and then we had the problem of moving him upstairs. He weighed about 16 stone.

My intention was to burn the house down. As far as I knew there was nobody indoors. We would get a couple of gallons of petrol, soak the lot, let it go and it would be dismissed as just a normal fire. I went out into the passageway, but as I reached the flight of stairs I saw two young children, aged about two and four, leaning over the stairs from the second floor. They immediately put an end to the original plan.

We finally got Jack up into the hallway. I had his legs and the others had the front of him. The idea now was to get him into the boot of his motor, which Ronnie Bender had pulled round from the side of the house. The offside headlight was broken.

We opened the boot, but it was full of junk and we couldn't get him in there. So we had to put him inside the car, on the floor between the front and back seats. It took fifteen minutes to get him there because people were wandering about: we were once halfway out the door when a copper came along, and we had to shove Jack back into the house. Once he was in the car we threw another cover over him and I went back into the flat to get his hat, which we put in with him.

Inside the flat Connie Whitehead continued cleaning, with another couple of people who had been called in, while we decided what we were going to do with the body. It had to be taken away from the scene, so we agreed to move it to the other side of the water, south of the river.

Nobody wanted to drive it. Whatever made me say it I don't know, but I agreed. 'All right, I'll drive it.'

Chris said: 'While you're driving the car, we're with you all the way.' Ronnie Bender drove the car which followed me, with Chris as his passenger. They were both armed. If anybody had stopped me that night, they would have had to go with Jack.

We drove down Evering Road into Clapton, along Mare Street, Hackney, into Cambridge Heath Road, through Commercial Road and into the Blackwall Tunnel. It was a quarter to two in the morning.

We came out the other side and about half a mile from there I parked the car up beside an old derelict church down a side turning. My intention was to report it to the twins to let certain people know where it was so that it could be taken away and disposed of. Little did I realise it was on another firm's manor, the Foreman manor, which could obviously cause problems for them if it were found.

I dropped Jack's keys into the Regents Canal. If you come up from Hackney Road through Queensbridge Road, Haggerston, to the canal bridge, they are in there on the right. If they sent a diver down there today, he'd recover them.

We went back to Blonde Carol's flat and carried on cleaning up. We finished at roughly five in the morning. There would be another clean-up the next night when Albert Donaghue went round and the place was completely redecorated and fitted out with new furniture, as though nothing had ever happened.

Chris and I went back to our Dad's house. He got out of bed and knew something was wrong. We were sitting there, the old man, Chris and I, with a cup of tea and we said: 'Something very, very bad's happened tonight.' The old man didn't want to know. He didn't ask us. I went home to my wife, who also realised that something was wrong but again didn't ask questions. That was an accepted thing. She knew I was involved with the Krays.

I could hardly sleep. I might have had a couple of hours, and when I woke up I didn't want to believe what had happened. There was nothing in the papers, so it seemed the body hadn't been found.

There were, at the time, five or six firms operating in south London, and I can say that while Freddie Foreman had absolutely nothing to do with the collection and disposal of the body, certain help was given, and it was done properly. It was picked up at about eleven o'clock on the morning we left it there and held until the early hours of Monday in a shed about three miles away from the church. The people involved said they were pleased it was Jack The Hat because he had caused trouble for them in the past.

When they picked him up, there was a fine white powder covering his body. No one seems to know what that could have been. Obviously, all the blood had drained out of him. The stink, apparently, was terrible. His car was crushed into a three feet by three feet cube in a masher. After that it was referred to as the Oxo. Then it was slung on to a scrap heap.

Jack himself is about three miles away from where the car went into scrap, and fifty miles away from where we left him. His body will never, ever be found. He and his hat were put into a grave which had been pre-dug, and covered with a layer of soil. A funeral took place the next day, and the grave was filled. So he did get a decent burial.

Chris and I next saw the twins on the Monday after the murder. They were in the Carpenters Arms with the Mills brothers, just sitting talking. Jack The Hat was mentioned only once. That was when Chris said, 'Tell me something, Reg. Was he a grass, was he a wrong 'un? Let's justify it.'

Reg said, 'No, he wasn't. He was just a nuisance.'

I hadn't in a million years expected to see anything like what happened. I thought Jack would be hurt, which he thoroughly deserved, and that would be the end of it. But set out to kill him? It just wouldn't have made sense. Where was the plan? There was no plan. Would we have been daft enough to bring the Mills brothers along to witness a murder? They, and the two young boys, would not have been in the room if anything like that had been predetermined. None of the details of that night point to any kind of conspiracy.

In my own way, I liked Jack The Hat. He wasn't a bad fella. He was a generous man and he had a very good sense of humour. He was flamboyant, loved to be the centre of attention and enjoyed having women around him. He was a total rebel, and he was fearless.

But overall, I never regretted what I did. I'm not for one minute saying murder was the answer to anything, but Jack was the one who made threats in the first place. The twins had not been threatening him in any way. And if he was prepared to take them on, he was also aware of the consequences if he came unstuck.

Let's not whitewash it. Jack McVitie was a man of violence. A lot of what has been written has painted a picture of him as mild, meek and helpless, a hard-done-by, innocent man. The girl he lived with got up at the Old Bailey, gave evidence against us, spat at the dock and talked about 'my poor Jack'. He had no respect for her, just as he had no respect for anybody else.

Reggie didn't do society such a bad turn. Jack The Hat was a known heavy man. He was six feet two and as hard as nails. He'd done a lot of imprisonment in his time. He'd been through the school and he'd hurt a few people along the way.

His stock-in-trade was crime, and he made money out of it. He was an active robber, he cared little for anyone and he was capable of anything. He was known to carry and use a gun. He would use a knife, and had no scruples about whether it was on a man or a woman. He would cause trouble and he would challenge people. He was on drink and pills and he was unpredictable. Where there was a good time, he wanted to be. If there was a row, he'd be in the thick of it. He'd be the first one over the counter. Even having a social drink, he could suddenly turn vicious for no reason.

He didn't have a care in the world. He didn't give a monkey for anything, but he should have done. That was his downfall. He became his own worst enemy. The twins only ever tried to help him: they put lots of work his way. But he started making errors, and he brought the trouble on himself.

He'd get into drunken moods and produce a gun, threatening to shoot the twins, which he was more than capable of doing. He'd mug the twins off – bad-mouth them – in front of other people. He'd pick up phones in pubs and pretend to be threatening them. He'd insult women who were with members of the firm. He'd go into clubs which the firm was protecting and cause violent scenes. I've seen him have a gunfight in the Regency: he issued threats there, he brandished a shotgun and he slammed an axe into the door, all on separate occasions. He burst into other clubs with guns. He shot out a bar in a pub because they wouldn't serve him. Usually the next morning he'd be sorry, but at night he'd had the bottle again and he'd be back. I mean that. Back.

All of these things were building up against him. Jack had been warned by myself and other members of the firm about his behaviour, but had paid no attention. How far could the twins let it go? He was persistently challenging their power, constantly trying to undermine their authority, and they could not allow it to happen. Men of their standing could not be seen to have someone like McVitie carrying on like that, particularly in the East End. Had I been in Reggie's shoes, I would certainly have done the same thing. And the tragedy of it all is that so many suffered for something which the victim himself decided to cause.

CHAPTER TWO

THE SEEDS
OF CRIME

L ooking back at my childhood in the East End, I don't believe
it's any wonder that a lot of us turned to crime. We went to
rough and ready schools where all that mattered was who the best
fighter was. We were always getting caned and whacked. When I
was in my early teens, a youth employment officer came to my
school. His report on the whole class was, 'No hope whatsoever.'
None of us really had a future. And when I say we were living in
times of poverty, I mean poverty. The money just wasn't there.

I was born in the middle of the Second World War, on 15 April
1942 in Bethnal Green Hospital. My Mum, Lilian, was a Geordie,
born in 1912, who came from Irish stock in County Kildare. My
father, Christopher, was born in Cyprus in 1899 and sold as a slave
to an Arab at the age of twelve. He was taken to Egypt, but ran away
a year and a half later and jumped on a ship with his sister Marie.
He hit these shores when he was fourteen, one of the first Greek
Cypriots to arrive in this country.

Dad made his base in London and took a job in a munitions
factory in Newcastle-upon-Tyne when the First World War broke
out in 1914. He later enlisted in the RAF, but remained working at

the factory. When the war was over, he returned to London and began work training as a chef, eventually building a solid career in catering. He was also a very good gambler and in 1927 he won about £12,000, which he eventually invested in two restaurants, both in Charlotte Street in central London; he bought the first one in 1938. His sister also went into business in Charlotte Street, with two dress shops and a café.

A few years before the Second World War started, my father was drafted back into the RAF. He travelled up north again to serve in the same munitions factory, which is where he met my mother, a very religious woman, a strict Catholic with a fiery temper. My eldest brother Chris was born on Christmas Day, 1938. Leon came into the world during an air raid, inside Chalk Farm tube station, in September 1940. At the time I was born, two years later, the family base was in Mornington Crescent in north-west London.

With my father in the RAF and the restaurant in business, we enjoyed a relatively good standard of living during the war years, although we were frequently shifted about. We were evacuated up to Newcastle, returned to London, and then sent off to Leicester before coming back down south for good. My father was stationed in Newcastle throughout, but we saw him often: he had quite a bit of leave, and when there was heavy bombing, they would close the factory.

In 1944 we moved to Howland Street, off Tottenham Court Road in the centre of London, near where the Telecom Tower stands today. My brother Jimmy was born on 14 April that year. The baby of the family, the fifth son, Nicky, arrived on Boxing Day, 1946. Ironically, in view of what happened later, we were all named after saints.

My earliest memories go back to the age of three. I remember visiting my grandfather, Arthur, on my mother's side. He had a small farm in Consett, outside Newcastle, with a cow and a couple of pigs. He had a fireplace in the house, a great big thing with an inglenook. My grandfather had his chair on one side and my grandmother had hers on the other. I sat on a stool in the actual fireplace, next to my grandfather, and I was crying because he tried to pick me up. I could never, ever stand anyone touching me apart from my mother and father. I would always scream. And that's my only memory of my grandfather.

Certain things have always stuck in my mind to do with the war itself. Again, around the age of three, I went with my brothers to Tottenham Court Road to get the accumulator, which was used to keep the radio running, charged up. And I'll never forget seeing a crater in the road with a bus teetering on the edge of it, and a couple of bodies lying in the street.

My mother used to grab us and whack us on to the floor when there were doodlebug attacks, and when there were air-raid warnings she would take us to the tube stations at Mornington Crescent, Camden Town or Tottenham Court Road. The house next door to us in Howland Street was bombed.

She always used to tell us about the day she was hanging out the clothes in a field in Consett while my father was in the RAF. I was in the pram and Chris and Leon were playing around at her feet. Out of the mist, she suddenly saw a German bomber coming down really low, so she threw us to the ground and waited for a burst of machine-gun fire. It never came.

All of these things, in their own way, alerted me at a very early age to violence of a certain kind, which probably hardened me up to a lot of what happened afterwards.

In 1945, my father acquired his second restaurant. But even though the war was at an end, rationing and the black market carried on. I remember my mother giving me a coupon and a sixpence for two ounces of sweets at the little shop near our house.

There were no televisions in those days, and families were more like families. The mothers used to be out chatting to each other while the kids played around the streets, and this was how I first came to hear about the Bentley murder. It involved two young kids, Derek Bentley and Christopher Craig. Craig shot a policeman, but because he was sixteen and not old enough for capital punishment they hanged Bentley, who was eighteen but innocent instead. It was a major topic of conversation at the time. I remember my Mum talking about it to a neighbour and saying, 'What that boy's mother must be going through, poor woman. . . .'

She was a very maternal person, my mother, very protective, very proud of her sons, and she was desperate with worry when I was taken to Middlesex Hospital with yellow jaundice as a toddler. They didn't expect me to live. Another major family crisis came only a couple of years later, in 1947, by which time I had started school at St Marylebone Convent.

Chris, Leon and I were in one of my father's restaurants one day when my father caught a rat. If you run a catering business and you find a rat, what do you do? You kill it. He put it on the pavement and scalded it to death with boiling water. An RSPCA inspector happened to be passing by at the time. My father wouldn't apologise for what had happened, and it all ended up with him being taken to court for cruelty to a rat. He was kept in Brixton Prison for a short while, an experience he never forgot, and he had to hire a lawyer because he couldn't speak very good English.

It went as far as the High Court. The whole case hinged on whether or not you could be cruel to an animal which was classified as vermin. In the end, they ruled that you could. My father was heavily fined and that, combined with the lawyer's costs, left him penniless. He had to sell the restaurants to pay the bills, and from then on things got very bad for the family financially.

My father went on to do some relief work as a chef in hotels and restaurants, and he started selling ice cream off a trolley. My Mum was working as a part-time home help. I can never stress enough how hard it was for them, with five sons to bring up.

In the summer, when he was selling the ice cream, he used to keep his trolley in the ground-floor passageway of the derelict house next door, the one which had been hit by a doodlebug. Chris, Leon and I used to get into the house in the morning before school. We'd nick some of our Dad's ice cream and my two brothers and I would walk down Howland Street to Marylebone Road, to the convent. One morning, we went to the floor upstairs to see what was there, and we found a pile of tinned fruit. We'd never seen anything like it before. Obviously, it was in storage for the black market.

But beside these tins of fruit was a dead baby, all wrapped up in a shawl. It couldn't have been more than two or three days old. It looked like a doll to me. We told our Mum and the police were called. They questioned us about where we found the baby, and that was the last we ever heard of it. Whether anybody ever got nicked over the baby – or the fruit – we'll never know. It was my first experience of police questioning.

I was about five then, and Chris, Leon and I were all altar boys. I used to carry the mace, wearing my white surplice. The only thing I ever won in my life, apart from the odd bet, was a Bible. Whatever happened, our Mum always made sure we were Catholics. Every week, no matter what, she would see that we had a shirt and tie on to go to Sunday school. She was very strict about that, and so was my Dad. While we lived in Howland Street we had to go to St Peter's church, Marylebone. The other mothers and fathers didn't like us because we were the 'ruffians', and they used to tell their kids, 'Don't mix with them.'

At that time we were just young tearaways who got into a bit of trouble now and again like any other kids, and I look back on my time in Howland Street as some of the happiest days of my life. We used to love going to the stables in the mews and back streets of the area. Bertram Mills, the circus impresario, used to hire out a stable there, and Chris, Leon and I used to exercise his ponies round the yard. One of the highlights of our year was the Easter horse parade in the Inner Circle at Regent's Park.

But in 1948 our lives were suddenly disrupted when we came home from the convent one day and found that the locks on the door had been changed. Our parents had been evicted because they couldn't afford the rent and we wound up in one of the old workhouses in south London. It was at the Elephant and Castle, and we spent four months in this place; everything smelt of disinfectant and the food was filth. We then moved to a rest centre, which was the next step towards being rehoused, in Sloane Square for another nine months. The facilities were slightly better but, like the workhouse, it had rules which did not allow the father to live there with his family. We kids were taken away from the convent and the nuns and given places in a school beside Victoria Station for a while. We used to make a few bob by carrying cases for passengers at the station. We went out there and we became the Artful Dodger.

In 1949, we were rehoused in the East End. We got a five-roomed flat in a block called Belford House in the Haggerston area of Queensbridge Road, London E8. It was bounded by Bethnal Green, Hackney, Hoxton and, in the north, Clapton and Stoke Newington. My parents were to stay there until they died. I was enrolled in Laburnum Street Primary School where I remained until the age of eleven. All of my brothers went there except Chris, who was by now a bit too old. He attended Scawfell Secondary Modern. At Laburnum Street we became very friendly with a schoolmate called Frankie Shea, the brother of Reggie Kray's future wife, Frances.

We quickly made a name for ourselves there – Chris was already known to be trouble. Junior school was where you started earning a reputation. Maybe we didn't know exactly what we were doing at the time, but this is where the reputation of the Lambrianou brothers, in some small way, began to take shape. Once again, but with more reason now, the kids around us were told: 'Keep away from those boys.'

We got kicked out of everything, including the Cubs and the Sunday school. After we moved to Haggerston, our mother had seen to it that we went to All Saints' Church and its Sunday school. We used to steal the collecting trays from both. Chris did it three times, and I stole the church tray once. When anything went missing, it was us who did it. The stage in the church hall used to be hired out for fêtes and functions. We were told on one occasion that we couldn't come unless we were dressed properly, which we considered to be an insult, so we set fire to the stage to get back at the church authorities.

When Chris was eleven, going on twelve, he fell foul of the law for the first time. He went out with Leon, broke into a local factory and stole some property. I remember my mother breaking down and crying, begging the officers not to take her sons away. They kept saying, 'No, they've gotta go.' They spent two or three weeks at Stamford House boys' remand centre in Shepherds Bush. When it came to court, Leon got off and he never went back to an institution of any kind. Chris was convicted and sent to approved school for two years at St Vincent's in Kent. He behaved himself throughout that time and came home on visits every Sunday.

By this time in my life we were really bleeding poor. Everything my mother earned was spent on us. I saw her crying because she was worried about where the next meal was coming from, but somehow she found it; somehow we always had our bellies full up. She never, ever went out, and she never drank. My father I only ever saw in a pub on Christmas Day, with the family. He'd have a drop of wine now and again, or if a bottle of whisky came along he'd have a little drink, but it was rare.

I remember the winter when I was nine, and my parents couldn't afford a Christmas dinner. My mother cried and my father went out and brought back kebabs. On Christmas Day, the only presents we ever got were an apple, an orange and some nuts in a sock. I never had a Christmas toy. In fact, I never had any toys at all. Our playthings in the East End were bricks, and our playground was the bombsite.

One day I was sent home for having a hole in my shoe. It had been pouring with rain and I walked across the assembly hall leaving muddy footprints, which showed up the hole. A teacher stopped me, and I had to stay off school for three days. In the end, my father found 3s 6d to buy me a pair of pumps.

It got very bad, but we weren't the only ones by a long shot. There were three sisters in that school who used to wear the same clothes every day. Each one would wear what one of the other two had been wearing the day before.

My Mum used to buy shirts and trousers for us at second-hand shops, and sometimes on credit. Everybody lived on 'the tally' in those days because they couldn't afford cash. You would pay the tally man a deposit and then a certain number of shillings a week, when he came round to the door, for clothes or other goods. We had two tally men, a big Jew and a little Jew. My mother could never afford to pay both of them, because that would come to 4s a week. The first one to turn up got paid, and the second one didn't. In the end, they were racing each other to get to us first.

The first suit I got, a gaberdine jacket and slacks, was on the HP. It cost £11. The proudest day of my life was the day I first wore it. I thought I was one of the boys then. I'd grown up. Later, I remember my mother crying because the tally man took Chris's suit away, for the sake of 2s a week.

My mother lived for her five boys, and I saw her fight for us. I've seen her knock out more women than I've had hot dinners. If anyone had a go at one of her sons, she took it personally. And when she could, she'd give us treats. With Chris back from approved school, she used to take the five of us to the pictures at the Odeon in Hackney Road on a Monday night when my Dad was out working as a relief chef. The best seats cost 9d. We used to have to queue for the cheap seats, which were 3d. She took us to the circus, too, and we all shared a quarter of sweets.

I was already working in my spare time, humping bags of coal and coke. From the age of eight I had to be out there earning on Saturday mornings, and I carried on doing it until I was twelve or thirteen. I used to get up early in the morning and take orders from all the people who lived around us. I'd go to the yard in Queensbridge Road and to Albert Usher's depot in Nuthall Street, Hoxton, and bring the bags back. In the winter it used to be freezing but I'd get 6d a bag and I used to give nearly all the money to my mother. My share I spent on doughnuts, a real luxury.

We also went round on race days selling sheets with the dog results on them. We sold them by the gross, and our payment was to keep forty-four out of each gross, which we could then sell for 5d apiece. Everybody who'd had a bet wanted to know the results, and we'd do two gross a night if we were lucky.

Another few bob I used to make came from Bert The Horseman, who had stables at Lea Bridge Road by the canal, under the railway arches. We used to take horses from there to the Elephant and Castle to be sold, most of them to the knacker's yard. The journey would take us about two hours, stopping at the horse troughs to water them along the way, and we used to be paid 5s an hour, half a crown for half an hour and 3d for fifteen minutes. Any horse going down there was worth at least £15. One day a mate and I took two ponies and a foal to the Elephant. We sold all of them, got the receipt and kept £15 of Bert's money; we told him some story about losing it. Then there was the Saturday morning he sent me to fetch his tea at a café by Regents Canal. He gave me a fiver. That was a lot of money at the time, and a shop wouldn't accept it unless it was signed for. I got Bert to sign it and rode to the tea room on a pony called Nelson. I bought his tea, a sandwich and ten weights. I then drank his tea, ate his sandwich and smoked his fags, and had it away on my toes – ran off home. I left the pony in a field. I couldn't resist the money.

People were so short then that very few ever had a holiday, but if they could afford it they'd go picking hops in the fields of Kent, a very East End thing to do. Our family never had a holiday together, and the first one I ever had I went on my own. I was taken to Eastbourne at the age of eleven by a family called the Hopkinsons, who lived above us in Belford House. There was Flo and Dan and their children, Danny, Terry, Rita, Maureen and Jean. We went away in his lorry, all eight of us, and slept in hammocks inside it. I had no new clothes to take with me. I was wearing Leon's, washed out. My mother scraped together £2 for me to spend, which for a kid then was quite a lot of money. The Hopkinsons were always considered to be 'better-class' East Enders, with that little bit more money to spend on enjoying themselves. They moved out several years later and they're all in America to this day, doing well.

It was around this time that the police called again on the Lambrianou family. One Sunday night when Chris was fifteen, he went out and broke into a newspaper factory in Hoxton.

I was at home with my mother, Leon and my two younger brothers when there was a knock on the door at eight o'clock. Two plain-clothes police officers came into the house with Chris and a package of paper. They had arrested him for breaking into the factory and stealing the newspaper.

I remember my mother in tears, saying, 'Why are you taking him over a package of waste paper?'

He ended up before the London Sessions and was sentenced to three years at Borstal in Hollesley Bay in Suffolk. He escaped from there a couple of times: once he was caught in Ipswich, the second time in Woodbridge. While he was there, he represented the Borstal at boxing. He fought at the US Air Force base in Woodbridge and he was the middleweight champion of the county throughout those three years. It didn't take him long to build up a reputation as a 'daddy' – the top man. And on his monthly visits home he was inviting characters that he'd met there, all the East End wide boys, who were a big influence on me. His attitude was becoming more aggressive – an 'I'm gonna beat 'em up' type of thing. That was Chris all over.

I was fourteen when he was released. And as soon as he came out, they stuck him in the Army. They put him in the Pioneer Corps, which meant that he was considered to be an uneducated no-good, only fit for dogsbody jobs. It was the dustbin of the British Army, for all the dregs they didn't really want there. He joined on a Thursday, and on the Saturday night there was a knock at the door. It was Chris, in his uniform. He sat at home with a hammer, breaking his toes, to get him out of the Army – to my mother's horror. She had to see things at that time which weren't very nice. The Military Police came and carted Chris off. Next thing we knew, he was in Shepton Mallet army prison, which is where he met the Kray twins for the first time. He got a dishonourable discharge from the Army.

Shortly after this Chris, Leon and I went to see a film called *The Blackboard Jungle*; the title music was 'Rock Around the Clock' by Bill Haley. That was the start of rock'n'roll in England. Nobody had heard of it until they saw *The Blackboard Jungle*. It was all about kids in America with flick knives, drapes and tight trousers, and I'd never seen anything like it. Suddenly, teddy boys were on the streets and everybody, everywhere, was saying what a bad influence they were. I'll never forget the day Chris came home with the drape, the velvet collar and the drainpipe trousers. He paid fifteen quid for the suit, which he bought from Woods the Tailor in the East End. The twins used to use him. They bought all their suits from his shop in Kingsland Road.

My father didn't like the image, and he went absolutely potty. He got this suit, he cut it up and he got the big stick out. . . . The way we were brought up, in typical East End – and Greek – tradition, the old man was head of the household and nobody, including my mother, ever questioned his authority or decisions. Even when we were grown up and married, he still kept the big stick by the dinner table.

But the teddy boy influence had taken hold of us. Chris used to have rock'n'roll music blaring out round the house. We had a radiogram by this time. A van used to come round and you could buy singles off the van for 2s 6d each.

By now I was at Queensbridge Road Secondary Modern School, where we all went except for Chris. One day, a schoolmate called Peter Robertson turned up to class wearing the drape and drainpipes. A teacher whom we called Clinker told him to go home and change. His answer was 'Fuck off'. It was unheard of to say that to a teacher, but it was very much our underlying attitude. School was just a big joke. To me it was a waste of time: there was no future in it. Half the pupils didn't even know the alphabet. The teachers felt that if they managed to teach you the 'Three Rs', if you could read and write when you left, then they'd done their job, but they were up against it.

We used to play pitch and toss, throwing money up against a wall. The person who threw the nearest coin to the wall would pick up the kitty. We got involved in petty crimes like stealing milk, or bullying kids in the school playground if we thought they had pocket money. We all gambled.

On Friday afternoons, they used to beat us up. There were three PT teachers: Mr Donnelly, Mr Leary and Mr Eldridge. They'd all have tracksuit bottoms on, and they'd walk round the classrooms, pick you up by the lapels and lay into you. None of us ever complained. We accepted that as part of our life. If I'd gone home and complained, I would have got a right-hander off my father.

They were schools for crime and I think the teachers accepted that that was how it was going to be. Some 'better-class' schools would take their pupils on organised trips to the museums and that. Not us. We were taken out on a sightseeing visit to Wormwood Scrubs, about twenty-nine of us. We walked around the prison, and then the teacher lined us all up and said: 'This is where you lot are going to wind up.' We thought it was a big laugh, but it wasn't so far off the truth. Many of the pupils went on to become well-known villains, Hoxton boys like Tony 'Tubbsy' Turner and George Murray, who ended up controlling the local lorry hi-jackings.

I did do something useful during my schooldays, though. At the age of fourteen, I represented the school as a boxer. My father's best mate, Eddie Phillips, had fought for the British heavyweight title between 1938 and 1944. He was known as the Aldgate Tiger, and he'd fought Joe Louis and Tommy Farr. He worked at Spitalfields Market on the fruit and veg, and he saw the potential of Leon, especially, as a fighter. Chris had done his bit, too, representing his approved school and borstal.

Another man my Dad knew was Prince Monolulu, the black racing tipster from Charlotte Street. He used to wear an Indian outfit and a headdress with big plumes, and they used to go to the races together. He would say to me and my brothers: 'You could be boxers or you could be villains.' And he'd tell my Dad, 'Your boys are fighters, one way or another.' I don't think my Dad understood it.

Chrissy and Leon had been recognised as fighting boys among the schools in the area where we lived. They'd been in plenty of street

fights. Leon was a good scrapper, and even as a young fellow Chris
had a reputation for being a bit of a lunatic. It was, 'Leave it out a
bit, don't get involved with him.'

He wasn't a bloke you could push. He would turn. He had a very,
very explosive temper and didn't know what fear was. He was
dangerous. When Chris had a fight, it didn't stop at a fight. He was
never one just to use his fists. He'd want to pick up a tool as well.
He'd think nothing of picking up a knife or anything else that
came to hand. There was always something different about Chris
and his fighting.

As a kid, Jimmy was the only one of us with curly hair. It was jet
black. He was a good-looking boy, and even as a young adolescent
he always wore a suit. He was a quiet fella, but if you upset him, he
wouldn't forget it. He was an out-and-out street fighter who
believed in settling his arguments with his fists. He was always very
proud of the family name.

Nicky, the baby of the family, had a wild streak as far back as I can
remember. He was reckless and he had a temper second to none. If
he got something in his mind, he would be right and that was the
end of it. He was influenced by the East End and by the brothers and
the people around us, so I suppose he was destined to go the same
way. He was to become the best money-getter of the lot of us.

It was obvious to us at an early age that you didn't survive by
being quiet. You survived by your fists and your boot. On Saturday
nights, we used to watch the brawls at closing time. People used
to come out of the bars fighting fit and the women were worse
than the men – two women fighting, usually about their kids, is
something to see. And if you didn't have a family of brothers with
you, you were nothing. Brothers were your strength. Apart from a
rare few one-offs, all the major villains of our generation were from
families of brothers. There were the Richardsons and the Frasers
from south London, the Regans from west London, the Foremans

from Battersea, the Nashes from the Angel, us from Haggerston and the Krays from Bethnal Green and Bow.

Most of them were boxers. They came from that type of background, all the time fighting each other in schools and at national level. Football was another important part of life in the East End. Ron 'Chopper' Harris and Alan Harris of Chelsea, and Bertie Murray of Chelsea and Brighton & Hove Albion came from the same school as me. Career opportunities at that time were very limited. The markets were a family thing, a closed shop. Tailoring and French polishing were very big, and if you could get into printing it was a bonus. Other than going into these trades, your only hope of rising above the poor conditions of the East End was to be a boxer, a footballer, a showbiz celebrity, a thief or a villain.

At thirteen, I had become very well aware of the Kray twins when the story of their fight with the dockers spread round the East End like wildfire. They had walked into a pub, the two of them, shut the doors, taken on a whole bunch of dockers and walked out. I was very impressed. If you were a docker you were a tough man, the bee's knees. But even the dockers stood back and said, 'These two are something else.' They were fearless, the twins. That was the difference about them, and that was important in their careers.

From my early teenage years I was increasingly drawn towards the same criminal path, like Chris before me and Jimmy and Nicky after me. But Leon, following his first early brush with the authorities, was two-thirds straight throughout his teens. He would later clean up his life completely, to become a good and honest man. In the period after his borstal, Chris was known to be up-and-coming and good at what he did. By the time he was eighteen he tended not to get involved in the things that we younger brothers were up to. He was a loner, Chris. There were several little gangs around Haggerston, and Chris moved about from one to the other. He spent a lot of his time involved in dubious dealings in the West

End, and he really started to take off. The rest of us, too, were becoming more and more notorious in the local area, especially in Hoxton. Where previously other kids' fathers had smacked us round the earhole, now they wouldn't. But we weren't all bad. If we ever saw any women struggling along the streets with heavy bags, we'd carry their shopping. I went into the twins' house many times, helping their mother Violet, without ever realising they lived there.

I left school early, at fourteen, and took a job at the Sleepy Valley Bedding Company in Hackney Road, Bethnal Green. I got it through a youth employment agency, where I didn't have much choice. I used to knock holes with a machine into the edges of the beds and I was paid 2s an hour. I gave my mother £2 10s a week. One day I came out of work and saw Frankie Shea at the junction of Hackney Road and Weymouth Terrace, which is where his family came from. His sister Frances came along. She would have been about twelve or thirteen, very quiet and very beautiful with big eyes. It was the first time I'd ever seen the girl who would grow up to marry Reggie Kray. The bedding company was one of the longest jobs I would ever hold, and I worked there for nine months. And from that period onwards I started getting into villainy. Properly.

CHAPTER THREE

GIRLS, GANGS AND GUNS

About this time Leon, Jimmy and I began to hang around the local dancehalls, places like Barry's in Mare Street and the Royal in Tottenham, as well as various arcades and cafés. A lot of similarly minded local boys were around: the Venables brothers from Hoxton; Terry Smith, who was a gunsmith; Johnny Dallison, later to be one of the Wembley bank robbers grassed up by Bertie Smalls; Roy Ewes, who went on to do the Baker Street vaults in the seventies; and the Nash brothers, Jimmy, Johnny, Georgie, Billy and Ray, who would each wind up convicted of a murder.

We teamed up with Terry and Jimmy Venables and started causing the occasional fight in Barry's. We'd go down there to take on the local tearaways because it was something to prove. I think we were on an ego trip: other gangs from different areas would be challenged, and we would always do what we wanted. We didn't fight clean: Chains, knives, anything that came our way we used, which is a trademark of the East End.

Eventually we discovered that there was money to be made from the fighting. Barry himself was a very nice bloke, a gay; he had a couple of bouncers there keeping a bit of order, but they couldn't cope with us lot. He asked us to stop the fighting, and in the end he propositioned us: he gave us £10 a week to keep the peace, but it didn't go very far among five of us.

After a couple of weeks of this, more trouble started. We put it to Barry: 'If you gave the boys £5 each, this wouldn't happen.'

Then we started to spread to the Royal. The manager said, 'We're going to bar you.'

'You'll get more trouble than it's worth,' I said.

One of the bouncers, Jim, went and had a chat with the manager, who then said: 'As long as there's no trouble caused, you can come in here for nothing.' It reached the point where he was giving us £50 a week.

This was our first little taste of protection, which was to expand greatly at a later stage. I was also going into a bit of thieving. By the time I was seventeen, my Dad saw the path I was taking. He never managed to speak English well, but he was no one's fool. If he saw me in what he thought was bad company, he'd say, 'What do you bring a person like that round the house for?' Leon was courting a girl called June Veal, his future wife, and my Dad would say, 'Look, Leon's found a girl and quietened down, what about you?' I did meet a girl, although I wasn't about to quieten down for anybody.

I first saw Pat Strack in 1959 with three of her mates in Barry's dancehall. She was a local girl from Bollo Road, Bow – very pretty, one of the best-looking girls in the East End. She was then sixteen, about five feet two, with blue eyes and naturally fair hair coloured auburn. What attracted me to her was her short, urchin haircut; she looked like a little doll. Pat wore the rock'n'roll era clothes, the billowing skirts and all that. She was an apprentice hairdresser at the time, working in Kilburn in north London, but she left after a couple of years.

I walked her home that night, down Mare Street and along into

Bollo Road. I took her to the door and said, 'I'd like to see you again.' She said yes, and we arranged a date for the next night.

I was seventeen, out to impress but I was skint – I had only a pound on me. I took her to the pictures, and from that day onwards she only ever had one night away from me while I was in freedom. That was the night she did her Aunt Gladys' hair.

Her mother, Maisie, came from a well-known family in Bethnal Green and her father, Charlie, who was nicknamed Flip, was a cab driver and an ex-docker. He knew everyone, including the Kray twins. I think he objected to me pretty strongly in the beginning, but in later years we were to become close. Pat had a younger sister, Anne, and a brother, John, who was the youngest of the family.

I remember the first time I brought Pat home. Everybody took to her, my Mum and Dad, and my Leon who was there with June. They virtually moved Pat in with us. She loved her parents, but she was with us all the time now. My parents idolised her: she was the daughter they never had, and that's the way they treated her. Our courting days were nothing spectacular, but all the same she quickly became one of us – a Lambrianou in all but name.

And then I got nicked. I was making quite a lot of money at the time by breaking into shops and wealthy houses, and in August 1959 I went off to the Midlands with a Shoreditch bloke called Phil Keeling and a couple of other local lads. Keeling had a nice car and he always had a few quid around him, and that was how I judged his success. He was a lot older than me, which was an advantage because if anything came to court my representative could always play on 'the influence of the older man' to wiggle me out of it.

We travelled with him doing jobs in Coventry, Sutton Coldfield, Nuneaton, Hinckley and Leicester, staying in bed and breakfasts or sleeping in the car. In the end, the police caught up with us in Coventry, where we had stayed the night with a friend of ours. I woke up to hear the door coming in. The police surrounded the house and took us to Nuneaton, where we were held for two days. Phil had apparently left a thumbprint at the scene of one of the crimes, and I'd left prints of a thumb and index finger.

I spent five months on remand in Leicester and Winson Green prisons. It was my first experience of prison. Winson Green was a dingy, filthy place in the worst part of Birmingham. There were three of us in a cell, locked up twenty-three hours a day. I felt a long way from home and my visits were a bit restricted. Pat, my mother and my father came to see me when they could, every Saturday and sometimes during the week. I would look at people doing fourteen years and think to myself: 'If that was me, I'd hang myself.' Little did I know what the future had in store for me.

I appeared at Warwick Quarter Sessions after doing a deal with the authorities. I was told that if I pleaded guilty, and saved them the cost of a trial, I would be put on probation. There were so many charges against me that they decided to make do with a nominal two. Pat and my father were waiting for me when I walked out in January 1960 with a two-year probation order.

In April I turned eighteen; by now we had reached the stage where people knew better than to rub us up the wrong way. As we got older, the tally man got bashed up, and there were incidents when the neighbours came to us for help. One day, my old man said to us: 'Joe Sylvester in Orme House wants to see you.' Joe was a well-liked man in Haggerston, and he asked us to sort out some people who had caused problems for his daughter. It was the first time we had ever been called on like this, and it certainly wouldn't be the last.

Jimmy and I and the Venables brothers drove over to the address Joe gave us in Lewisham, knocked on the door and duly bashed up these blokes. Joe was so impressed he gave us £75 and told us that some of his friends might be able to use us. Another neighbour came home one day and found out his wife was having an affair with someone. He offered us £100 to beat the geezer up – which, again, we did. From smacking us round the earhole to paying us to bash someone up was obviously one big step. We were starting to be treated really differently: 'All right, Tony? How are the boys?' People knew we were getting useful. It didn't take long for these things to get around.

My mates and I were ready for anybody and anything. We had built up an arsenal, with weaponry like you've never seen. We had shotguns galore, three rifles and half a dozen hand guns, a Thompson sub-machine-gun, a couple of grenades and numerous knives and swords. A lot of these we were able to get through our connections with Terry Smith, the gunsmith, who would steal them out of the factory bit by bit, the barrel one day, the stock the next. We also knew a trading place for guns, old wartime relics, called Port Road. A lot of dealers kept souvenir weaponry, which could easily be converted back to what it was.

The machine-gun had been taken off a plane used during the First World War and renovated privately by Terry Smith. We decided to test it out in the Venables' back garden in Hoxton. Terry Venables let the chickens out: one burst and they were all dead. It was always kept nice and clean and oiled, the machinegun, but it was never used against people. Nor were the grenades. We exploded one in a field in Epping Forest and it blew a tree right out of the ground. The other one we threw in the sea, just to see what would happen. About thirty fish flew up, dead.

The nucleus of our gang was Terry and Jimmy Venables, David Sadler, Terry Smith, my Jimmy and myself. By now we had started to go to town on the dancehalls, the arcades and the cafés, and we were always tooled up when we were around them, in case we came up against another gang. The swords were stored in the boot of the car, and we carried a gun and daggers and knives. People didn't mess about with us, but at the same time they never took a lot of notice of the weapons. On a few occasions we fired shots into the air in certain places, but the reaction would be: 'No one hurt, let's keep this quiet.'

We were taking weekly payments from the dancehalls and we started making money from a string of amusement arcades run by a man called George Fairey and his partner Paddy. They had four businesses in Hackney and Dalston Junction. We'd go in and, all of a sudden, bang! A machine would get done or one of his customers would get knocked out. I'd say, 'You'd better keep this lot happy.' And eventually he started paying up. We used to get a lot of money out of him.

Round the corner from his arcade in Dalston Junction was a club called Chez Don, which was doing well. I walked in there one night with a friend called Timmy Reynolds and it went off – an East End expression for trouble starting. We said to the manager, 'If you don't let us in here again, there's going to be more.' In the end, they were paying us £50 a week to stay away from the place.

Fifty yards away was Lou's Café, which was owned by a Jewish couple. We used to get a few quid off Mr Lou: he didn't want his business turned over. One Saturday afternoon I was in there with Terry Smith, Jimmy and Terry Venables and Davy Sadler. Five Irishmen who were doing roadworks outside came in for a meal. Somebody handed me a packet of three. I took out one of the condoms and chucked it into the chip pan. It expanded more than a bit, but because it was that pale, fatty colour Mrs Lou didn't notice it. She served it up on one of the Irishmen's plates.

He said, 'What's this?', and all of a sudden he grabbed her by the throat and tried to throttle her, at which point her husband dived underneath the counter to hide. The place was in uproar. We just broke up.

When we went back after that, Mrs Lou wouldn't serve us

although old Lou himself would. He used to call her the dragon –
'Don't come in when the dragon's here.' I think he was scared to
refuse us – he was very wary of us. He had another café in
Shoreditch. One day about a year later I walked into this café and
there she was, Mrs Lou. She yelled, 'Get out, you animal! Get out!',
and chased me down the road.

I was doing well for an eighteen-year-old. I was earning about
£130–140 a week from all these rackets and the thieving. The other
boys viewed it all as a bit of a joke. I didn't. I saw the opportunities,
the openings and the advantages. My mother, naturally, wanted us
all to settle down, but I was drifting in and out of odd jobs, doing a
lot of driving with the aim of nicking a load when the right one
came along. I was always one to keep my eyes open for an easy
chance. Looking back, it was pretty reckless.

I remember working for a firm called Blue Star Sheets Ltd. It was
run by a little Jewish man, Manny. It was all very Jewish in the East
End in those days, although the Maltese were coming in and
opening lower-calibre cafés and bars. I took the van out, loaded
with sheets, and drove round the corner, where a couple of my
mates were waiting. We unloaded the van and its contents. I went
back to Manny and said, 'I think someone's stolen the load out of
the van.' I got the sack, obviously, and a couple of days later we
shared out the load.

My brother Nicky had become heavily involved by this time, and
Nicky was good. You could always rely on him to get a few quid. He
would think nothing of jumping a lorry, pushing the driver out
and driving off. Jimmy, however, had drifted back out to the
fringes of it all – and, thank God, he was to go on and do greater
things in life; Leon, too, was more or less straight. They still joined
us on the occasional job, but it was getting rarer and rarer. So it
was Chris, Nicky and I who were coming through as not the best
boys in the area.

It was also during this period that I started having a bet. Bookmakers were illegal at the time, but street-corner bookies would operate out of a house. There were always two runners, whose job it was to watch for the police. When the shout went up, the bookie would lock his door. The street-corner bookie was very much part of the atmosphere of the old East End. I remember one Grand National day when I was eleven or twelve. All the old girls were putting on bets of 6d and a shilling, but this bookie, Harry, did a runner with the takings. Some of the Hoxton mob got him in Southend, brought him back and gave him to the old girls. They whacked the life out of him.

From having bets myself, I started working for one of these bookies in Haggerston. He paid me good money to run for him, and I soon found out that ninety-nine times out of a hundred the police were aware of what was going on and were being paid back-handers. I used to see the local copper go in there and come out smiling.

Throughout this period, people kept saying, 'You should be with the twins.' The Krays' name was very big then; everybody knew of and respected them. They were very, very powerful men, at the top of the tree. They were known to be ruthless: they didn't threaten – they did it. They weren't men who messed about. No one in the local criminal circles ever referred to them by name. It was always 'they' or 'the other people' or sometimes 'the firm'; an expression which at the time specifically referred to the twins' gang but has since passed into everyday language to describe any band of villains.

The minute Reggie and Ronnie walked into a nightclub, you knew instantly. You didn't even have to see them. The atmosphere would change. People would stop talking; some would leave. Their presence alone gave out certain messages: be careful what you're saying; don't barge in; never touch them; always be polite. They were treated with the utmost respect. I never saw anybody pat them on the back or use bad language around them. If someone was out of turn they wouldn't stand for it, and everybody knew that. As fighting men they were unchallengeable, and it was no shame to say that if either of them hit you on the chin, you went down on the floor. And they were always on the look-out for up-and-coming material. Of course, we were nowhere near their league in those days and all that was still something in the future. I'd only just met them.

I was standing on a street corner just outside the Cornwallis pub in Bethnal Green Road when an American car drove by. Reggie Kray and Frankie Shea were in it. Frankie shouted out at me, 'Okay, Tone?', and I yelled back, 'Nice car, Frank.'

He shouted, 'It's Reggie's.' Then he said something about me to Reggie.

Three weeks later I was in Bethnal Green Road again, in Pellicci's Café, which was one of the places that the twins used to hold their afternoon meets. I'd seen them there on and off since I was a boy, two very smart young men who always had a few people around them. Neville, the guv'nor of Pellicci's to this day, often jokes about the number of people Ronnie knocked through the window. On this particular day I was sitting in there with a mate of mine, Timmy Reynolds, when Reggie and Ronnie walked in with several characters I would later come to know as Big Pat Connolly, Teddy Smith, Tommy Cowley, Sammy Lederman and Harry Jew Boy.

Reggie came over to me and said, 'You're Tony, a friend of Frankies. He's going to be my brother-in-law.' He added, 'Don't forget us, come and see us . . . and I'll do this, Neville.' With that, he paid our bill.

They were good-looking men, obviously very fit, and well known for being clean-living. That day I sensed an aura about them, a certain danger. You instinctively knew they were something different, and you knew they were men you didn't take liberties with.

Chris and I often sat and talked about them. We began to see more of them in Bethnal Green over the next year, and we got to know them well enough to have occasional dealings with them. If we went to the twins, we could always get a little bit of help. They had an open door, and all they asked in return was a bit of trust and a bit of respect. They worked on a basis of: 'Look, if we can do a good turn, come and see us, and if you can ever do one in return, fair enough.'

They had so many car dealers in their pocket it was untrue, and they could use their influence to get you a motor. You paid a deposit on it and signed up legally. Then it was yours, and you would just forget about the following payments. Only when the case went through the civil courts could they order a snatch-back on it, so you would keep it for two, three years until the finance company repossessed it. The twins would send you to certain car dealers who would sign you up straightaway; you couldn't do that without their help. Sometimes you didn't even need a deposit.

But our connections with the twins at this time were very slight. Chris was off doing his own thing, and I was doing mine. He was always a bit aloof, Chris, and never went out of his way to get on with us like brothers normally would. For example, if we were all playing cards he had to win. He always wanted to show that he was the tough one among us, and Leon and I were a challenge to him. I had a fight with him one day and he threw a knife at me. It went in my leg, so I let one go at him with a shotgun. Luckily for him, I missed. It took a bleeding great lump out of the wall.

Chris was capable of doing anything. He was a man of very changeable moods, and if someone upset him he didn't think, he acted. He wasn't a man you could turn your back on, and he would hold a grudge badly. He was big, about six feet two, well-built and very smart – a Savile Row man. He had to have the best things in life, and he had to have them right away. If he wanted something, he just went and got it. While I was growing up, I always looked up to him, because he was the livewire of the family.

Despite the fact that we usually worked independently, in 1961 Chris and I joined forces in a disastrous escapade. He wanted to do a post office. He'd got hold of some explosives and he was talking about, blowing a safe. We decided to go to the post office in Stoke Newington. I went round to the alley at the back to keep a look-out while Chris broke in. He got inside and rummaged around, but we must have made a noise and disturbed somebody, because the next thing was that the police arrived.

They decided to let me go and to charge Chris with breaking into the post office and having explosives in his possession. They just wanted Chris: they saw something in him, and the Old Street and Dalston police had it in for him. My mother was convinced that Chris was being picked on. He was the one my parents doted on: for them, Chris could do no wrong. I saw the other side of him. He was sentenced to two years in a corrective training centre in Verne prison, Portland, a small island joined to the Dorset coast by a causeway.

Chris was at that time courting a girl called Carol. He'd met her about six months before he went away. She stayed on at Queensbridge Road with my Mum and Dad, Jimmy, Nicky, Pat and me. Leon had moved out to a flat in Blythe Street, Bethnal Green, after marrying June that year in Bethnal Green church. Carol visited Chris regularly and so did Pat and I, in a car which Carol bought me, a Mark I Zodiac. Carol went on to marry Chris when he came out, two years later.

Meanwhile, I'd started making money in the West End for the first time, along with my Jimmy, the Venables brothers – Terry and Tiny – and Terry Smith. We knew a Greek who had a basement snooker place in Soho, in a narrow alley running between Wardour Street and Dean Street. He was known as Nick The Greek, and he was the only man I ever met who could bend a penny with his fingers. His brother was on the door of the Society Club in Jermyn Street. The girls from the clip joints around Frith Street, Greek Street and Dean Street used to go in and out of there and we would get talking and have a laugh with them. I remember three in particular, called Carol, Dawn and Kim, and it was through meeting them that we got the openings.

The set-up in every clip joint is the same. The customer, or john, picks the 'hostess' he wants to sit with. The man buys her drinks all night, and the promise is that he gets sex afterwards – he makes a private arrangement with the hostess. The whole operation is geared to making as much money as possible in a very short time. The drink is usually watered-down scotch – the john could be paying more than £500 for a bottle's worth – and each drink is served with a stick. The girl returns the sticks at the end of the night and cashes them in for money. Some of the men would spend a fortune on alcohol and cash gifts to the girls.

Afterwards the girl would tell the punter she would meet him down the road in ten minutes. She didn't, of course. Our job was to have a car standing by to get her away from the club. For this, we received 50 per cent of what she had earned. I can only once remember a girl actually going with a bloke, when she happened to meet a millionaire. I took them to the Russell Hotel in Russell Square. But the biggest coup I ever knew was when a girl called June clipped a wealthy old farmer for about twenty grand. He'd come to London for the Agricultural Show at Olympia and he was so delighted to be promised a night in a hotel with a pretty girl that he lavished her with cash and champagne, for which she later picked up the rewards. Needless to say, she did a runner before the farmer even saw a hotel. They did need protection, the girls. If any of the men got troublesome, we'd give them a kicking. We were always four- or five-handed.

We began to build up a lot of contacts in the West End, and we became known in the clubs round there. I started to see quite a bit of the twins, especially Reggie Kray, who was always around. He was very active at that time, very smart, a man about town. The twins were running Esmerelda's Barn, a gambling nightspot in Wilton Place, Knightsbridge, and they were into all the best places. I used to bump into them in the Regency in Stoke Newington, in the City Club in the Angel and generally around the West End in the Pigalle, the Bagatelle, Churchills, the Stork and the Society Club. I joined their company on these occasions, and I came to know virtually everybody around them.

In October 1961 I got nicked again, and again it was with Phil Keeling. He was a gelly man – a gelignite expert – and he drove me to the West Country, where we headed for two small Somerset towns called Ilminster and Chard. Phil was into blowing safes, and he had heard of one in the Ilminster Co-op department store. It was like a post-box: people used to post their money into it.

As we were driving along, Keeling pulled out a packet of three. I thought, 'What does he want them for?' That's when I learned that French letters and balloons are ideal for keeping gelignite in. When you do a safe you have to put the explosive to the weakest point, which is usually the lock. You have to get a thin layer of gelly round the door, you have to goo it up into the keyhole itself and you've got to get as much as you can into the safe. When you're laying the gelly, you pierce the end of the rubber and squeeze it out in a thin line like you do with pastry or icing. Then you can cover it with Plasticine. You set it off through a detonator, a battery with a wire on it. You cross the circuit, and that's what causes the explosion. But you've got to know what you're doing.

We got into the store at midnight and ran round the different departments, picking up fur coats and carpets to cover the safe with so as to muffle the bang. But gelignite has got to be kept cool and dry, and the heat was making ours start to run. It was too dangerous to use – we would have blown half of Somerset away. So we had to find another way.

I went for a walk around the Co-op and found a 14lb sledgehammer. But the safe had a steel door, solidly built into concrete. The counter was built round it. I was smashing this hammer into the concrete and making no impression whatsoever. Then we went right to the back of the store, by the railway, where we found an oxy-acetylene bottle and a flame gun. So we set about cutting the safe. We were half an inch away from getting the door open when we ran out of gas. . . .

We read in the next issue of the local paper that the safe had contained nine grand, which was a lot of money in those days. Before we'd left the store, however, Keeling had picked up a little jewel box with two diamond rings in it. When we arrived back in London, he gave one to me and one to a girlfriend he was having an affair with. She put it on, not realising it was worth £6,000. She was in a café one day when the guv'nor, a Jewish guy called Day, said to her, 'That's a lovely ring.'

She said, 'Phil gave it to me.'

Obviously he knew a bit about jewellery, so what did he do? He picked up the phone.

Just after this I walked round to Great Eastern Street, near the City, where Keeling lived. His wife was in tears, saying, 'The police have taken Phil away.'

I went home, got my ring and immediately had it valued: it was worth £2,600. I got rid of it through certain channels, and two days later I was nicked. Keeling's wife had obviously mentioned my name.

They picked me up at my father's house in Queensbridge Road and took me to Cannon Row police station. I was brought to the Flying Squad offices and from there I was taken by train from Paddington to Taunton, cuffed up to an officer throughout the journey.

I was held at Taunton police station for two days pending an appearance at Ilminster Magistrates Court. Keeling was charged with the explosives side of it, and I was charged with shopbreaking and breaking and entry. Keeling was pleading guilty, which left me nowhere. His girlfriend pleaded guilty to receiving stolen property. I was kept in custody for another week without bail. Then I was granted bail, and finally I was given three years' probation.

But that wasn't quite the end of the story. Two officers involved in arresting me turned up at the house not long afterwards in a grey Rover. The heavy one was an out-and-out bruiser who was as bent as a nine bob note, as was publicly proven later.

They said to me, 'We want you to go and pick up some insurance money.'

What happens when property is stolen is that the insurance companies pay a reward when there's a conviction. It's supposed to be paid to the person who gave information to the police, leading to the conviction. In this case I committed the crime, the two officers solved it and now they were putting me up as a beneficiary so I would sign for the money. Then I was expected to hand it over to them.

I didn't know what was going on at the time. I just went with them to the insurance claims building off Albert Embankment and received an envelope with money in it, which the policemen took off me. They couldn't claim for it because they weren't allowed to. They were supposed to give it to the person who put them on to the recovery of the property, but it ended up in their pockets. That's how naive I was in those days. I didn't realise what was happening until it was over.

Just before they left me, they said: 'Thank you very much for your help. You got *your* result in court. . . .'

And so I walked away from the whole episode a wiser man, at least as far as the law was concerned.

Life carried on as normal with the rackets and the clip joints. I was running around in my own Zephyr, I was always dressed smartly and I was never short of a few bob, but my parents never asked any questions and I never felt that I had to explain where I got my money from.

My mother and father were straight people. My brothers and I, on the other hand, had our fingers in the pie. If my mother had known we were giving her money gained from crime, she wouldn't have wanted it. Yet she wasn't a fool. She saw the type of people we were mixing with, she saw that money was coming into the house and she knew that we were up to no good in some way. But she just never said anything about it because I feel, deep down, she didn't want to know.

I think my Dad knew a little bit of what was going on but, like any father, would tend to ignore it until we brought the problem home. He'd voice his opinions, especially if he didn't like someone in our scene, and we'd argue with him, but at the end of the day we respected and listened to him.

But by and large he wasn't a man to interfere. His sons were six feet tall, looking for trouble all the time, fearing no one. Because of his lack of English he didn't understand a lot of it. But he understood it when we got into trouble, and if trouble came, he was there regardless of what. We were his sons and that was it. He was very, very proud of us. Same with my mother. She believed that her boys were being singled out by the police, that there was a vendetta going on about getting Chris put away, and she lost a lot of respect for authority.

My mother and father were people who would help anybody. Sometimes it would involve criminals. If Chris had been in a fight with a couple of his pals, my mother was the first to dress their wounds. I have never known my parents refuse anybody a cup of tea and a meal. They were as good an influence as they could possibly be under the circumstances, and we brought them a lot of heartbreak. Yes, we did that. And there was more of it to come.

CHAPTER FOUR

CASHING IN
ON CHAOS

I was nineteen when my brother Jimmy went to work at a refrigeration depot which had opened about a hundred yards from where we lived in Queensbridge Road. It was owned by a man called Carlo Gatti, who was known as the Ice King of the East End. He had originally made his money selling ice to fish stalls and shops. The depot was purpose-built and it contained four massive stores, each set at a different temperature. If you had turkey for Christmas from his deep freeze, you could bet your life it was seven years old. Meat traders from all over London used to store their goods at the depot, and various frozen-food firms had contracts to put their fish and pies and other foods in there.

Jimmy and a couple of his mates were taken on as porters, and he said to me one day, 'Why don't you go over there and get a job?' So I did. And before long we had about nine of our pals working with us. We used to have to come to work with donkey jackets, thick trousers and socks, steel-capped boots, hats and gloves because it was so cold in there. But we were on to a good thing. We were stealing meat, topsides, silversides, steaks . . . half the stock was disappearing, and we were earning bundles.

Jimmy and I had the power in the workforce. If there were any problems in the firm, Jim the manager and Pete the assistant manager would come to us and we'd sort it out. Inevitably we'd cause trouble every now and again; so they had further reason to ask for help, and we would end up getting more out of them. One day one of the lorry drivers from Smithfield Meat Market pulled in and asked, 'Are you organised in here?'.

I said, 'What do you mean, organised?'

'Union,' he said.

Once you're in with the Meat Market, you've got a job for life. So of course we were very interested.

He said, 'If I talk to one of our boys, perhaps we can enlighten you on how to get a union here: Any problems, we can back you.'

Jim and Pete got to hear that the union was becoming very interested in this cold store, and they didn't like it. As things stood, the management could pay lower wages and sack the staff, and they could continue hiring out storage space to frozen-food companies, which would be in contravention of the union rules: the Meat Market handled meat, and meat alone.

We appointed a bloke called Ted to be our union official, the puppet who did what we told him, and a few days later the same driver came to see us. He said, 'You know the Meat Market have been trying to get this place in the union since it opened, but we won't go in there while it's handling frozen food and all that. Go away and think about it. . . .'

The prize was a Meat Market ticket. Ten of us were strong for the union, and six, led by a half-gypsy called Spike, were against it. We called a meeting, at which I said: 'We're on strike, call the management in and tell them we want to join the union.' We had already told this lorry driver we intended to come out, and the Meat Market had trucks parked up and down Queensbridge Road. We set up a picket line straightaway – me, Jimmy and the boys, and

Leon too. A union representative gave Carlo Gatti the message: 'The boys are definitely not going back. Not a lorry is going to pass the picket.'

Gatti wasn't giving in. He thought that he could beat the unions, but he was a doomed man. The six employees who were against the strike were just standing around doing nothing. Four of them were told what would happen to them if they went in there again, and immediately left their jobs. Spike and his brother were not so easily intimidated, but after we bashed them up they left too.

We had support from everywhere. No lorries attempted to cross the picket lines, except for a few frozen-food firm vehicles. We approached them, threatened the drivers and punctured the tyres. Other than that, we didn't take a lot of notice of them. They had no power anyway. The strike lasted for five months, during which time the Meat Market was having a whip-round for us, plus we were nicking food from the cold store.

It all ended up with us getting our tickets into the Meat Market, so Jimmy, Leon, Timmy Reynolds, Ted and I and a couple of others left the depot and started work at Smithfield. We left Carlo Gatti to pick up the pieces of a completely ruined firm. He lost all his contracts, and the strike sent him virtually bankrupt.

It was during our time at the Meat Market that we became involved in the Oswald Mosley riots in London. We were approached by a friend of ours who was a minder at a dancehall in Dalston and also a Meat Market man. He was very friendly with Mosley; a Nazi who was notorious for his anti-Semitic rants and the violent confrontations they provoked with members of the Jewish community. This bloke said to us one day, 'You know the area really well. Mosley wants to do a bit of talking in Dalston. You could have a few mates up there to create a fracas while he's talking.'

Mosley was a guaranteed crowd-puller, and he'd have heavies

scattered throughout the gatherings to get everyone going. His aim was to attract publicity.

Next thing, we were in Dalston Junction with the Meat Market boys in a crowd of about a thousand; there were riots going on, mass fights with all sorts of weapons, and Mosley was on the news. We weren't in it for anything other than the money. On that occasion, and on several others afterwards, we were getting £50 a time to be out there Jew-baiting. There's a lot of money in racial issues. Mosley was never short of a bob or two, and he always found money to throw around.

I have never, ever liked what they did, the Nazis. Anybody who could approve of the terrible things they were responsible for has got to be sick in the mind. It just didn't occur to us at the time that by being at the rallies we were supporting them. To us it was just a few quid. We treated these people purely on a financial basis – we were in it for what we could get out of it.

Jimmy and I and our friend Davy Sadler were also picking up a bit of cash for going on Nazi manoeuvres which were organised by Mosley's right-hand man, Colin Jordan. These often took place in Dorset, sometimes on the edge of Salisbury Plain. Occasionally, he'd have his fifty or sixty men marching around Dartmoor.

We got into this by accident; through Davy Sadler. He was a giant, about six feet seven, though his father Jimmy was a midget of four feet ten. We used to go round to his flat in Hoxton to play cards; we'd all be sitting there gambling while his father, this midget, would be running round getting teas and drinks.

A fanatical SS lover, Davy used to collect uniforms. You very rarely came across a genuine Gestapo or German uniform; if you did, it was a collector's item. His bedroom was covered in SS flags, and he had dummies dressed in all these Gestapo uniforms. He had machine-guns and pistols in there too. One day, he dressed himself up and went marching up and down the heavily Jewish area of Stamford Hill wearing the uniform, the boots, the lot.

Davy organised a holiday for me, Terry Smith and the Venables brothers down in Devon. When we got there, we were each given a .303 rifle, old army issue. He said, 'We're going for training.'

I said, 'I thought we'd come down here for a holiday.'

We stayed for a week, during which time we shot a cow in a field. Stories about the manoeuvres began to appear in the papers, so we disappeared and came back to London. Despite the fact that he lived, and really believed in himself, as a Nazi, I always saw Davy Sadler as a useful person to have around – 'We can always do with one of those.'

After this period, my Jimmy dropped out of things completely – just retreated into the background. He'd come out occasionally, socialising, or to offer brotherly support, but we never involved him in anything again. He went into legitimate business. Had he not, he would have wound up the same as us. By this time he'd met his wife-to-be, a Hoxton girl called Carol, who married him in 1963.

However, before that wedding there was another one: mine. I hadn't yet turned twenty when Pat informed me that she was expecting a baby, so we decided to get married. It delighted my parents, but I didn't like the idea of becoming a father one bit. It was a responsibility, and at that time I had no sense of responsibility.

We were married in the register office at Shoreditch Town Hall on 23 August 1962. Leon was the best man; Chris was still away on his Corrective Training. I wore a blue serge suit, white shirt, blue tie and black shoes. I remember buying Pat a nice dress and matching coat in beige.

I thought the whole thing was a big joke – I remember bursting out laughing when I took the marriage vows. Pat took it all rather seriously, but my view at that time was, 'If it keeps her happy, don't worry about it.' We got in the car and drove home after the ceremony, and my mother was crying, but that afternoon I went out as usual. Pat and I went out to the dogs in the evening, and then for a meal, with Leon and June: I won £800 at the racetrack, so that was a nice little start for us.

It was only later that the whole significance of the day occurred to me. I thought, 'God almighty, I'm a married man and I'm only twenty!' But being married didn't mean that everything had to stop. My brothers and I always tended to do what we wanted anyway, and I carried on going out and about with my mates.

I saw some pressure at home with Pat, though. We needed somewhere on our own, especially with the baby coming. Leon was living in a house in Blythe Street, and he introduced me to the landlord. Pat and I moved into number 22, the top flat next door, and Jimmy and Carol eventually took the flat above Leon. Nicky stayed at home in Queensbridge Road until he was nineteen, when he moved in with his girlfriend, Cathy Reilly, a Bethnal Green girl.

My daughter Karen Lee came along on 13 October 1962; she was born in Bethnal Green Hospital at five past midnight on a Tuesday morning. I'd been on the phone all Monday night trying to find out what was happening. When I found out that Pat had had a 71/21b baby girl, I rushed over with my mother to see her.

I felt absolutely great. It's yours, and nothing can ever take that away from you.

When we brought the baby home, my mother wouldn't let her out of her arms. *Now* she had a daughter, the first girl born to the family. And as the weeks went past, she took the baby over; my Mum almost brought her up. Everybody was thrilled about it. Leon and Nicky were always making a fuss of her, and she was spoilt rotten. She was a beautiful baby, my pride and joy, and this was a very happy period for me.

The happiness, unfortunately, came to a standstill for a while when Karen was a year old.

On 6 October 1963 I was sent away for my first term of imprisonment. I'd been arrested one night after going out drinking with Timmy Reynolds and two other blokes called Frankie Hawkey and Jimmy Cribbin. We were all walking along Bethnal Green Road, and as we turned into the top of Vallance Road we went down an alley to pass water. Two constables came along and accused us of attempting to steal a motor car. We were taken to Bethnal Green police station and charged with that offence. I was put up as the ringleader and kept in custody, while the other three were bailed out.

At that time there was a CID officer at the station who was determined to make life as miserable as possible for my brothers and me. His name was Sergeant Gray. If he could nick one or other of us it was great, so he was in his glory when they got me. Next thing, my Jimmy, Leon and a few of our pals turned up at the police station and Jimmy threatened to bash him up.

The arrest was on a Saturday night. On the Monday morning, Thames magistrates committed us for trial to the London Sessions, and heard our applications for bail. Timmy, Frankie and Jimmy Cribbin had no problems, but the police objected strongly to releasing me and said they believed I'd been interfering with witnesses. However, the magistrate, Donald London, said: 'I don't see how you can grant bail to three men and keep one in custody.' So we were all granted bail, and subsequently stood trial. Jimmy Cribbin and I were sentenced to eighteen months' imprisonment, Frankie was sent to a Corrective Training centre and Timmy received a Borstal sentence.

I found myself first of all in Wormwood Scrubs, but within a few weeks was moved to Eastchurch prison on the Isle of Sheppey. There was a lot of trouble in Eastchurch. A laundry burned down in mysterious circumstances, so they moved about thirty of us out to different prisons. I had nothing to do with the laundry, but I wanted to get out of Eastchurch anyway – it was like a military camp. I went to Canterbury and from there was transferred to Stafford. Several months into my sentence, another con in Stafford asked me: 'What are you nicked for?'

I answered, 'Stealing a car. But I don't know how I could have stolen a car that I didn't even move.'

He was like a barrack-room lawyer, this guy. He said: 'You cannot be convicted of stealing something you haven't taken.' I put in an appeal, and lo and behold, the Court of Appeal set me free over a misdirection of the jury. I walked out of that court in June 1964 saying, 'Never again.' It was Derby Day. My Dad, Pat and Leon were there for me, and we went back to the East End together to my parents' home. I was thinking, 'That was easy enough to get out of.' In a way, it was like cocking a snook at the law.

Chris, in the meantime, had finished his CT and married Carol, a Liverpool girl who worked in public relations and was earning a good living. Like me, Chris was anything but a stay-at-home type, and I was getting around with him. We palled up with a man called Eric Mason, a well-known villain of the time.

Eric had just finished a seven down the Moor – seven years in Dartmoor – and as an old friend of the twins, he went to them for a little bit of help when he came out. Typically, they gave him suits, some money, all the rest of it. With two men called Kenny Bloom and Maurice King, he then went into partnership in a West End club called the Brown Derby in Kingly Street. It was a drinker and spieler, or gambling club.

I was in the Brown Derby one night with Chris, Eric and another villain called Davy Clare when Reggie came in about ten-handed. I saw Big Pat Connolly, Tommy The Bear Brown, Tommy Cowley, Teddy Smith, Albert Donaghue and a few others. All of a sudden there was an argument. One of the boys whacked a geezer who came in drunk. The twins didn't allow drunken behaviour around them. I remember that incident in particular because it was the night that Reggie came over to me and said, 'Come and see us soon, Tony, you and Chris – but be careful of him,' meaning Eric Mason.

I hadn't realised there was any bad feeling there. Apparently Eric had been running around sticking their name up – using it in front of a lot of people in the West End for his own advancement. The twins weren't too pleased about it, and were even less impressed with Eric after a dramatic turn of events in another West End nightspot.

Maurice King, in addition to his partnership with Eric and Kenny in the Brown Derby, owned a club called the Starlight in Oxford Street; he was also legitimately involved in the early careers of many of the sixties' pop singers and groups, including P. J. Proby, the Walker Brothers, Shirley Bassey, the Rocking Berries and Jackie Trent. Jackie, who went on to make a fortune with her husband Tony Hatch as his songwriting partner (composing the *Neighbours* TV theme tune, among other credits), started her rise to fame as a barmaid in the Starlight. Her first husband, Drew Harvey, was very friendly with Maurice.

At this time the Brown Derby was like a Kray club, but the Richardsons had started getting into the Starlight. Everyone was aware that trouble was brewing, particularly between the Krays and the Richardsons, over the balance of power in the West End, especially with regard to protection in the clubs and businesses. The area was divided up among three or four firms, with the twins taking the lion's share, but the Richardsons were expanding fast and people were treading on each other's toes.

One particular night, Erie was in the Starlight with Davy Clare, a man named Boot and Maurice King, who was behind the bar. Frankie Fraser, a notorious villain from south London, turned up for a drink with some of the Richardson firm, and an argument broke out between the two groups.

It all stemmed from an old Dartmoor sore: Eric had apparently taken the side of a Scottish firm against the Londoners in the prison, which caused a lot of bad feeling and was surprising, since Eric was a south Londoner himself. The argument in the Starlight suddenly went off, and Eric wound up getting the treatment. He was dragged out of the club and badly done with pitchforks and shovels, after which he was thrown out of a car outside a hospital in north London. The police called it a gangland warning.

No one was quite sure whether the Richardsons were behind it or not. Assumptions cause trouble, but feelings were running high and Chris and I were ready to make one with him – to take his side – against Frank and the Richardsons. Eric, for some reason, didn't want to know.

At this time we were very active, the nucleus of our little lot being Davy Clare, another villain called Peter Metcalfe, Chris and myself. Peter, Chris and I went to visit Eric in hospital. He was all patched up on his hands, his legs and his feet, and his head had been slashed. He'd been cut up quite a bit, in fact. We told him we wanted to do something about it, but he seemed very reluctant.

When he came out of hospital, the twins called him round to their house in Vallance Road, Bethnal Green, and asked him what he thought should be done. Again he said, 'Nothing.' I think Reggie and Ronnie were putting pressure on him because they were looking for a row with the other firm – 'They've had a go at one of ours.' Eric's attitude left a bad taste, and the twins lost a lot of respect for him.

Chris and I had already seen at first hand what certain members of the Richardsons were capable of doing, notably George Cornell, who was later shot dead by Ronnie Kray in the Blind Beggar pub. Earlier, during this period with Eric, we'd heard of a long firm which was being operated in a block of offices in Great Portland

Street. A long firm is an outwardly respectable company which will build up good contacts with its suppliers and then suddenly vanish with the stock and the takings, leaving only unpaid bills. We were introduced to the two fellas who were running this long firm, Manchester boys called Bill and Derek. The Richardsons were running an operation on the floor below: George Cornell was working out of there with a man called Don Giles.

They had approached Bill and Derek about hiring some cars out through their long firm. The two Manchester lads phoned a contract hire firm and arranged to have four cars delivered to the offices, while the invoice would be sent on. The cars were duly sent round but two were illegally parked, and the council impounded them without anyone knowing it. When Cornell and Giles went out and found the two cars missing, they thought Bill and Derek had had them over (conned them).

We went round to the offices, Chris, Eric Mason and I, only to discover that Cornell and Giles had got these two tied up. Cornell had a golf club and about twenty balls, and he was lobbing golf balls into one boy's mouth while Giles held his head. The lad had lost nearly all of his teeth. The other fella was on the floor with bits of paper stapled to his body. It was a nasty little business.

As we went in, Chris said, 'What the fucking hell's going on here? It's a liberty.' He then decided, 'We'll make a few phone calls here.'

We rang to find out if the cars had been put in the police pound, and the police said, 'Try the council compound.' The council confirmed they had the cars and for a fee would release them. Meanwhile, Bill and Derek were trussed up like chickens, black and blue, which made Cornell and Giles look a bit stupid. He was a stocky character, Cornell, and an arrogant man. His main pal was a bloke called Roy 'Little Legs' Hall. I met Roy in Hull prison in later years. While I was away with him and the rest of the Richardsons none of the outside troubles between us were mentioned, and no old wounds were brought up. Charlie Richardson, in fact, did most of his sentence with Chris and me.

But that was well into the future. For the present, my brother and I were looking at a new career as mobile criminals, the first of our kind in the country. And the key to it all was Eric Mason, who moved away to Blackpool after his fall-out with the twins.

CHAPTER FIVE

A TRIP
TO BLACKPOOL

I t was late summer 1964, and with my prison sentence well behind me I travelled to Liverpool with Chris and his wife for her sister's wedding. I wasn't really all that keen on going to the wedding, but I was hoping that we could combine it with a trip to see Eric Mason, who was living in that part of the world. He'd told Chris that he had it all his own way up there, and that there was a lot of opportunity. As it happened, we did pay a visit to Eric, but it was more than a social call: it lasted for six months, and it came about as a direct result of Chris bashing up all the in-laws at the wedding and turning the celebrations into a shambles.

All of the bride's family were football-mad, and fanatical Liverpool supporters. Chris was a Spurs man. Liverpool were playing at home on the afternoon of the wedding, and her relations all left the reception, which was held in a drinking club, and went to the football.

The reception was still going on when they came back, and they were all ready for a drink-up. Chris had a row with her father and her brothers over Spurs and Liverpool, and next thing all of them were going up in the air. We went back to the caravan site where the immediate family were to stay. Chris, his wife Carol, her brother and I were all expected to stay in this one caravan which was the size of a cloakroom. Chris said, 'I'm not staying in that.' And we went into Liverpool to try and find a hotel – but with no luck. It was then about eight o'clock at night.

We came back to the site and Chris towed the caravan into a take. The police were called, and we disappeared. We rang up Eric Mason, who said, 'Come over right away.'

Eric was living in Lytham St Annes, just outside Blackpool, in a road where singing and variety stars used to rent houses while they were doing the summer season in the seaside theatres. He was staying with the Clarke Brothers, who were tap dancers appearing at the Queen's Theatre, Blackpool. We arrived at the house to find that our neighbours were Dave Clark, Freddie and the Dreamers, the Bachelors and Stan Stanwick, who went on to appear in *Coronation Street*.

Peter Metcalfe flew up from London to join us. A bloke who had to do things in style, he was always immaculately dressed. At about five feet ten he was a tubby fella, clean-shaven with neatly trimmed mousy hair and Italian-type features. Peter was into karate.

The other member of our team, Davy Clare, was in Manchester on the run from the twins. There was a rumour going around at the time that he had been asked to take some action in London against George Cornell, who was becoming increasingly troublesome, but hadn't done so. It was also said that before he went into hiding Davy Clare went to see his bank manager, handed him a letter and said: 'If anything happens to me, you're to give this to Scotland Yard.' Chris and I later found Davy in Manchester accidentally, when we bumped into his girl in a casino one night. We went round to where he was living. He must have seen us coming because he had his head in a gas oven and he was saying, 'I know it's all over, you've come to get me.'

Chris said, 'Don't be stupid. Get up. If I was you, I'd go and see the twins and straighten it up with them.'

But at the time we arrived in Blackpool we had no idea where Davy Clare had gone, and we were anticipating nothing more than a couple of nights out with Eric Mason. He was a stocky chap, Eric, with fair hair cut in a similar style to Reggie Kray's. He was known as a hard man, he had a great knowledge of boxing, and he knew everyone who was worth knowing in our circles, but what he wanted more than anything in his life was stardom.

He introduced Peter, Chris and me to the Clarke Brothers and invited us to see their show the next night. We went on from there to a nightclub called the Embassy, where we were given the best table. Sitting with us were the Clarke Brothers, the Bachelors, a singer called Twinkle and Bill Heaney, the owner of the club. They gave us the full treatment, and even put the spotlight on us. It hadn't taken long to get around that we were East End gangsters up from London courtesy of the Krays, which was totally untrue. But Eric was trading on the twins' name, just as he had in London, and was having a good life, thanks to them.

I saw an opportunity, so a couple of nights later I approached this Bill Heaney and asked him to lend me a couple of grand. I said, 'We need it until our expenses come up.' It's a way of asking for protection money without using the threat.

We had no trouble. He said, 'You want it now?' He put two grand in cash in a bag and slipped it on to my lap.

Not long afterwards, he called me into the foyer and introduced me to a very pretty woman he was obviously having an affair with. He pulled out a .22 pistol and asked, 'What do you think of that, Tony?'

I said, 'What are you trying to do – impress me, Bill?' I took it off him, put it in my pocket and told Chris. It was Heaney's little test. He then realised we were into it 100 per cent.

It reached the stage when we were going there every night, and every night we were at his throat for more money – a grand here, £1,500 there. Chris, Eric, Peter and I used to cut it up between us. Dominic Pye, the doorman, all dressed up in his gold braid uniform and top hat, used to salute us when we walked in. We had to straighten a few things out, though, like the time the head waiter, Jimmy, handed me a bill. I said, 'Don't embarrass us,' and he never troubled us with the bill again.

On a later occasion, Jimmy made a proposition. He said: 'If you look after me, I'll tell you what's going on with the law if they start to make inquiries, or if I hear of anything like that coming up.'

It looked to us as though we were on to a good thing in Blackpool. We could get anything we wanted and were having the time of our lives – we were getting five-star treatment everywhere we went. We were also into one or two other clubs, a bank manager and other leading citizens from the area. The fact that we were so-called underworld characters attracted a lot of business people – straight people who loved the image of it around them. They wanted to say they knew us. Bank managers, company executives, show business personalities, sportsmen – they all loved that mystique, that danger, and the strange prestige they thought it gave them to be seen associating with us.

The bank manager, when we met him, was rotten drunk. He said, 'Look, if you're thinking of investing money up here, come and see me.' If I wanted a loan, who better than the bank manager? We got about four grand out of him, and he wasn't going to get it back. For his part, he could come out and be entertained and sit at our table. No doubt he was a hen-pecked husband.

But although we were spreading our wings in Blackpool, working our way into various different businesses, we still used the Embassy as our base. Heaney was making it worth our while. One day I had to go down to London immediately. At a suggestion from Chris, Bill

Heaney offered to lend me his black E-Type Jag. I told him, 'I might as well have the log book too.' I said it jokingly, but at the same time I didn't mean it as a joke. He went to the safe and gave me the log book. Obviously, by doing that he was giving me his car.

Eric Mason was continuing to drop the twins' name, more than we knew at the time. He was always careful to hide it away around us, but we caught him out when someone said to me one day in the club, 'He's the twins' right-hand man,' pointing at Eric. 'What are you talking about?' I said. It turned out that this was what Mason had been telling people.

He loved to be the centre of attention. In London, he'd had a flat with a woman dancer in Jermyn Street. The way he felt about her was neither here nor there: it was a relationship of convenience. He just liked the image of having a young girl around him. He only ever used to wear one suit, the serge one Reggie had given him when he came out of the nick. One day my brother found him putting black polish on the patches where it had gone shiny. And it was a blue suit! Then there was the time we went out to spend a couple of grand Bill Heaney had given us at a nice men's store. Chris and I were looking at the £75 shirts, and Eric was at the sale counter where they were getting rid of three for £1. Yet, despite all this, he always looked presentable.

Chris and I went to another club one evening at the invitation of a man called Mitzi Walsh who had an involvement in it. He was from a family of brothers who were very big in Blackpool at the time and who made us welcome there. We arrived there to find Eric holding court. He had all the dancers from the Blackpool Tower sitting round him, and he was ordering champagne as if it was going out of fashion. He had a £20,000 cheque with him, made out to himself, and he was waving it about, getting all the credit in the world. He had the bank manager with him too – anyone who was anyone in Blackpool. . . . But he knew and I knew he hadn't got a tenner on him.

He threw the cheque on the table: 'Where can I cash £20,000 at twelve o'clock at night?'

Mitzi asked me, 'Can he meet the bill?'

I didn't know what to say. I looked at him as much as to say, 'Don't ask me.'

Chris, Peter and I enjoyed all the hospitality in the world at this club, like every other, but people were starting to become suspicious of Eric over his so-called connections with the twins. Yet, because there was an element of doubt, Mitzi couldn't go against Eric. He had to write the money off, and it did cause a bit of aggro.

Meanwhile, Eric was becoming more and more ridiculous in his bid to grab the limelight. Take the night we were invited to go and watch Gerry and the Pacemakers at the Queen's Theatre. We got VIP seats right at the front. Eric made sure that he had the spotlight put on him, and he was introduced as 'Eric Mason, that well-known club-owner from London.' On another occasion, we went to a Tom Jones concert. When the singer reached the request spot, Eric shouted out, 'Tom, what about my number?' as if he knew him. He'd never even met him.

He then went over to Gordon Mills, Tom Jones' manager, and said: 'What's up with Tom tonight? He didn't seem to recognise me.'

Mills looked at him vacantly and said, 'What are you talking about?'

There was yet more embarrassment, thanks to Eric, when he, Chris and I accepted an invitation to the Grand Order of Water Rats' charity ball at Pontin's Holiday Camp, just off the Golden Mile. We each had a ticket, but Eric brought along a girlfriend who hadn't. Most people wouldn't get through the doors without a ticket, but Chris decided just to walk straight in. We plonked ourselves down at the finest table in the room.

A little geezer came over and said, 'Excuse me, but you're sitting at our table.'

Eric retorted, 'If you don't fuck off, you won't be fit to sit at a table.'

Without further ado, the bouncers came running over. They tried to be polite about it – 'Look, boys, the management are prepared to make up another table for you.'

But Eric was insistent. He took the place cards which were sitting in front of us, crossed out the names, including Eric Morecambe and Sophie Tucker, and put ours on them. Chris and I had to force him to sit down and then move to our own table with us when it was ready.

We decided it was time to keep out of Eric's way – it wasn't good to have him around us. He was a likeable character, but he caused himself a lot of problems. He had a million pounds, but he didn't have a penny; he was a poor millionaire. He liked the style, but he couldn't back it up with what he had. Eric tried to be friendly with everyone, which put him in a very difficult position. He was a worrier; never without something on his mind. He was continuing to crack the twins' name around all over the place, and it was getting back to them. It was common knowledge in London by now.

I decided it was time to go to Vallance Road to have a talk with Reggie and Ronnie. I asked them, 'How do you feel about Eric?'

They told me to tell him that they wanted him to come down to London as soon as possible.

I phoned Chris and told him the twins wanted to see Eric. Eric himself was very wary about it, so Chris agreed to come down with him. The instructions were that he was to visit them on his own. Give him his due, he did keep the appointment, and Chris and I waited for him in the Cornwallis pub at the top of Vallance Road. He came back a bit shaken. They'd had a go at him for sticking their name up.

I went round to see the twins the next night on my own. They said, 'Anything untoward goes on up there, let us know, or anything that we might be interested in getting into.'

I told them about the club, but they were busy with other things and weren't really that concerned about it.

When we got back up to Blackpool, we had a talk. Eric had nothing without the twins. Whatever he had, he'd built it all because of them. And now that we'd stopped being seen around with him, he had zero form, no weight. He decided to move to Nottingham where he would later meet a woman club owner. Chris, Peter and I stayed on in Blackpool.

But we had problems ahead. One afternoon when I was passing by the Embassy, Jimmy, the head waiter, waved me in. He invited me to sit down and have a drink, and then said, 'Look, the police have been in here asking for glasses that you, Chris and Peter have used – glasses with your fingerprints on them.'

I went back and told Chris and we had a row about it. I said, 'I think we'd better make a move out of here. Things are getting a little bit hot.'

He said, 'You're paranoid.'

Then the CID chief, Superintendent Leach, started politely putting it about that it would be in our best interests to leave town. But you've got to bear in mind that we were having a marvellous time up there: we were able to do just what we wanted. So we decided to move into new accommodation for the time being.

We met two bouncers who invited us to the club they worked at on the Golden Mile. We got chatting, and they said we could stay in their flat, which was also on the Golden Mile, any time we wanted. But what we wanted was their flat without them in it. We arranged to go and stay there. We got Peter Metcalfe to drive the car round into the back courtyard where there was parking space. Peter was carrying a huge bundle containing three shotguns, an axe, two swords and other weapons. He called them down to give him a hand upstairs with the stuff, knowing full well that they'd look to see what was inside the bundle. They left there and then, these bouncers, and decided never to come back. And we just took the flat over. Later, we had the cheek to go to their club, have a drink with them and ask how they were doing.

And as for Bill Heaney we took everything he had; we took him something terrible. He wound up sweeping the streets: We were active and we had to be that way.

Unfortunately, before long people began taking a really big interest in us. Obviously, the twins' name was still getting mentioned a lot around the town. One of the Nash brothers, our old friend Johnny, came up, and he was inviting all the boys from London to Blackpool. We'd been there for five or six months, trading on our reputations, so it had to come to general attention sooner or later. Trevor Aspinall of *The People* started making enquiries about criminal activities in the area, and one Sunday morning Chris came screaming into the bedroom. There, in the paper, was an article about lawlessness in Blackpool, and about London gangsters taking complete control of the town..

Our policy was to keep one step ahead and, bearing that in mind, we decided it was time to leave Blackpool. Our plan was to move to other cities, to Liverpool, Manchester, Birmingham, Stoke-on-Trent, Leicester, Cardiff, Bristol and Plymouth, and do the same thing all over again in each one. In other words, take them over.

We'd already got into quite a few places, including Liverpool, Manchester and Preston, which were next door to Blackpool. Normally we'd know people in every town we went to, through prison or reputation. Chris would go in and do the groundwork, making the contacts and gathering information, and I'd follow on, sometimes with my Nicky. Obviously violence did come into it along the way. If it was necessary we would take out the local villain, make him the target and belittle him. That pulled everything into line. You don't start at the bottom when you can start at the top. It didn't often come to that, though. We were known for our association with the criminals of London; who was going to threaten us?

It was Chris and I who came up with the original idea of getting out of London, making money across the country. We were very mobile. Nowhere was too far to go for a pound note. And up to the point where we started taking off in Blackpool, it was an independent operation. However, we soon began to realise the potential advantages of having the twins' backing. We wanted their name. At that time, a lot of people were going round England sticking their name up without permission, with the result that they were being associated with crimes they knew nothing about. This was a sore point with them. They saw it as a liberty, and became very touchy about who used their name and in what way. But they gave Chris and me their official blessing. Reggie said, 'Put us up, but put us in.' By this, of course, he meant that we could use the Kray name for a price.

So with these words ringing in our ears, we exploited it to the full. That name was worth money on its own. It opened doors for us wherever we went, and did us vast favours. From then on, the twins got a cut of most of the stuff we were doing. Not all of it – they had enough coming in as it was – but we never did anything behind their backs. We always went to them with news of what was going on. Sometimes they'd say, 'We're not really interested, but go ahead, do it.' At other times, they'd want to know the ins and outs of it and want some cash, or ask us to carry out some justice if they had the hump with someone. It was called Kray justice, and it was more feared than the lawful variety.

Things began to move very quickly for us. But my own involvement came to an abrupt halt when I was sent back to prison in the New Year of 1965.

It all began in a Wimpy bar in my old stamping-ground of Dalston Junction. I was on one of my visits back to London from Blackpool and I was sitting at a table by the window, keeping observation on a bank for future reference. Another man was with me who shall remain nameless because he wasn't caught. We had our eye on this Wimpy bar, too, because the takings in there must have been coming up to £1,000 a day, and we decided to do it there and then.

So we went downstairs into the office. I got the manager by the scruff of the neck, put a knife up to his throat and asked him to open the safe, which he did. I then pulled a gun on him, and when he gave us the money we disappeared. But the paper seller on the corner recognised me. I was well known in the area through my dealings with the amusement arcades, Lou's Café and Chez Don, and this man decided to point the finger. Even more to my surprise, he couldn't be straightened out.

I went to see him and I asked: 'Are you going to give evidence against me?'

He went, 'No.'

I said, 'Good-day.'

The next thing I knew, I was being warned about approaching witnesses by the police, who came to pick me up at my parents' house. Despite the fact that I was married and living with my wife and daughter at Blythe Street, when I wasn't away earning money in Blackpool, I always considered Betford House to be my home; and, like all of my brothers, I spent a lot of time there. Detective Sergeant Robeson, who later claimed he nicked the Great Train Robber Bruce Reynolds, and Detective Sergeant Terence Day took me to Dalston Lane police station, where I was charged.

The trial went on for five days at the Old Bailey. I expected to be acquitted, because the case against me was very weak. The witnesses – the Wimpy bar manager, his assistant and the paper seller – were contradicting each other all the way through, and the police officers' notebooks didn't match. One claimed that he had made his notes at the same time as the other, but his colleague said something completely different. But unfortunately I wasn't very well represented in court: my QC wasn't putting the case over as I would have wanted.

I was in front of Judge Maud, who was known as the Lagging Judge – he was always giving out three-year sentences, as if that was all he knew. I suppose I should have counted myself lucky: on 29 January 1965 I was sentenced to thirty months' imprisonment for assault with intent to rob and for being armed with an offensive weapon with intent to rob. I was acquitted of having an armament in my possession.

While my case was going on I was sharing an Old Bailey cell with Frankie Shea, Reggie Kray's brother-in-law. He was being tried for robbery with John McVicar and Roy Nash in one of the other courtrooms in the building. On the day of my sentence, I spent some time in the cell with Frank while the jury was out considering his case. I remember giving him my dinner because I thought he was going to go down. He was acquitted. And I wasn't.

I was taken back to Wandsworth prison in a van with McVicar and Nash, who had been sentenced to eight and five years respectively.. I thought back to the last time I had seen McVicar, when I was walking along Essex Road in the Angel with Chris. We saw Frankie Shea there too. Frank waved us on, and we knew immediately that something was up and we should get out of the way. It turned out they were in a robbery – the same crime which brought them to the Old Bailey where, unfortunately for all of us, I saw them again.

John McVicar, at that time, was in his prime. He was about twenty-three or twenty-four and was probably one of the top men of his profession. Strictly a robber, he had built up a solid reputation and was very well liked among the criminal fraternity.

But he's lost a lot of respect lately over his writings and articles. He sees himself as a professor of criminology, talking about prison reforms and pointing the finger at other people about their past. Considering the things he was involved in and the sentence he served, I believe he should keep his views to himself. He will be remembered more than anything for being one of the hard men of London and one of Britain's most wanted villains, after his escape from Durham prison and the film *McVicar* which documented it. If I was a member of the public, I would view John McVicar not as a campaigner but as an ex-criminal.

There were quite a few cons in Wandsworth at that time who were, or would later be, 'celebrity' criminals. One was Ronnie Biggs, a likeable fella who always had a smile on his face. Everyone used to point at him – 'That's Ronnie Biggs' – and I think he liked that little bit of glamour within the prison. But I don't think he expected for one minute to become what he is today. I was pleased – everybody was pleased – when he escaped. I'd only like to see him able to return to freedom in England.

But the odd character apart, Wandsworth prison was the most doomy, gloomy place I could imagine being in. I was devastated enough that I'd been convicted, but this made the misery worse. Wandsworth was a law unto itself. There's no other nick in the country like it.

I immediately lodged an appeal, and while an appeal is running you're still technically innocent. But the authorities failed to take note that I was an appellant. In the meantime, I was transferred to Chelmsford prison, and further charges were brought against me. It was said that I was in breach of the probation order imposed after the Ilminster Co-op case because I had broken the law again. But I could not have been said at that point to have broken the law again, because I was to all intents and purposes an innocent man until the Court of Appeal decided I wasn't. But this didn't occur to me at the time. I was sent back to Bristol on the breach of probation order charges and sentenced at Wells Quarter Sessions to two concurrent sentences of six months, added to the end of my two and a half years. This made three years altogether.

I stayed in Bristol to carry on with my sentence and did my best not to think about the extra time I'd been given. Then one day I came across another barrack-room lawyer. I was in the prison tailor shop when a con said: 'They can't do that. They can't sentence you for breaking a probation order through criminal activity when you haven't finished going through the channels of appeal.' They'd jumped the gun. So I decided to petition the Home Office about it, petitions being the one form of protest always available to the prisoner.

If you don't get an answer within forty-two days, you can try to expedite it on Governor's applications. My petition was in for seven months, and I kept going down to the Governor's office, trying to get it hurried up. I was told it was with the Home Office's legal department. Eventually I was called up and told I'd been given six months off my sentence over this mistake. The original appeal, over the thirty months, was chucked out because the authorities felt I had no grounds for it.

It was while I was in Bristol that my mother died. It happened on a Friday the thirteenth, in August 1965. I woke up that morning and – I don't know why – I put on a jacket and tie, and had a shave. I was walking round on exercise with my mate Johnny Peebles, a Portsmouth boy, and I said to him, 'I can feel there's something wrong at home.' Just before midday, I was working in the prison tailor's shop when I was called out by a screw, taken into the main wing and shown into the Governor's office. He said, 'I have some very bad news for you, Lambrianou. Your mother has passed away.'

There had never been any bad news in my family before, and I just didn't believe it. Without realising what I was doing, I dived across the table. I just wanted to grab hold of the Governor and batter him.

We'd all lived around my mother, the five of us, and all of a sudden she was gone. End of. It was a terrible blow. She had died in Newcastle, in the house she was born in, the first time in thirty years that she'd been back to it. For three years she'd lived on half a lung and never known it. She was a heavy smoker, one after the other, and her lungs had burnt out. And she worried a lot. She'd had a bleeding hard life.

The night before she went to Newcastle Chris had a blazing row with her, and I always used to blame him in a little way for what happened. Throughout our long years away for the McVitie murder, I would always bring it up when we were arguing: 'I blame you for the old lady.' It was the one thing that would shut him up. I suppose, in my way, I was looking for some excuse for my mother's death.

Today we never, ever talk about my mother. We all feel a lot, but she's never mentioned. She was a very basic, pure woman. What life had she had with the five of us? And when we were eventually in a position to do something for her, she wasn't there. Chris and I were to make a lot of money from our criminal dealings, which would have made her life much easier; she would have gone short of nothing. But time didn't give us the privilege of being able to do it for her, and that's one of the biggest regrets of my life. Not a day goes by that I don't think about her.

My mother was going to be buried in Newcastle the following Monday. I was told at lunchtime that day that, because of my connections with the London underworld, I would not be permitted to attend. The authorities believed my brothers would make sure I didn't return to prison. They denied me the dignity of being with my brothers at my mother's funeral.

I was released in December 1966, having served almost two years. I would have been out before that if I hadn't lost some remission for bad behaviour. I lost fourteen days for illegal bookmaking in the prison, and I had to serve two weeks without privileges and without associated labour – that is, labour involving the other men. For three days of this time I was on a number one diet, which was literally bread and water – a punishment that no longer exists. A bloke called Billy Thomas was also down the block – the punishment or isolation cells – for cutting another geezer in one of the workshops. He was on a normal diet; and he used to leave boiled eggs and other bits of food for me wrapped in paper behind the toilet.

While I was away, Chris was out and about all over the country, getting up to all sorts of villainy. He would check into London from time to time, but he still preferred to be out of it. That's how he acquired the nickname of London Chris. By the time I came out of prison he had set up a base in Birmingham, but I decided to stay in London and go to Chris, if and when he needed me.

It turned out that I was to spend a lot of time up in Birmingham with him throughout 1967, while together we scaled dramatic heights of criminal activity. But I was also around the East End for long enough to become heavily involved with the Kray firm.

CHAPTER SIX

GETTING DOWN TO BUSINESS

I came out of prison to discover that my brother Chris had been having an affair with the girlfriend, Barbara, of a well-known villain called SP. Chris didn't know SP, but when he finally did meet him it was in a violent confrontation which would put the Lambrianou brothers even more firmly on the map.

On his periodic visits to London Chris was active in the heavy game, which is how we referred to armed robbery, and was working on and off with a well-known firm at the Angel in north London. They were known as the Odds and Sods, but they were good at what they did.

One day, after he'd been on a successful bit of work with them, he went round to Barbara's house. She knew he'd had it off with a nice few quid, and she said to him: 'Where's my fur coat, Chris?'

'What do you think I am, a fucking idiot?' was his reply. You don't start flashing money around the minute a job is done. They had a row and Chris drove off.

He went back to pick her up that evening, but in the meantime she'd been in touch with her boyfriend. What she said I don't know. She'd obviously wound him up against Chris, because when he pulled up in his car SP was waiting. He put a blade up against my brother's face, and he said: 'If you come round here again, I'll open you up.'

Chris said, 'You'd better do it now, because if you don't I'm coming back to shoot you.'

SP said, 'Yeah, I've heard it all before.' He may well have done, but he didn't know my brother. Chris was definitely coming back.

He went home, filled up a .38 revolver, a Smith & Wesson police special, and returned to the girlfriend's house. As he pulled up, SP came walking down the front path.

My brother said, 'If you feel that much about her, you can have her. She ain't worth the aggro.'

With that, SP came at Chris with a knife and yelled, 'I warned you about coming here.'

Chris pulled out the .38 and shot him three times, once in the stomach, once in the chest and once in the thigh. He then tried to run over him in the car, but the kerb was too high to reverse over, and Chris couldn't hang around. People had heard the shots. He should have been dead, SP. He was nearly dead, but he did survive.

Three days after I was released from prison, I was in the Regency Club in Stoke Newington with Nicky and a friend called Paddy Dinnear. When I went downstairs for a drink I saw this bloke looking at me. I knew it was SP. I said to Nicky and Paddy, 'Watch my back,' and I went into the toilet. SP followed me in.

He said, 'You're Tony Lambrianou, aren't you? Your brother did this to me.' He lifted up his shirt and I saw these big holes. I said, 'I know all about it. You came unstuck once. Don't let it happen again, or this time we won't fuck about with you.'

I went back to my parents' house, and who was sitting there cleaning his guns but Chris. He used to sit indoors every night doing this. He'd oil them up and then bury them in the ground where the earth would keep them moist. It was a ritual called 'Oil it, bury it'.

I said, 'I saw a mate of yours tonight in the Regency.'

'Who was that?' Chris said.

'SP,' I replied.

Chris said, 'I've got something for him. I owe him something.' And he went out to find him and finish him off. But SP had left the Regency and Chris had no idea where he lived. SP escaped with his life that night.

The reaction to the whole episode in criminal circles was this: 'They're not mugs, those Lambrianous. They'll go all the way.' The twins, particularly, had an eye for people who could be useful to them, who could be good allies, and we fitted in. They started to take a lot more notice of us after that incident. It didn't take long for the story to get around, and people from all walks of life started approaching Chris – 'If we ever need a bit of help, can we rely on you?'

We were offered a lot of work. I was approached in the East End one day by a bloke called Mark. Somebody had taken a liberty with one of his brothers, and they weren't really strong enough to get back at them.

I said, 'Well, what do you want done?'

'I want this man's legs broken,' he answered.

I asked, 'How much are you prepared to pay?'

'I'll give you two grand,' he promised.

He gave me all the details, which I passed on to my pal Paddy Dinnear, telling him what was necessary. The man we were supposed to do lived in Loughton in Essex, just on the outskirts of London. We went out there and knocked on the door. The father opened it. Paddy said, 'Can I see your boy?'

Not only did Paddy do the son, he did the father and the sister as well. If I hadn't pulled him out of there, he would have killed them. I didn't want to see the woman hurt, so of course I stopped it. The trouble with some women is that they won't stay out of it. They jump into the middle of things, and they can be a nuisance.

My own experience of this was the day I stole a big brass till out of a shop in Roman Road. I had information that there would be around £2,500 in the bottom part of it where the paper money was. I went to the shop in a car with three other people I can't name, and we parked outside. I walked in and tried to pull the till off the counter, but it was bolted on. The driver stayed where he was in the car and the other two came running in to help me.

We had to demolish the counter to get at the till, and while we were doing that the women in the shop were pelting us with cans of peas and beans. I spent quite some time recuperating from the injuries I received.

Unfortunately, as we came out of the shop a young girl who was passing jumped on my back and tried to wrestle me to the ground. I wouldn't like to face her in the ring – I couldn't come out of the house for days because of the injuries she caused me. My mate tried to grab her by the hair and she turned and jumped on him. She had to be thrown to the ground.

We never wanted to see women getting involved in this sort of business, but Paddy Dinnear didn't even think about it. That day in Loughton, he was more than capable of killing the sister when she launched herself into the fray.

Paddy would use violence at the touch of a button. He was a man of very few words, but when it came to the action he was the man I always wanted there. I never stopped using him, and he never forgot us all the time we were away on the Kray convictions.

He was a boyhood friend of ours and later a bus driver who worked the 149 route from Liverpool Street to Edmonton. Often he flew into fits of temper. One day a cabbie tried to cut him up at Dalston Junction. He completely demolished the cab with his bus, he tried to kill the cabbie, and then he aimed the bus at a bus stop.

The bus inspector was terrified. Sadly, Paddy's brother Tommy committed suicide a few years ago, and I haven't seen Paddy since.

These were the sort of people I had around me in London at that time. My Nicky was always with me; he was very useful. We also had another five or six other reliable friends around us, plus the firm in general. I was going with the twins full whack and, at the same time, keeping busy with our interests out of London. We accidentally discovered a profitable way of combining the two, and on the basis of this we built up the most unusual public relations enterprise I've ever heard of.

It began when a car dealer in Birmingham approached Chris and said he would pay £2,000 for the opportunity to meet Reggie Kray. I contacted Tommy Cowley, a short, smart man with a red face and ginger hair, who was big on the business side of the Kray firm. He was an earner, always negotiating deals and involving himself in the protection; frauds and long firms rather than the villainous end of things. He wasn't a violent man, and he wouldn't have jumped into a fight. Certainly not.

Cowley rang back with a message from Reggie that we were to bring this car dealer down to London. In due course we introduced the man to Reggie. They shook hands and Reggie said, 'How are you getting on? Have a drink.' That was all there was to it. Yet the man was so impressed at having met Reggie Kray that he went away very happy and considered his two grand well spent. It was incredible.

We soon realised that there were criminals, club owners, all sorts of people in Birmingham and other towns who were willing to pay large sums of money to meet the twins. There was no reason why we shouldn't take their cash when it was offered. So we started bringing all these people to London to see Reggie and Ronnie. The fee would vary, depending on the circumstances. The clients would deal initially with Chris. He would contact me in Birmingham or London, depending on where I was, and I would get in touch with the twins. They would tell me where they were going to be on the night of the meeting: Only I knew. I would then meet the clients at another venue and take them on to where the twins were.

This was all good public relations for the twins, because it added to the strength of their reputation. The clients would go back to their home towns and circulate starstruck stories of their night out with the Krays. It was also good PR for Chris and me. These people would do our groundwork for us: they would make it known that we genuinely were with the twins, and it would carry by word of mouth, thus increasing our influence in whatever town they came from.

One day Chris phoned me in London and said, 'I want you to meet a couple of boys from Birmingham and introduce them to the twins.' They'd offered my brother £10,000.

I said, 'Bring them down.'

The money was split equally between Chris and me and Reggie and Ronnie.

The two men, who were car dealers, came to my father's house in Queensbridge Road. They parked a yellow E-Type Jag and an AC Cobra, which they'd bought while they were in London, outside the door. I asked if I could take a spin in the Cobra. They said, 'Be careful, it's a bit nippy.'

I didn't know what I was driving. I took it down Queensbridge Road; along Hackney Road and Cambridge Heath Road, across the Bethnal Green Road junction and Roman Road, driving along towards the Blind Beggar. As I came to the lights outside the Beggar, I changed gear and shot forward, right underneath a lorry. All the lorry driver felt was something just touching the underside of his vehicle. He jumped out of his cab and there was me sitting beneath the lorry in an AC Cobra, a car which would cost at least half a million pounds today.

I reversed the Cobra back out, which ripped part of one wing off and tore the side. I exchanged numbers with the lorry driver and contacted Leon. He had a big old Ford truck, which he reversed into the Cobra. He then 'admitted' the accident and his insurance company paid out £15,000 for the damage. My brothers and I cut it up between us and gave the car dealer a 'drink' – a small sum of money – out of it. We had the car repaired privately and returned it to this car dealer who was so rich he didn't even blink an eyelid.

The night of the accident, we took the two dealers over to meet the twins. All the meeting consisted of was a handshake, 'Good evening' and 'Are you enjoying yourselves?' They went back to Birmingham happy as sandboys.

Another meeting we fixed up with the twins had a less happy outcome. This involved a man called the Tank, a forger who was operating in Birmingham at the time. He wanted to see what the scene was like in London, and was invited down by the Mills brothers in late 1967 – not long after the murder of Jack The Hat. This Tank was six feet four or so and weighed about twenty stone. He looked like a typical thug: he wore a Crombie overcoat with a velvet collar, like something out of *The Godfather*.

We were all in the Carpenters Arms that night; there was a big meet going on. When you drank with the twins, it didn't matter whether you had money. Those who did would put a minimum of a tenner into the pot, but guests would never have to put their hands in their pockets. Regardless of how little you had, you drank. The scene in the pub that night was what people imagine when they think about the underworld, a word I don't particularly like. It was a typical East End pub, not very big, with a long L-shaped bar going right the way round and plush red carpeting and seating. Everybody was suited and booted. The phone was placed on the bar, cars were pulling up and people were coming and going.

We'd all totally forgotten about this Tank, who was at a table beside the door. He'd been sitting there saying nothing, hardly moving, and the drinks were piling up in front of him.

All of a sudden, one of the Mills brothers, Ray, said to me, 'I think the Tank has soiled his trousers.'

I said, 'What are you talking about?'

He sniffed. 'Can you smell it?'

The Tank had met Ronnie Kray, and Ronnie had shaken his hand. He'd heard so much about the twins that he imagined they were going to chuck him in the Thames, concreted up. He did actually soil his trousers. He never, ever got over what he saw. When he went back to Birmingham he became a straight man.

Some of the meetings we arranged for the twins did Chris and me more good personally than others. One followed an incident in a Birmingham nightspot called the Cedar Club, in Constitution Hill.

Chris, Nicky and I were there one night with a bloke called Patsy Manning, who was of Irish descent but living in Birmingham. We were drinking with a firm who were active locally. They controlled the gambling up there, and the prostitution, which was not our scene. They were also running protection rackets within their own community.

My Chris was talking to two particular members of this gang, whom I'll refer to as X and Y. Suddenly, he called me over. He said: 'Did you ask X for £50 a week protection money to drink in this club?'

I turned to them and said, 'Ask you for £50 a week? You ain't even got five bob in your pocket.'

What was going on here was a deliberate confrontation on their part, a challenge. They wanted to see how strong we were. It was something that had been coming to a head, but we were prepared for it.

Patsy Manning had this pump action shotgun. I said, 'If anything happens here, don't stop pulling that trigger.' I had a .38 police special with me. I liked that one because it was accurate: a great stopper. It would stop anyone in their tracks. I think Chris had a .45 pistol, an American service one, and Nicky had a sword-stick.

Before anything could happen, Y, who was the leading member of the firm, said to me, 'What are we all arguing about? We should all be in this together. Let's have a drink.'

Then he said: 'We'd like to meet the twins.'

'Right, I'll see what I can do,' I said.

I knew, and so did Chris, that they wanted to see how powerful we were. I explained to the twins what had happened, and they agreed to hold a meet in a pub near Vallance Road.

This firm came down to London, and they went home very impressed. We enjoyed very good standing in Birmingham after that. We saw members of Y's gang from time to time, and if we were in company they would send over a drink and leave.

However, we didn't usually have to go to these lengths to win all the little challenges that were coming at us up there. One argument involved a boxer called Johnny Prescott, who was well respected and well liked in Birmingham, but he had upset Chris by letting him down on a meet. Shortly after this, Chris, Nicky and I were in the Elbow, a local club. Johnny Prescott sent us over drinks, and Chris slapped them back down on the bar. A slanging match broke out, which ended with my brother offering Prescott out to the car park.

One of his associates shouted, 'You people don't fight with your fists. You fight with guns and knives, and an argument is never forgotten.'

Nicky jumped up and said, 'I fight with my fists. You want it with me?' And he threw his coat off. The other lot backed out of it then. Most people did.

But we were always ready and able for violence in the face of a challenge. It was vital for us to protect and promote our reputation and that of the twins. This was our priority, and it sometimes meant that we had to dish out a little bit of Kray justice. The twins could not, and would not, allow anyone to get away with taking a liberty.

There was an incident, for example, with Patsy Manning. The

twins took the hump with him after giving him money to go visiting a certain individual in Parkhurst prison. Patsy didn't bother going to visit this man, but went out drinking instead. We didn't know anything about this at the time, but the twins found out, and Ronnie said to me, 'Tell that Patsy Manning we want to see him.'

I went to Birmingham and spoke to Patsy. I said, 'If there's anything wrong, tell me, and I'll talk to them.' He didn't say a word about it.

One night, back in London, I went out to a pub called the Old Horns in Bethnal Green. When I walked into the pub, the twins were there with a couple of the firm and Patsy Manning. He was standing well away from them.

I went over to say hello, and Ronnie said, 'Invite Patsy Manning round to a party.' If the twins were upset with anyone, an invitation to a party was a very dangerous thing. But Ronnie was right to be annoyed. Patsy was collecting money to visit the prison and he wasn't doing it, even though he knew what he was dealing with.

I summed up the situation. 'Look, Ron, with all due respect, I don't think you should have to dirty your hands with this one. Leave it to us and we'll take care of it up in Birmingham.'

Ron agreed: 'As long as it's taken care of, we'll leave it to you.'

A couple of nights later, Chris and I came out of the Cedar Club and got into the car. We pulled up at the traffic lights, and Patsy Manning drove up alongside us. We hadn't been making ourselves busy to find him. We knew where he lived and we knew his brother Alan, who owned a well-known club called the Wheel. We didn't want to make an issue of it. If we came across him, he would get a right-hander and that would be the end of it.

We both stopped at the lights and Chris jumped out of the motor saying, 'Look who's here.' He got in beside Patsy, and they followed me to Patsy's flat. We went indoors and Chris gave him a dig which bust his eye open, telling him, 'You know why you're getting this, over the man you should have been visiting, and you're taking the dough.' We gave him a right kicking. Later, we told Ron about it and that was the end of the matter.

We were becoming very big indeed in Birmingham and thereabouts, and it seemed we could get away with anything, despite the personal attention we were receiving from the police. We had a special squad of policemen watching us, and we felt their presence. They would openly drink in our company. It was pleasantries all round. They'd say, 'Good evening, boys, we're hoping you don't have a late one tonight.'

And then there was an incident in the Piccadilly Casino in Manchester, the night we bumped into Davy Clare's girlfriend. I was in this little casino with Chris, Peter Metcalfe and Eric Mason, who'd turned up again. Chris and I were watching the action on the roulette when a man suddenly walked over to where we were standing. Without saying a word he got out these little books, opened them and let us see that they contained photographs of the four of us. He then said, 'Good evening, gentlemen,' and promptly walked out of the club.

It was like playing a game. The police were letting us know we were not going to get any control of the North or the Midlands. But in a sense they'd missed the boat: we were already established there. And any attempts to undermine our position were quickly dealt with. We were once told that five club owners in Birmingham had got together and decided to impose a blanket ban on us. We immediately sent out a wreath to each of them, with a message saying, 'Sorry to hear about your recent loss. Our sincere condolences.' That put an end to any notion of barring us from the clubs, and we found doors open wherever we went. That's the power of fear. One night, someone threw a bottle in one of the clubs and it hit Chris on the head. The person who chucked it didn't realise at the time who the bottle struck. He did later. From what I understand, he immediately left Birmingham and went to live in Canada.

Fear is one thing, but continuing to command it is another. You must be known to be capable of carrying out whatever you threaten. We were known – and seen – to be more than capable of it. The customers at a Birmingham casino-diner called the Ambassadors could vouch for that, as well as the six bouncers on the door. At the time, I was using a brand-new American Mustang which I'd acquired through a long firm, while Chris was driving a Ford Galaxy 500. We pulled up in the driveway of the Ambassadors in these cars, Chris and I got out and marched into the building, straight past the bouncers in their dinner suits. We were looking for someone. In front of a whole crowd of people we dragged the man we wanted out of there. No one did a thing. We gave him a right thumping there and then. We'd supplied him with money for gambling, and he'd tried to have us over.

It wasn't the first time someone had tried this, although it was unusual. For the most part we made a killing from gambling, financing the games and then taking our percentages. One man, however, took a £500 loan from us on the understanding we'd see him three days later in the Albany Hotel in the middle of Birmingham. Up there we always used to have our meets in hotel bars, never pubs. But he didn't turn up. We then heard that this man, Graham, had won a large amount of money. We always had one of the girls in the casinos straightened out, giving her money to tell us what was going on. He'd obviously done a runner.

Some time later, I booked into the Albany for a short stay. I came out of my room one day and there in the foyer was Graham with a girl. He didn't see me. I discovered he was in the next room to me, and I immediately informed my brother. Up came Chris. We knocked on the door, the girl opened it and we burst in. Chris ripped the television off the stand it was sitting on and threw it at Graham. Then we gave him a pistol-whipping. We confiscated the money he owed us, which was more or less all he had in cash in the room, and told him to leave Birmingham and never come back. He went abroad.

It wasn't as though we were picking on an innocent person. People like Graham approached us, they knew we were criminals and they knew the rules. If they broke those rules, they knew what to expect, and they couldn't go to the law for sympathy. Our attitude was either they paid us or we paid them. Everybody accepted that from the beginning, so nine times out of ten violence was never necessary. But if anybody was stupid enough to try and take a liberty, we would stop it automatically, even if some of what we had to do was unpleasant.

At this stage in our career, as I have mentioned, we didn't have to tout for business. People from all walks of life were coming to us with propositions, like the two Jewish car dealers in Birmingham who wanted to talk to us about a Rolls-Royce. They were very peeved because they'd been ripped off by another car dealer called Nick, who had a business in Harrow, northwest London.

This Nick, whose surname I can't divulge, was a very rich man. He had picked up a paper one day and seen an advertisement for a Rolls for £8,000, so he sent a young guy of nineteen to Birmingham to put a £2,000 deposit on the car. The young lad also offered a cheque for the outstanding amount. It wasn't even a legal deal – you couldn't have credit unless you were over twenty-one – but the young guy was very sharp and the Birmingham dealers went for it hook, line and sinker. Then the cheque bounced, too, so they were fucked for £6,000.

They gave us all the details, but what they didn't tell us was that they had had Nick over a year or so earlier for a car out of his company in Harrow. What Nick was doing was getting one back at them.

I asked, 'What's in it for us?'

They said, 'If you can recover the car, we'll give you half its value.'

We took the job on condition we were given £500 expenses up front. They came to London with us, booked us into the Russell Hotel in Russell Square and took us to Nick's pitch. It was lovely. He had Bentleys, Rollers, all sorts of expensive cars there. You could tell at a glance that he was loaded.

This is where we called our old bus driver friend Paddy Dinnear in again. Chris and I had a talk with him and we decided to pile up to this place in Harrow four-handed. We gave Paddy a pick-axe handle and told him to run into Nick's office, smash it across his desk and say, 'You fucked us out of £6,000. We want it now or you're in trouble.' We agreed that Chris and I would follow within a couple of minutes and hold him back.

He did exactly what we asked. Chris and I went in, pulled Paddy away from Nick, who was on the floor in a terrible panic, and said, 'We want the car or we want the money.'

He was whimpering, 'I'll give you anything you want, but don't hurt me.' Then he asked, 'Can I talk to you?'

I said, 'You can talk to us all day long, but we still want the car or the cash.'

He then gave us his side of it, and told us about the Jewish car dealers having him over. 'The car doesn't mean a thing to me,' he said, 'I just don't want *them* to have it. If you boys want to make a nice killing I'll give you the value of the car, and I'll also give you a cheque – which the bank won't pay out – for you to give the Birmingham men.'

And he did. He gave us our money, and he wrote a cheque for £8000, making a deliberate error so that it would not be paid. We went back to the dealers in Birmingham and told them we had the dough. I waved the cheque in front of their faces, put it away again and said, 'You're not getting this until you give us our half of the money in cash.' One of them came to the bank with me and paid over £4,000. Then I handed him the cheque, which he immediately put in his pocket. Five days later, he realised he'd been had.

So we made £12,000, plus expenses. Nick lost £8,000. And the Birmingham car dealers got burnt very badly, to the tune of £18,500. The whole issue was this: they went to criminals. As the saying goes, you live by it, you die by it.

But the story didn't end there. This Nick from Harrow got in touch with me and Chris and said: 'I've always got a use for people like you two. I'm willing to put you on a retainer and, should I ever need you, I'll call upon your services.'

I replied, 'I do a lot of work for the Kray brothers. I'll have to see what they think about it, and we'll take it from there.' When I mentioned it to the twins, Ronnie said, 'Keep it for yourself.'

From then on, I started meeting Nick at the bar of the London Hilton Hotel every Friday to collect a retainer of £800. Chris and I would have £300 each and my Nicky £200. Nick, through his wealth and through paying out money at that rate, was leaving himself open to a lot of things. I phoned him up one night from a call box fifty yards from his house and told him I wanted to see him immediately. He said, 'I'll see you in an hour.' I got there within five minutes. Chris was waiting outside, round the corner, because Nick claimed my eldest brother made him feel uncomfortable.

A young boy wearing a white pinny answered the door. I said, 'Is Nick there?' I walked in and went straight into the bedroom. Nick was in bed with another young boy with a pinny on. I said, 'It's not my thing, what I'm looking at here, but I have to stay here to tell you that we need £5,000 right away.'

'I'll have to give it to you tomorrow,' he answered. I said, 'We need it urgently.'

He asked me to wait outside the room. I did, but I was watching what he was doing through the crack in the door. He got out of bed, and I saw he was dressed as a woman. Then he moved the bed away from the wall to reveal a built-in safe. I saw him count out £5,000. He called me in five minutes later, by which time he was back in bed.

'Thanks for the cash,' I said. 'By the way, we'll see you again next week.' And we upped his money to £1,000 a week. I was still drawing it six months after I was nicked for the McVitie murder. That's what a violent reputation can do for you.

He knew we were connected. He knew he was being had over. He knew what we were up to. It was protection money. Protection he never even needed.

Cars and car dealers were a recurring feature of our time in Birmingham. Another one who fell in love with the romantic idea of bringing criminals into his life was a man called Tony Hart, who acquired my Mustang and Chris's Galaxy 500 for us.

Hart, an ex-club bouncer with the gift of the gab, was the proprietor of a garage and car wash company which was virtually on its knees when he invited Chris in to help revive the business. I went to Walsall, just outside Birmingham, to meet him. He wanted to slaughter the garage, make a quick profit out of it and then get rid of it. He asked me, 'What prison sentence would I get if I ran this as a long firm?'

'Between four and seven,' I replied.

He was prepared to accept that, and he started ordering large amounts of goods. He wanted Chris and me to run the car wash firm, the legitimate end of his business, which was making a good profit. We agreed to keep it ticking along, mainly for our own amusement. Every night we'd cut up the takings, and we'd make about £200–300 a week out of it. He would also give us a little whack out of what he was defrauding from the garage.

But we knew that something wasn't right about him. Overnight he changed the way he dressed from suits and boots to a black Crombie overcoat with the collar turned up, and he started telling people that he was a friend, a dear friend, of the Krays. In the end, Chris and I had to have a talk with him; I whipped him with a pistol and whacked him round the head a couple of times. To our surprise he loved it, and then started putting it round Birmingham that he had been pistol-whipped by Ronnie Kray. Just for the glory of it.

He wanted to be a nine-to-five gangster. At the end of the day he went home to live a normal life with the wife and kids, but at work he revelled in his imagined image. He even started to cultivate prison mannerisms. Long-term prisoners form certain habits: they walk around with their hands behind their backs, shoulders straight and eyes down, and they whisper out of the corner of their mouths. He began doing this around the garage forecourt. Chris said to me, 'He thinks he's on exercise.'

We were living like kings, though. We got Hart to book us into the Albany Hotel through the company, and we were still involved with the car wash when we got nicked with the twins. Then we forgot about him straightaway.

But he started to visit Chris in Wandsworth and me in Brixton while we were on remand. I was called up for a visit one day, and when I walked into the visiting room Hart was standing there in a trilby with tears streaming down his face, his collar rolled up and his hand on his chest. He shouted across the room, 'I should have been in the dock with you boys. It was all my doing.' This was the type of person that you could attract if you weren't careful. Eventually he went into debt to the tune of about £180,000, at least some of which was down to our extravagant hotel bills.

After our trial, a spate of stories began to appear in the papers about what we had got up to in the Midlands. Who was the author? Tony Hart. According to him he wasn't scared of us – although he kept a shotgun under his bed – but his wife lived in utter fear. We apparently asked him to bury people for us, and he was all the time in contact with the Birmingham Regional Crime Squad, tipping them off about what was going on. It was a pack of lies from start to finish.

He wound up getting a few years for the garage long firm, and unfortunately he served some of his time in Leicester prison while I was there. I was in the maximum security block and he was on a level above it. He kept throwing pieces of paper with messages over the exercise cage – 'Anything I can do for you. . .' I was forever picking up little notes with Tony Hart's name on them.

Another bizarre character from the Birmingham era was Richard Forbes, a multi-millionaire whom we came across one night in the Cedar Club. Chris and I were having a drink with one or two of the boys when all of a sudden bottles of champagne started coming up. We were then told that everything we wanted was on the house, down to this Richard Forbes. Chris had met him somewhere along the line. I never had.

I didn't really pay him a lot of attention that night because we were in female company, just out enjoying ourselves. But the next morning I woke up where we were staying in Harts Hotel – nothing to do with Tony Hart, I might add! – and outside in the grounds was a brand-new white Ferrari. Chris said, 'It belongs to that Richard. He seems all right.'

Richard duly came down to breakfast drinking a bottle of vodka. He went, 'Look, my father owns a steel works and he gave me half a million pounds, five horses, a flat in Birmingham and a cottage in the country to stay out of his life.' He was also drawing on a pension fund set up by his father. He never carried cash, only cards, and he was a raving alcoholic. A couple of days later he came round again, this time in a powder-blue Aston Martin DB6, a James Bond car. He changed cars like they were going out of fashion.

In a way, Richard Forbes was courting us. He loved the atmosphere around Chris and me. He obviously didn't need us in a financial way, but we needed him. Here was a man who thought it would do him favours to be connected to criminals, and he was prepared to spend large amounts of money. If someone comes up and wants to give you money for nothing, why refuse? There are some people in this world who want to give money away, and I never saw anything wrong in taking it off them.

One day he turned up at the Albany in a new Jensen, phoned me in my suite and asked me if I would like to go riding. I agreed. I was wearing jeans, a shirt, a jacket and ordinary shoes. He was dressed up like Prince Charles with a topper, a red hunting jacket, breeches and boots, and had a whip in his hand. What I found more fascinating, though, was the bottles of vodka sticking out of his pockets. We came out of the stable and were cantering along this road when he insisted on stopping at an off-licence for yet another bottle of vodka. Needless to say, it wasn't long before he and his horse started disagreeing with each other. . . . .

Sober or drunk, Richard Forbes would always insist to me and Chris: 'If you want anything, just ask me for it.' I always found, after entering into professional as opposed to amateur crime, that there was no such thing as a demand for money (except if it was owed), and I personally never uttered a direct threat in any of the situations I profited from. It was mainly a matter of persuasion. But Forbes, like many others, didn't need any persuasion. He was one of those people who wanted to be on the right side of us at all costs, for the 'glamour' as much as anything else. He paid everything. He paid hotels, he wanted to buy us cars. We had him around us purely and simply to pick up the tabs. He invited Ronnie Kray to his cottage in the country and he wanted to take him abroad on a cruise. He would have given Ronnie anything, but Ronnie didn't go. He didn't want to know. Ronnie was busy, anyway – as I knew from my other life in London.

CHAPTER SEVEN

FEAR AND FORTUNE

At the time I came out of Bristol prison, just before Christmas 1966, the twins were into having new faces on the firm. I was a young guy, smartly dressed, useful, reliable, and they wanted me to be around them. Within days, I became a party to one of their most closely guarded secrets.

I was asked to drive a member of the firm, Scotch Jack Dickson, to a flat in Barking. When I pulled up outside I saw another member, Albert Donaghue, open the door. I noticed he was pushing someone back, someone who was trying to stick his head out, and I recognised him straightaway: Frank The Mad Axeman Mitchell. I was shocked, and didn't want to know too much about it. Frank had been in prison for many years for violent crime. On one occasion, he had escaped and had terrorised an elderly couple with an axe while robbing them. He was subsequently recaptured, but now he was on the run again. It was common knowledge in our circles that the twins had organised Frank's escape from Dartmoor, but his whereabouts were being kept very quiet.

I knew Frank well. He was a simple man in many ways, a big man, very well built and immensely strong. You couldn't fight him

– he would just crush you up. Everybody knew about him: he was a legend.

I remember Frank arriving at Wandsworth prison while I was there, almost two years before his escape. He'd been brought from Dartmoor in a coach which was carrying two men called Mitchell, a little weedy one and big Frank. The prisoners had to leave the coach, which was surrounded by about ten screws, as their names were called.

'Mitchell.' The little weedy one stepped off the coach, and the screws started heckling him – 'So you're the Mitchell' – and pushing him about. All of a sudden a big hand came out. 'No . . . I'm the Mitchell.' That was a standing joke around the prison for months.

The screws came to realise that you couldn't give Frank a direct order and expect him to carry it out. It was physically impossible to punish him, so they treated him very gently. But he didn't always respond to this softly-softly treatment in the way they wanted. When the Governor came into the S1 shop – the high-security workshop – on his daily rounds, Frank used to like to pick him up and carry him around, to the delight of every con in Wandsworth. He made the Governor promise to behave himself.

Frank never knew what a normal life was like. He had spent most of his time behind bars from an early age, and rumour had it that he was never to be released. The twins had a great affection for him – they looked after him in a lot of ways and they got him out of prison simply to help him. The idea was to use the escape to bargain for a release date for Frank, while he remained hidden away. When it was given, he would return to Dartmoor.

But the authorities were not forthcoming with a date. And Frank wasn't a man you could control. He didn't see things in a rational way, and from what I understand he had his own ideas about what he wanted to do. The situation was getting dangerous, for Frank and everyone around him. Apparently this led to trouble between Frank and certain members of the firm. I was busy with other things, and nobody was talking too much about what was going on. Finally I heard that Frank had been shot dead, just before Christmas.

The twins had nothing to do with his murder, as was shown in court when they were acquitted of it. I did hear that Frank had been killed by Billy Exley, an ex-boxer who was on the fringes of the firm. He vanished from the scene after Frank's disappearance. That was the rumour at the time, and rumours carry a lot of weight. In criminal circles, rumours are usually correct. Exley's name came up quite a few times. The whole tragedy of Frank Mitchell is that he ended up dead over something that had started with the best intentions in the world.

It was often said that the twins could have two hundred armed men on the street within an hour if they wanted, and at that time they could, without any doubt. But the twins were an army on their own. There will never be another two like them. They took the lot on. They got London by the scruff of the neck and they didn't ask permission. They just went there and took it, because they knew they could.

The firm they gathered around them was composed of people who could be relied upon in the three areas they were concerned with: villainy, business and image. Image-making was a very important part of the operation. It became an essential part of the legend which was building up round the twins, and that legend gave them more and more power as it grew. The more fear they could inspire, the more successful they would be. If the Krays did something, it had become twenty times bigger by the time the story reached the bottom of the road. The twins were well aware of the advantages of this, and they knew that if there was going to be one big picture, then it had to be larger than life in every way.

They were good at putting out an impression of danger. Both of them had minders, even though they were the last two men in London who needed them. Some people on the firm, like Tommy The Bear Brown, were brought along for show on social occasions. Tommy was a gentle giant, a very likeable person and a good friend of the twins since they were boys. Standing at about six feet three, his eighteen stone of muscle dwarfed everyone: He was a handsome, white-haired man with a kindly face, except when the twins wanted him not to look kindly. But Tommy was never really used in any of the activities.

The twins could lay it on lovely when they wanted. They could have every major face in the East End in a pub on the same night, and all of this was particularly useful when Chris and I brought our clients down from other cities. They would see a very impressive show.

The whole of the Kray empire revolved around fear. That was the key to the lot of it. And it was a very real and deep-rooted fear, as I soon discovered. The more I became involved with the firm, the more my own friends became frightened of me. I didn't encourage this. I did try to have a bit of a separate life and go out on a Friday night with my mates to the Queen's Arms in Hackney Road. But I could see the difference in their behaviour; I could sense that their reactions to me were changing. They became wary of me. Sometimes I'd invite them to come over and have a drink with the twins and they'd shy off. Their attitude was: 'We don't want to fuck about with them. They're dangerous. They go beyond.'

Some characters' fear of the firm was so overwhelming that they were driven to acts of sheer lunacy and ended up bringing upon themselves the very trouble they had dreaded in the first place. One example of this happened after we made a meet with a man called Walter who had some plates for printing forged money. Chris and I went to see him in a pub in Notting Hill Gate with Peter Metcalfe.

Eric Mason and Davy Clare, who had established an uneasy peace with the twins, were there too.

Eric had been freelancing around the country, and he knew this Walter's firm. Because he also knew us, he became the go-between in our dealings. That night, he'd pulled Davy in for back-up. We wanted these plates, and so did various firms; they were worth a fortune, and they had been causing big fall-outs amongst a lot of people.

Walter wasn't there when we arrived, so we ordered a drink while we were waiting. We saw three Irishmen in the bar, navvies about six feet tall and built like the proverbials. They were with a woman who was wearing a pair of tight leopardskin trousers. Eric Mason, who always had an eye for the ladies, saw her at the jukebox. He walked over, put a coin in and said: 'Would you like to pick some records out?'

One of the Irishmen got up and said to Eric, 'You're talking to my woman.'

Eric replied, 'I'm very sorry about that, but I don't really see what it's got to do with you.'

Standing on the bar was a big red glass vase, and all of a sudden I saw Eric go to pick it up. The Irishman tried to throw a right-hander at him and Eric cut him to pieces – he did him in the face with the vase. All he had left in his hand was the stem of it.

The barman let the Dobermann out and came running round with the ice pick. The bar was U-shaped, and in the middle was a big, fancy glass display unit. Chris grabbed this barman, threw him straight over the bar into the unit, picked up the dog and sent him flying over as well. Then we completely demolished the pub. All the windows went.

Meanwhile Walter walked into the pub, saw what was going on, thought it was something to do with the plates because of all the aggro they had caused so far, and did a runner. That's fear of the firm.

We caught up with him at a flat in Brick Lane in the East End. Davy Clare knew where he was staying and took us there, and as we got out of the car we heard two loud bangs. I saw this Walter firing a pistol at us. One bullet went in the side of the car, and another missed Davy's head by an inch. We got hold of this geezer and we beat the shit out of him. He was stabbed up the behind and he had a tendon cut. He had to have about 150 stitches.

He didn't even have the plates, although he was supposed to have brought them to the pub. In later weeks we discovered that the plates had been broken and were therefore useless, so no one ever got their hands on them or the money. You can be a millionaire one minute and a pauper the next. . . .

In happier circumstances, the general fear of the twins could be turned to the advantage of individuals who needed help. One day a man called Peter who owned a café in Bethnal Green approached me and said: 'Can you get me a gun?'

I said, 'What do you want that for?'

'I'm hoping to have the basement done into a restaurant,' he replied, 'but we've already had tearaways going down there and smashing the place up.'

I told him, 'I can't just do that, but I'll go and talk to somebody.'

I went to see the twins: Ronnie said, 'I'll go down there on Saturday and have a meal.' He was famous for his bit of plaice, Peter.

I told him, 'I'm going to bring someone here on Saturday. Just look after him.'

Sammy Lederman and I accompanied Ronnie to the café, and we sat at a table for a couple of hours. Peter never had a problem there again, for which he was eternally grateful. It solved itself, just through Ronnie Kray coming in for his dinner.

That story illustrates yet again that it wasn't the use of violence, but the fear of violence that kept everything afloat for the twins. People knew what the consequences would be if they didn't play ball. The truth is that the twins never used violence unless they had to, because the fear was usually enough. They certainly never used it as much as people would like to believe. If anything they would avoid it to an extent, but if you crossed them you were crossing the wrong people.

Who in their right mind would want to take them on? I never saw anybody throw a punch at either of them. No one ever threatened them, because if you did you paid the price. It was well known that if they had to be ruthless, they were there to the limit. They were deadly. And I'm talking about violence like you've never seen.

Their whole reputation was built on their violence, so it stands to reason they were more than prepared to use it to safeguard their standing as the top men. Play the fool with them, and you would expect to get it. When they gave out a kicking, it *was* a kicking – inevitably a hospital job. When weapons came out, it was for something more serious. They'd cut people, or they'd shoot them in the leg. If a challenge was sent out, it was met with a challenge. If anybody played up with a person or property they were protecting, threatened or attacked any of their friends or the firm, adversely interfered with their business affairs or tried to cheat them, woe betide the one who was causing the problem.

The twins were always prepared. A lot of people around the East End were carrying artillery of some sort or another, and the twins had to live with all sorts of rumoured threats to their lives. It was said at one time that other gangsters were planning to shoot them from the railway bridge over Vallance Road.

But all of this was kept within the criminal community, amongst ourselves. It's been said so many times it's a cliché these days, but we never involved innocent people. I have no reason to lie now. I'm out, and it's all in the past. I can only think of one instance when someone who was not in criminal circles suffered injury. He came to a party in a flat in Manor House with friends, who, we assumed, had told him about the company and what sort of behaviour was expected.

Reggie, Tommy Cowley and I had been in the Regency Club to pick up some drink. We arrived at the party to see Ronnie steaming out of the flat, followed by a young fella and a model, who were friends of his. He was going: 'Fucking liberty!'

'What's the matter with you?' Reggie asked.

There was a geezer in there holding a towel to his face and three girls screaming their heads off.

It transpired that Ronnie had hung his coat up on a hanger in the hallway. Then these people arrived at the party. The bloke took Ronnie's coat off the hanger, flung it on the floor and put his own coat up. When Ronnie went out to get his Players from his coat, he saw it on the floor. He came back into the room with the coat which had replaced his on the hanger. 'Who does this belong to?'

The guy said, 'It's mine.'

Ronnie opened up his face.

If Ronnie let someone throw his coat on the floor, he was leaving himself open for others to treat him disrespectfully. Everyone who came unstuck asked for what they got, and not one victim ever complained or came back whingeing that they didn't deserve it. If the twins took action against someone who later on turned out to be in the right, they would be the first ones to make it up. I've never heard anyone accuse them of taking liberties. I'm not trying to justify the things that happened; I'm not saying that what the twins did was right; but it was right for them in their position at that time. It was villains among villains, people who lived by our code, people who knew the rules and were fully aware of what would happen if they chose to break them.

What the Krays actually did in London at that time was keep the peace. They kept all of the villainy under control. No one stepped out of line. They hated grasses, sex offenders, people who committed crimes to do with women and children – 'They'd better leave town.' They couldn't stand petty housebreakers. The twins would never have stood for muggings and the sort of street crime that's going haywire today. In those days the East End was a better and safer place for the general public to live in, and I feel a bit proud of that. The twins did a job that the police couldn't do, and there are a lot of coppers who would admit it. The twins should've been given a bleeding medal.

I was present on various occasions when Reggie and Ronnie had to administer their own swift form of discipline. There was a pub party one night in the Old Horns in Bethnal Green. Ronnie had just come back from a trip to New York where he had met some Mafia people and the boxer Rocky Graciano, who had given him a portrait. He was in good spirits; he had brought some American friends, the Kaufman brothers, back with him, and wanted to show them the real East End.

The firm was all present. David Bailey, the photographer, was there with his Roller parked outside. There was a Wakefield boxer called Johnny Guitar, and an Irish minstrel called Kevin O'Connor, as well as a couple of midgets whom Ronnie liked to have about. The Clarke Brothers were dancing on the stage.

I was watching their routine when all of a sudden I heard a bang, and I saw the Clarkes' eyes widen in absolute horror. Something had happened behind me. As I turned around, I saw a fella fall backwards off a stool and start writhing around on the floor. Ronnie had done him in the eye with a glass. We grabbed this geezer and chucked him out of the pub. What he'd done was march up to Ronnie and stare him straight in the eye. That was a direct challenge. He knew full well who Ronnie Kray was, and Ronnie couldn't let people do that to him.

Another night we went into this club in Knightsbridge, a little drinker. A man called Johnny Cardew was sitting in there, drunk as a sack. He came from a well-known family of brothers from the Angel.

He said to the waiter, 'Get some drinks over to that table, including the fat one.'

That was intended to be a reference to Ronnie, who didn't hear it. So we had a drink and left. We were in a car passing Marble Arch when one of Ronnie's friends said, 'Do you know what he said about you?'

'What's that?' Ronnie said.

We turned the car round and drove back there. Ronnie told us to wait outside the door. He went in there on his own, called Cardew into the toilet and never said a word to him, just gave it to him right down the face.

Afterwards, obviously, there had to be a meet with Cardew's brothers over it. Ronnie called them round and told them why Johnny got it. And they said, 'We accept that what he did was out of order.' And that was the end of it.

The Cardews used to come to the Carpenters Arms regularly after that to see the twins, and there Johnny would be, with a big, broad groove in his face. He was given a new nickname: Tramlines.

Ronnie said to me one day, 'He deserved what he got, Tony', and I understood. Someone was taking a liberty. If no one had taken action, he would have got away with it. But the twins had to be on top of things like that. It was very important.

A similarly insulting comment spelled trouble for two brothers called Billy and Jimmy Webb in another Old Horns drama. My Chris had known the Webbs during the late fifties, and we were all having a drink together when something was said to him. He walked over to Ronnie and said, 'If it wasn't for respect for you, Ron, I would have shot him,' meaning one of the Webbs.

Chris then left, and the next day when I phoned the twins they asked to see me. Ronnie said, 'What's the trouble with Chris and these Webbs?'

'I really don't know,' I replied.

The next night I walked round the corner from Blythe Street to the Old Horns and saw Ronnie, Reggie, my Nicky, Scotch Jack Dickson, Ian Barrie, Teddy Berry, Tommy Cowley, Sammy Lederman and the Webb brothers. Ronnie and the Webbs were on high stools at the bar, and Nicky was standing by them. At the other end of the pub was a man called Ivor, who was a sort of groupie around the villains. He said he knew the Richardsons. He came in with the Webbs but sat at a different side of the pub. He was always coming to me with little business deals that amounted to nothing. He really wanted to get in on the fringes of what was going on.

I walked over towards Reggie. He was talking to this Ivor, who was shitting himself. Reggie then turned to me and said, 'When it goes, I'll grab hold of him.' I knew it was going to be heavy.

By the time I got back to Ronnie's end of the bar, Ron had hit one of the Webb brothers in the face with a pint glass. He'd said to Ron, 'I was in the nuthouse, same as you was.' As soon as he said that, he was right off the stool. A couple of the boys were setting about the Webbs, and I turned round to see Reggie with a gun, telling Ivor, who was against the wall, 'You move and you're dead.'

The Webbs got a hiding and I dragged them both out of the pub and round into an alleyway. They were going to get it anyway because they'd upset Chris, and the twins would not let that pass. But the comment about the nuthouse sealed their fate. That was something you didn't say to the Krays.

The hanger-on, Ivor, had insulted Reggie earlier in the evening by getting over-familiar, which was strictly not on. Reggie had asked me, 'Do you know who this geezer is? He keeps asking questions.'

So it didn't surprise me to see Reggie giving him a good whack while, on the other side of the bar, Ronnie, Sammy Lederuran and my Nicky were kicking the hell out of the Webb brothers. Reggie had decided not to use the gun, but all of a sudden the knives came out – Albert Donaghue and Ronnie Hart wanted to cut Ivor to pieces. Ironically, they were two of the people who later stood in court pointing the finger at other members of the firm for violence.

Reggie stepped in when he saw the weapons: 'That's enough.' He was capable of dealing with the situation himself, in his own way.

I've seen Reggie hit numerous people on the chin, but I've never, ever known him to fight with Ron. They argued a lot, just like any brothers, and you were always convinced that something was going to happen – but it never did. However, Reggie did come to blows with their brother Charlie at least once that I know of.

There was a party in Mansell Street, Bethnal Green, for the firm and the Kaufman brothers. One of the guests was the nephew of Billy Hill, a gangster who, with his partner Jack Spot, had controlled London in the early fifties. The nephew was a bit drunk, said something to Reggie, and Reggie pulled him up on it. The next minute Charlie and Reggie were arguing, and they disappeared outside to have a fist fight.

A girl, who was with one of the boys at the party, was standing nearby. She said to me, 'Separate them.'

I said, 'If you feel that strongly about it, separate them yourself.' I knew better than to step in between two brothers. Charlie was indoors with a black eye for three or four days after that.

If you were called round to see the twins, you went – otherwise you would be visited personally. Because they could be so easily offended, if anybody ever did them wrong my advice to that person was always, 'Straighten it up with them as quickly as possible. If not, don't ever bump into them.'

Someone once said to me, 'You don't fight them, they fight you,' and that was how it was.

Reggie was more accessible than Ronnie, more open to an discussion about problem situations. To upset Ronnie was to bring things down on your own head. He had his morals and he acted upon them as a matter of honour; I've always respected him for that. He saw things one way only. There was no in-between with Ronnie. If he had the needle, you knew it, and there was no reasoning with him. If he had the hump with someone who was in a crowd of a hundred people, he'd go in there and do what he had to do, regardless of the odds against him.

Ronnie was well known for his unpredictability, and could be spontaneous with his violence. You knew just to meet him that there was something different about him. He was a sociable man, a mixer, but at the same time he was aloof. He had an air which seemed to say, 'Don't approach me too closely'.

The stories about him were legion. It was said that he branded a man on the cheeks with a poker in a pub called the Grave Maurice. He may well have done, but I never saw it. And then there was his famous hitlist, the list of people he was going to do. Around our circles, they used to say that it was easy to get on it and very difficult to get off, but I never saw any list.

When they did their villainy, the twins didn't hide it. It's been written that when Ronnie killed George Cornell in the Blind Beggar in March 1966, he did it openly because he wanted everybody to know he was the murderer. Ronnie actually did it on the spur of the moment because he was angry. Same with Reggie and the McVitie murder. That moment of anger, and it was done.

I often advised people in our company to leave a club if I saw any danger signs. I'd say, 'Don't get invited to the private bar downstairs for a drink.' Some of them went against my advice and took a drink and a beating. Even worse, of course, was to be invited to a party at a private house. That was a serious business. As the saying went, 'You go there, you walk through the door, and you're carried out. Feet first.' On the other hand, if you were invited round to the house in Vallance Road, or to Braithwaite House in Old Street, where Reg and Ron later lived with their parents, you knew you were safe. They never carried out any acts of violence at the family home.

You couldn't fool the twins, couldn't pull the wool over their eyes. They had a grapevine second to none. People reported everything back to them, usually to curry favour. I'd go somewhere one night, and I could bet my bottom dollar Reggie or Ronnie would say to me the next day, 'We hear you were in such-and-such a place with so-and-so.' They never directly asked you not to associate with certain people, but if they disapproved of somebody you were friendly with, they'd say, 'We don't particularly like him.' And you got the message. You stood by their rules.

In my own personal experience, they were never bullies. On the contrary, the twins were scrupulously fair. There have been all sorts of rumours about them – that they took the flowers off the flower woman, that they had to have their whack out of every job that was done locally. It's not true: it wasn't in their nature to be like that. They didn't go charging round the East End insisting on half of every load that fell off the back of a lorry, or percentages out of robberies committed by other firms. I never saw that happen. It wouldn't have been political. It would have made enemies. They were all for making friends, because it was important that while they were feared, they were also respected.

It was all done very diplomatically. I never once heard them make a direct demand for money off anyone. They had a way of handling people tactfully, never with a violent attitude. They didn't just march into places demanding 30 per cent of the takings. Most of the protection business they did came to them. They never had to ask for work. People wanted them because they were the best.

Club owners, publicans, restaurateurs and arcade proprietors were people who knew that their premises naturally attracted trouble, the wrong 'uns, the 'Friday night gangsters'. There were a lot of these people who worked five days a week for a wage and on Friday night would go out drinking with their mates and want to tear the place up, to wreck the business. The only way to stop that was to protect it with heavy people. The fact that the Krays were known to be involved in a business was enough to prevent any further problems. We did a lot of good in that way. It was in everybody's interests to have the twins about. Publicans, club owners . . . they were guaranteed safety. They had no aggravation.

Once they got into the heavy game, the scene of involving known criminals in their businesses, obviously they had to pay for it. But it saved them money in the long run. It was a good investment. Because the East End was like the Wild West, and the twins' word was law. They were the sheriff and the gunslinger rolled into one.

CHAPTER EIGHT

A FAMILY AFFAIR

W alk anywhere in the East End with the twins, and everybody knew 'em. 'All right, Reg?' 'Lovely day, Ron.' As much as they were feared in criminal circles, they were very well liked by the local population. The twins were genuinely pleasant and polite and, towards women, charming and respectful. When they moved to Braithwaite House towards the end of the sixties Ronnie used to come out every Sunday for a stroll, impeccably dressed as always, and walk up towards City Road and across into Ironmonger Road. Every person he passed would call out a greeting.

Much has been said and written about the so-called Robin Hood syndrome and, yes, it's an accurate parallel. Although the Kray twins pursued a legitimate career in clubland, they earned much of their living from crime and violence, and most of what they got they gave away. They gave so much that people must have thought they were potty. They were very generous men, very charitable indeed.

They never forgot that they came from a working-class background, and they were determined to put as much back into the community as they could. A lot of people in the East End have reason to thank them. The twins handed out a huge amount of money every Christmas. They looked after women whose husbands were in prison, and they insisted on certain ways of going about it. For moral reasons, you never knocked on the door of a woman whose old man was away. You put the money through the letterbox in an envelope, or you passed it to her via a third party. On one occasion I was driving along the road with Ronnie Kray when he pulled up, took off a brand-new Crombie overcoat and gave it to a dosser.

People have been suspicious in the past about the twins and their charity work, suggesting that it was designed to gain them a good image in the press. No. If they took up a cause, they genuinely got involved in it. When he was later questioned about it in the Old Bailey, Ronnie refused to blow his own trumpet. He said, 'I don't think I want to talk about that.' They were very sincere with their charity. I'm not trying to paint them white, but if we're going to talk about the truth of the Krays, it has to be said that there were good intentions as well as bad, kindness as well as villainy.

They raised a substantial sum for the Aberfan Disaster Fund, set up after a slag heap engulfed a Welsh village school and killed the children; and they kept the Hackney Road Queen Elizabeth Hospital for Children in funds and donations. They also did a lot of work amongst the old people in the East End and they supported all the boxing charities. Members of the organisations were invited to one of the twins' clubs or pubs, where the money would be handed over. The twins never had a tanner of it.

Reggie and Ronnie were fascinating people, very moral men in many ways. They had a code of ethics which stated that you didn't interfere with other men's wives, although it did sometimes happen in our circles and it caused a lot of friction. You never stole off your own. Sex offenders, heroin dealers and ponces were not acceptable.

The twins also believed in a certain honour among thieves, something which has gone out the window today, and were prepared to help any criminals suffering hardship. They had a pension fund for ex-cons – a protection fund, if you like. It was known that if you came out of prison and went to the twins, you'd get a bit of help with no ulterior motive. It was sometimes said of the twins that, once they'd done someone a favour, they'd hold that person in debt. That was never the case. The only thing Reg and Ron ever gained from helping former inmates was the chance to expand their grapevine. They were running a business, after all, and it was in their interests to know what was going on.

They were happy to lend, as well. Various celebrities and society figures borrowed money from the twins to get themselves out of trouble, so all in all a fairly wide cross-section of people had cause to be grateful to the Krays.

In a social setting, they were very friendly and likeable. They were always the first ones to buy a drink for the company. If you were ever short of a few quid in the pub, they'd take care of you. When they went into a pub, the guv'nor would place the phone on the bar for their convenience, and a buffet would always appear. He knew he'd get good trade and no aggro – unless something drastic happened.

Ronnie was the more flamboyant of the two: he had a very dry wit, and he could be quite eccentric. Sometimes he'd say, 'I'm having one of my parties tonight', and you'd turn up to find that dwarves, giants and big fat women were the star attractions. He used to sit one of the midgets on a stool, put his hand behind him as if he was a dummy and pretend to be doing the talking.

I found Ronnie's humour hilarious. He used to keep an Alsatian, and one day when we were about to leave the house I said, 'Are you going to feed the dog, Ron?'

Ron went to the cupboard, picked up a tin of dog food and threw it out the window. He said, 'If he's that fucking hungry, he'll open it himself.'

But at the same time, you knew you had to behave around Ronnie. You knew you were dealing with someone *different*. You were on your toes. With Reggie you could relax a bit more, especially if he was on his own. I remember one night at a party in the pub, a young geezer was trying to get past old man Charlie Kray and he just pushed him out of the way. Luckily for the young guy, Ronnie Kray didn't see this. But Reggie did. He let him off with a warning because he was a boy. Reggie went about things in a more considered way.

In their personal habits they were clean-living men. They were early risers who used to work out regularly. They liked a drink, but they never had anything to do with drugs; they stayed well away from that scene. And their home was spotlessly clean: you could eat your dinner off the floor in Vallance Road.

They were two of the smartest men London ever turned out, and a lot of people copied their style. I only ever saw Ronnie once in casual clothes. I was walking up to my mate Peter's café on the corner of Blythe Street one day, when all of a sudden a car pulled up alongside me and in it were the twins with an old friend of theirs, Dickie Morgan. Reggie and Dickie were both wearing blue suits, but Ronnie was dressed in a pair of blue slacks and an open-necked shirt. It was a rare occasion.

The twins were meticulous in their dress without being flash. You would never see the same suit, shirt or tie two days running. They were very influential on me that way. I took my cue from their dress sense, and they would be the first people to come up and say, 'I do like that suit, Tony.' We were all expected to be smart around the twins, especially in company. They hated scruffiness. They also used to call the barber over to the house to cut their hair, and I took a leaf out of that book too.

The whole style of the twins was sure to draw women. Women were never involved when we were out drinking on business evenings, and they would not be invited into the company, but if we were holding a purely social gathering then they would join in, know their place and be chivalrously treated. A lot of girls liked Reggie, but he paid very little attention. He loved his wife, Frances, and he was inconsolable when she died. Reggie was more of a man for regular relationships.

Some of the men, however, and I'm thinking particularly of Albert Donaghue, regarded the more obvious of these women as 'fringe benefits', and used their status as members of the firm to succeed with them. Albert was not the most faithful husband in the world. He was a handsome bloke, always with different birds, and he had an affair with Lisa, the girl who was called in to keep Frank Mitchell happy after his escape. Albert always liked club-type girls, the ones who were well known in our circles. Today they'd be called gangster groupies, for want of a better term, and we attracted quite a few of them. They were typical of the period, with beehive hairdos and black eyelids.

A great many women found Ronnie Kray very attractive. He was a good-looking man, and had he wanted, he could have had girls every night. Ronnie was not ashamed of his bisexuality, but he made no big deal of it. It was a personal thing and he kept it that way; he never forced his opinions on anyone. He wasn't a camp person by any stretch of the imagination. Quite the opposite: he didn't like 'gayness'. He was a man's man. He would knock himself, sometimes, in a joking way – 'I like the boys over in America' – because that was his personality, but none of us would ever volunteer any wisecracks. Ronnie's preferences were his own business, and that was respected throughout our circles. The subject was only ever mentioned if Ronnie brought it up himself.

When George Cornell called Ronnie a 'poof', it was a direct challenge. This was one of various crucial incidents leading up to

Ronnie's killing of Cornell. In many people's eyes, Ronnie had no choice but to do what he did after that.

Occasionally, Ronnie would have young men round him. I wouldn't call them boyfriends, I'd call them friends. Sometimes there might be three or four, and whatever relationships they had were kept exclusively within that private circle. It didn't involve anybody else. Ronnie would think nothing of buying one of these friends a suit or a piece of jewellery. He was as spontaneous in his spending as he was in everything else. Whatever he had, he would give you.

The twins' mother, Violet, was invited to all the dos and functions, although old man Charlie wasn't always encouraged into the pubs. I don't think the twins were too happy about their father's drinking habits. On family nights, or when the twins invited women or personal friends to join them in the pub, you knew that nothing unpleasant was going to happen – not even bad language was allowed. You always knew how the night would be by the people who were there. No matter who the twins had the hump with, they would never do anything in front of Violet. Whatever they did, they never brought it home. Their family ties were very, very strong, and we got to know all the Krays well. I liked old Cannonball – the twins' grandfather, Jimmy Lee – and I was friendly with their Aunt May and her husband, Albert. They were a lovely couple, who always had a smile and a good word.

I used to see Violet often at May's house in Vallance Road. She was a very quiet, easy-going woman who always made you welcome: 'Hello, how are you? How's the family? Would you like a cup of tea?' When the twins had their mansion, 'The Brooks', in Suffolk, she always did a Sunday dinner, no matter how many were invited. She idolised the twins.

Smallish, with blonde hair, and always smartly dressed, she was a real East End woman. First and foremost she was a mother who loved her family – very homely, always in and out with her shopping bags. I never saw her lose her temper. She wasn't like that. The twins adored her, and the boys on the firm respected her greatly. We'd all have a little chat with her when we saw her.

Old man Charlie was the guv'nor, because in any East End family the husband was the head of the household. He was always very aware of the twins' standing in the community, but I doubt if he knew exactly what was going on. When we were all nicked, I think his reactions were much the same as my father's. They didn't want to believe what had been happening around them. Same for Violet. What mother would want to believe it? She didn't say a word about it in public after it happened. She never commented, just looked the other way.

Charlie Kray, the twins' brother, was very well liked indeed and got on with everyone. He had a nice personality about him and he was a socialiser, a man who liked a good time. He was always smiling. You could have a laugh with Charlie, whereas Ronnie and Reggie you had to take seriously. Charlie's wife Dolly kept her distance from the Kray family. She seemed not to be part of them. He's since split with her and is now with a lovely, friendly, outgoing woman called Diana.

When the firm was at the height of its power, Charlie never took an active part: he wasn't seen around, except on social occasions. He had his family, he had his own career as a businessman and he only ever helped his brothers on the business end of things. But he was aware of the twins' position, and he was loyal to them. I always got the impression he was closer to Reggie than he was to Ronnie.

They were very staunch family people, the Krays, and the twins were always fiercely proud of their roots. Much has been made of all their nights out clubbing with celebrity friends, but the twins liked nothing more than to be among their own people. They'd sooner spend a night in the pub in Bethnal Green than glam it up in the West End of London.

Any celebrities they came across, they brought into their own areas of life, not the reverse. Contrary to what has been written about them in the past, they didn't seek to glamorise themselves, although they eventually became glamorous because of their show business connections and their club ownerships. They never forced themselves on showbiz people; it was the other way round. Many celebrities knew the twins could open doors for them socially because of their legitimate club interests and sought their company, although when the cameras came out Reggie and Ronnie undeniably saw the opportunity for good public relations. Other well-known personalities, of course, were aware of the twins' notoriety and wanted to know them for that reason. Wealth and crime tend to mix, and showbiz and crime mix even better; wealth, crime and stardom are an eternal triangle.

Entertainers, actors and actresses and sportsmen spent hours with the twins in clubs. I met Sonny Liston, whom I found to be a little bit aloof, among a host of champion boxers, and I shook hands with singers Lenny Peters and Joe Brown, both very likeable chaps. Christine Keeler, who sparked the Profumo political crisis of the sixties, was photographed with Reggie and Ronnie.

Some lasting friendships did grow out of these celebrity liaisons. Diana Dors and her husband Alan Lake were very, very nice people who had a real fondness for the twins, as did Barbara Windsor, another East End girl who never forgot her roots. Judy Garland was a genuine friend who was proud of her connections with them; she was the guest of honour at one of their pub nights in Bethnal Green.

You never knew who you were going to bump into next when you went for a drink with the twins. One night I had a meet with them in the Old Horns. Two Scottish guys were in the company, one of whom was destined to become an extremely well-known criminal: Jimmy Boyle. At the time he was on the trot from the police and, like most villains, was more interested in seeing the East End than the West End. Jimmy was the same age as me, and he was very well regarded in Scotland at the time. My Nicky and I showed him round a few pubs at Reggie's request, and he turned out to be a very polite fella, nothing like his reputation. A few weeks afterwards he was nicked and charged with murder in Scotland.

It was around the same time that I met Freddie Foreman, at a party with the twins. He had his own pub, the Prince of Wales in Lant Street, south London, a minute's walk from where I live today. Of all the people I've met in my life, Fred had had the roughest end of the stick. He was charged with three murders he didn't do, and was acquitted of each one. Every other serious crime there is he was accused of at one time or another. He had a great love of children and family life, Fred, and he was a big fan of boxing and sport in general. I always knew him as a man of integrity and honour. Recently, there was a disgraceful attempt to belittle him when he was dragged on to a plane in Spain and sent back to England to appear in court. He was subsequently found not guilty of participating in the £26 million Brinks-Mat gold bullion robbery at Heathrow in 1983, but he was convicted of handling money from it and sentenced to nine years – an outrageous sentence. Had it been anybody else, it would probably have been two years.

Ronnie Knight, Barbara Windsor's ex-husband, has also been suspected of an involvement in Brinks-Mat. I first met Ron in the Kew Club in Paddington around 1967. He was the archetypal 'likeable villain', a rough and ready man who liked a party. He owned a club, the A & R, in the Charing Cross Road in partnership with Fred. Another one from a family of brothers, Ronnie has had his share of tragedy in life. One of his brothers was shot dead in an arcade in Soho. Ron was accused of murder in what was said to be a revenge attack, and acquitted. Now he's in Spain and feels that, if he came back to England, an injustice would be done to him regarding Brinks-Mat. Again, it's a case of 'give a dog a bad name'. I hope to God his problems sort themselves out.

The twins' nose for the law was second to none. Sometimes we'd be in company when, out of the blue, Ronnie would announce, 'The law's about, we're leaving.' Everything would stop and we'd move out immediately. Nine times out of ten, he'd be right: the strangers he'd noticed would indeed be coppers. Every pub Reg and Ron went into was thoroughly checked over by members of the firm before they arrived, as a security measure against the police and other villains. If you saw Albert Donaghue, for instance, you knew the twins weren't far away. They would take over the door and put their own men there so they could keep tabs on who was coming in and out. Photographers in clubs frequently had the film in their cameras taken off them, and anyone who came over, making themselves busy in a drunken state, would get a right-hander. A drunken man can be a dangerous man, and the twins didn't like that.

I had my phone taken out because it was bugged. If I rang Ron from a call box, he'd keep it short and sweet. He'd say, 'Come round', and slam the phone down. If he was in one of his humorous moods, he'd often say, 'You may as well go and have a tea break,' before the phone would go down.

We all began to get paranoid about police surveillance. A friend of mine, Billy Taylor, told me that he once set up a meet with the twins and they were so convinced they were being set up they made him sit in the Grave Maurice until their solicitor came and reassured them that everything was all right. In my experience, if they weren't sure of someone they would shun that person.

We never really looked upon it as a personal vendetta with the police. The twins were not men to slag off the law; they were polite, not ignorant or insolent. They had a certain respect for the law as a foe. I'm not talking about the local bobby on the beat, who I suppose puts up with the brunt of the flak, but the gangbusting squad which had by now been set up especially to investigate us. That squad, I'm certain, developed a reciprocal respect for the twins, whether the officers admitted it or not. I think the twins did expect to be nicked at some time, but none of us had any idea of the scale of the operation being mounted against us. Much less did we anticipate the consequences of its eventual success.

I felt safe around the twins at the time. Being in their firm gave me a sense of security, a feeling of being amongst my own. In many ways, we were just like all of the other gangs we dealt with. They also had their characters, they were in it for the money, they relied on who they knew, what they were capable of doing and what went out over the grapevine, and at the same time they were mostly men of principles and respect. You gave respect and you got it back, inside and outside of criminal circles.

But beyond these areas of common ground the twins were different, and people knew it. They were often called upon to solve disputes between different firms, and they were very good at it. Their leadership, through sheer personality and character, was all-powerful – so capable you couldn't imagine anything going wrong. They were the organisers and we worked under their umbrella, which we trusted.

Everything was done properly. When they were having a business meeting, Ronnie would listen to the basics and the prospects, then Reggie would take over and discuss the finer details. For the most part, they conducted their affairs in the same orderly, efficient manner. It was reassuring.

The twins weren't people who would take orders off anybody: They never backed down and they didn't pretend. If Ronnie Kray said he would do something, he would do it, come hell or high water. If he gave his word, he kept his word, whether he was making a threat or a promise.

Not many would go to the lengths they did, in every respect of life. They had their own very keen sense of right and wrong. They would always take the side of the underdog, if they thought that someone was intimidating or taking a liberty with a weaker person. My brother Chris could never stand a bully, either. He was very much in the same mould as the twins, and they recognised that in him.

Their loyalty to members of the firm was absolute, and they expected the same in return. They gave their men a good living and a lifestyle which included all the fringe benefits you could think of. But certain people abused the twins' trust, took the benefits and then took advantage, long before the final betrayals at the Old Bailey. If you had an animosity with someone else in the circle, it would have been easy to go to the twins and say, 'He's a wrong 'un', and wait for them to take action against that person. This did happen. They were used by people whose word they trusted to hang out some dirty washing that they should never have been involved in. Scotch Jack Dickson, a man few of us liked, engineered one or two such episodes.

Scotch Jack was fat, with pug features and dark hair pushed back off his face. He'd been in the army with Ian Barrie, I think in a tank regiment, and they'd come to London together – much to Ian's later disgust – to put themselves up for the firm. The twins always liked a Jock around them.

Ian, who had been sent down by a Scottish firm, was worth his weight in gold, as the twins would subsequently discover. He became Ronnie Kray's right-hand man. Jack, however, ended up just doing a bit of running around for them, and he used to stick their name up everywhere.

Scotch Jack was a very unsavoury character, the sort of person who would beat someone up for their social security money

Above: The Kray twins boxing when they were boys.   ©*PA Photos*

Below: Ronnie and Reggie (*left*) with their mum, Violet. I used to help her carry her shopping when I was a lad.   ©*Getty Images*

Above: Ronald and Reginald with their brother Charlie (*second from right*) at the Kentucky Club after the Premiere of *Sparrows Can't Sing* in 1963. ©*Getty Images*

Below: With heavyweight boxer Sonny Liston, signing autographs at the Kentucky Club in 1965. ©*Getty Images*

Above left: Reg and Frances Shae at their wedding in Bethnal Green in April, 1965. They were married for two years until her suicide at just 23. She was the only woman he ever loved. *©Getty Images*

Above right: Ronnie on holiday with a friend in 1965. *©Getty Images*

Below: Me (*far left*) with my brothers Christopher (*far right*) and Nicky (*second right*) in a West End club, just about the time that Scotland Yard were closing in. *©Getty Images*

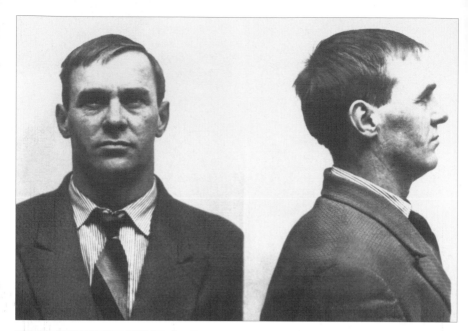

On March 9, 1966, Cornell (*above*) and a friend were drinking at The Blind Beggar pub. Cornell, an enforcer for the Richardson gang, sneered 'Look who's here' when he saw Ronnie, who pulled out a pistol, shot him in the forehead and walked out. A police photograph (*below*) clearly shows the blood on the floor. Cornell died in hospital (*inset*).

Above left: Jack McVitie, better known as Jack The Hat. We called him that because of the bowler he wore to conceal his baldness. ©*Getty Images*

Above right: 97 Evering Road, Stoke Newington, where Reggie murdered Jack The Hat with a carving knife. I saw the whole thing; death has a terrible, terrible smell that never leaves you. ©*PA Photos*

Below left: Reg and Ron at their family home in Vallance Road. ©*Getty Images*

Below right: Police Inspector Leonard 'Nipper' Read, who led the investigation into The Firm. I never thought he was a bad man. I even wrote to him from prison and he replied saying he'd back any parole application that I might make. ©*Getty Images*

Reg gives Ron a light, shortly before the trial. ©*Getty Images*

Above: Reg (*left*) and Ron (*right*) at their mother's funeral in 1982.   ©*Rex Features*

Below left: Charlie (*left*) and Reg (*right*) at Ron's funeral in 1995.   ©*PA Photos*

Below right: I do have regrets about my past, I must admit, but I'm not ashamed of it.

©*PA Photos*

Above: At Charlie Kray's funeral in 2000 with my Wendy. She brought stability into my life at a time when, after my release, I was confused and disorientated; it's not impossible that I might have drifted back into crime. But with her around, keeping my feet on the ground, I'd never be tempted to go back to my old way of life. I first saw her in the pub The Florist, in Bethnal Green. We were making eyes at each other for months before we started talking properly. *©Rex Features*

Below: Me and Freddie Forman in 2000. He's often had the rough end of the stick, having been accused of almost every crime under the sun at some point in his life. But he's a man of integrity and honour and I've always found Freddie to be a good friend, very well liked and respected. *©Rex Features*

without a thought. He would violently injure people, ponce money off those who couldn't defend themselves, and once beat up the local milkman because he wanted his girl off him. Surprisingly, he got her. He later married the woman, Stella, and they deserve each other.

One night at a party, when things were dying off, Scotch Jack walked around the room picking up all the boxes of cigarettes, taking any which were left in the packs and filling them all into one box for himself. He didn't feel that he should have to put his hand in his pocket, not even for a drink or a cigarette.

Because he was connected, he thought that was his passport to live on Easy Street. 'Here I am on the firm, I can do what I like.'

He frequently went to the Regency, and he used to wait for people he knew in there to buy Stella a drink. He wouldn't think of buying it himself. I saw him beating up a kid one day, while Stella sat there laughing and drinking. That's the sort of people they were. If the twins were ever accused of being liberty-takers, it was never their own fault. It was down to people like Scotch Jack doing things in their name.

On one occasion Scotch Jack Dickson had an argument with Connie Whitehead, and Whitehead rightly stuck a glass in his eye. Dickson went whingeing to Ronnie. On the strength of what Scotch Jack had said, Ronnie wanted to do something about it; but he was persuaded by other people to change his mind.

On another night, Dickson got a right-hander in the Regency from a man called Johnny Shea. So Dickson went whining back to the twins about Johnny. He said, 'He called you a pair of mugs.' It was a pack of lies: Johnny Shea never said it. We all knew him, and he was a sound man. I liked him. In a drink, like anyone else, he might say the wrong things, but he was a nice bloke.

Ronnie Hart, the twins' cousin and another less agreeable member of the firm, was ordered to shoot Johnny Shea because of the remark he was alleged to have made to Dickson. Hart was instructed to hit him in the body and not kill him. He burst into Shea's flat and shot him in the hand. It wasn't warranted, but I must add this: Shea never held it against anyone. He was the first one to come to the Old Bailey in defence of us lot – to stand there and do what he could to help us. At the same time, the man from our firm who had set him up, and the one who shot him, were busy giving evidence against us.

If Dickson ever achieved anything in his life it was this: while he knew Reggie and Ronnie Kray, he was granted some type of respect. They invited him in and they fed him. After all they did for him, he manipulated the support they offered to suit his own purposes, and when it came to getting nicked he was one of the first to stab them in the back. The twins used to hear some bad things about him, but because of his connections with the firm they wouldn't want to believe it, partly because he'd come down from Scotland with Ian, who was greatly respected. They were very loyal. They protected him to an extent, but even they got to the stage where they said, 'Enough is enough,' and pulled him up about his bullying.

Scotch Jack wasn't the only person around the twins to take advantage of their loyalty. And in other ways, things were not entirely happy within the firm. There was a lot of mistrust between us all, and there were various people stirring up trouble, trying to curry favour with the twins and score points off the rest of us. I find that sad now. The twins were aware of a lot of what was going on, and they were good at juggling it about when it suited them, keeping one in favour and another out. On the surface, everything was sweet. Underneath, it certainly wasn't.

CHAPTER NINE

A PERIOD
OF TURBULENCE

Ian Barrie and Ronnie Bender were the only two members of the firm who became personal friends of mine. Most of the others were easy enough to get along with, purely through our common working interests, although I disliked Scotch Jack Dickson and I never had a great regard for Ronnie Hart.

Hart was roughly the same age as me, not a bad-looking man, smartish, fair-haired and a bit of a ladies' man, like Donaghue. He was a cousin of the twins, and his real involvement with them began when he escaped from Eastchurch prison on the Isle of Sheppey; they took care of him then because of the blood connection. He let it be known that he was a Kray and took full advantage. He thought he had a licence to go anywhere in the twins' name and do what he liked. He'd cut people, knowing full well that, because of his connections, they could do nothing about it. Hart saw himself as some sort of third in command, and he tried to give orders out to members of the firm. Obviously, it was to be laughed at – nobody took it seriously. He would have been nothing without the twins. Technically, they let him get away with it for a while. He hung around them more than I suppose they wanted him to, but they put up with him because he was a relation.

He came to me and Chris one day with a deal. He had taken money to shoot – but not kill – somebody in Romford Market. He went to the market with Scotch Jack, they fired a shot in the air, and Hart reported back to Ronnie that it had all gone wrong.

Ronnie called him a liar, and said he'd see someone else about it. That's when Hart asked me and my brother to do it. The deal was, Hart would say he'd done the job and he'd cut the grand with us. I went to see Ronnie Kray and he couldn't believe it. He said, 'Forget all about that, we'll take care of it in our own way.' I think the twins were a bit amused by it.

Certainly, the rest of us treated Hart as a joke. But he wouldn't prove to be so funny later on when it came to the arrests. When the going was good he was first past the post, but when the going got tough he was last. He told lie after lie to save his own skin when the police picked him up.

That didn't surprise me in a big way, but Albert Donaghue's betrayal certainly did. He was Reggie's personal minder, a very deep bloke and one of the few we all felt we could rely on. Everybody respected him. I liked him as a person, and on a few occasions I went out with him socially. Albert was on the East End payroll; collecting protection, and I did the rounds with him a couple of times. We'd visit around forty pubs, stopping every now and again for a drink, and an envelope would be passed to him in each one.

All in all the twins had a good income, not only from the protection rounds but from their legitimate club interests in the Kentucky, Esmerelda's Barn and El Morocco. Charlie had a business too, a tie firm in Mare Street.

Protection payments were known as 'pensions', a word which became famous through our trial, and most of the firm were given what we called 'sweets'. You would have a pay-out from one particular place, and what you got out of it was your business. It was yours – in the twins' words, 'Get your own sweets.' It was a wage of sorts. I personally never got involved in the sweets because I was earning commissions through my public relations work. I made my money my way.

The twins eventually promoted Albert to the West End with Tommy Cowley, collecting from club owners like Pauline Wallace, who ran the Pigalle, the Stork and the Society among others. She was one of the best-known greyhound owners in England. One night on the round, she said she was going away to the States for ten weeks and wanted to pay all the protection up front, which amounted to a lot of money. She eventually moved to America for good and settled in Florida, a multi-millionairess.

Albert Donaghue lived in Bow with his wife Pauline and a couple of kids. He was a dangerous man, feared in the East End: I saw him stab a couple of people. He had to be good, because of his personal job with Reggie, who was very explosive at the time. In my mind there were no two ways about it: Albert was more than capable of killing a man.

On one occasion Dickie Morgan's girlfriend, Sally, invited a bunch of us round to her ground-floor flat in Bethnal Green. There was Dickie, Albert Donaghue, my Chris, Nicky and I, Ronnie Bender, the Cardew brothers from the Angel, and two other men called Billy Thomas and Micky Bailey. I gave Nicky a .38 pistol to hold on to for me. We always had one near us. Always.

Suddenly an argument broke out between Billy Thomas and Dickie Morgan's brother, Martin. One of the Cardew brothers poked his nose in too. As it developed, a secondary row started between Albert Donaghue and Billy Thomas, who was a good friend of his.

Billy said, 'Albert, you're a slag,' at which point Albert said to my brother, 'Give me the gun, Nick.'

As soon as I saw Albert with a gun in his hand, I knew he would pull the trigger. He let two or three go off, and shot Billy in the leg. I pushed Micky Bailey over the balcony to get him out of the way.

Chris, Nicky and I got hold of Albert and took the gun off him. We had to dig the bullets out of the wall and the floor. I was in the middle because I knew all the parties concerned. Billy was a good friend of mine, so I pushed him out the door, telling him, 'I think you'd better fuck off.' Which he did. I saw him a couple of weeks later when he came round to see me and Chris, wanting to know how he stood on it.

Albert was also rumoured to have stabbed a man called Billy Amos, who later became a supergrass, in Smithfield Meat Market over a deal involving some clothes. Albert was the buyer. Amos claimed to have been visited in hospital by some of the police who were investigating the Kray firm. He told me the police said: 'If anything happens to Donaghue, this is yours.' Meaning, if there were any revenge attacks on Albert, the police would fit up Amos. So obviously Albert was already co-operating with the police.

At this time, though, the only one of us who didn't trust Albert was Reggie Kray. A couple of years before, Donaghue had fallen foul of the twins, and Reggie had shot him in the leg. I remember Reggie telling me: 'I never really trusted him after that. How can you ever trust a person you've shot?'

Albert wasn't the only member of the firm to be shot in the leg by Reggie. Another was Nobby Clarke, a villain who'd been with the twins for years. He was about five feet one, Nobby, a real character with a bad little temper, ducking and diving all around. He did a lot of running about for the twins, and he looked after one or two places, but he was really more of a companion for them. We all had a liking for Nobby. He never complained or bragged about the fact that he had been shot by Reggie. It came out of a nothing incident that blew up out of all proportion when Reggie had the hump about something.

So although the general impression of the firm was of one fearsome and united front, we had our own internal troubles every now and again. Additionally, there were undercurrents and needle matches which never actually boiled over into violence but were still very much a part of the atmosphere around the firm at that time.

Connie Whitehead, for instance, was a whipping boy for the twins, even though he'd been with them for years and was a close member of the firm, involved in everything and very capable – the typical Cockney villain who was going places. He was involved in frauds, violence and helped after both the McVitie and Cornell murders, to an extent. Chris and I both liked Connie. When we got to know him, he was a go-between for us in our early dealings with the twins. He used violence only as a last resort, but when he did, he was very useful. For some reason, Ronnie always used to take his rages out on 'that rat Whitehead', and the twins always wanted to know where he was – 'Get hold of Whitehead.' He would show at the last minute, always looking uncomfortable.

Ronnie Kray kept Tommy Cowley on his toes, too. Tommy, along with businessmen like Leslie Payne and Freddie Gore who fronted companies for the twins, worked on the financial side of the firm – strictly on deals, never violence. Ronnie would always be saying to him, 'Go out and get me some money.' Once there were about ten of us in a Turkish club in Liverpool Street, and Ronnie was on about Cowley all night – 'I hope he's out there getting me some fucking money.'

All of a sudden, Cowley appeared. Ronnie said: 'Where the fucking hell have you been?'

Cowley replied, 'What the fucking hell's it got to do with you?'

It's the only time I've ever seen anybody other than Reggie or Charlie Kray get away with having a go at Ronnie. He just looked at Cowley as if he didn't exist.

Cowley was lucky. No one stood a chance against Ronnie Kray, least of all him. I recall one night in a club when a big argument broke out, involving Tommy. I saw words being exchanged. A geezer was having a go at Tommy, and Tommy didn't want to know. I had to step in on his behalf and do the other bloke with a big glass ashtray.

Outside the small and turbulent world of the firm, bigger problems were beginning to pile up. For Reggie Kray, life turned into a nightmare with the death of his wife Frances from an overdose of barbiturates in June 1967. He went through a very, very bad time within himself, the lowest ebb of his life. For a while, I don't think he could believe that Frances had gone. He managed to remain in control of everything that was going on, but he was very vulnerable: he was on the bottle, and people in the firm were able to influence him, whereas previously that could never have happened. It may well have been a combination of these things that led him to murder only a few months later.

Reggie had loved Frances and treated her well. After her death he thought a lot about what had happened to her — the bad circumstances under which he had lost her. At times he became virtually unapproachable. He suffered terrible remorse, although there was no way he had anything to do with her dying. It wasn't his fault: you can't be responsible for what another person's going to do.

There were accusations coming from her side of the family, and bad feeling between Reggie and Frankie Shea, Frances' brother, who had long been a friend of all of us. It was a very awkward situation, but it was understandable: you've got two brothers-in-law, and you've got a sister and a wife who's died. Frankie had introduced Frances to Reggie, and I think he thought, 'If it wasn't for Reggie, she'd be alive today.' Reggie was trying to handle the loss of a wife he adored as well as the flak from the Sheas, particularly Frances' parents who had tried to keep her away from him after they first separated at the end of 1965. They disapproved of Reggie, and involved Frances in what Reg later referred to as a 'tug of love', putting pressure on her to leave him. When she did, she suffered a nervous breakdown and attempted suicide twice, but she was about to go on a reconciliation holiday with Reg at the time of her death.

A lot of people have tried to blame Ronnie Kray for the split in the first place. But to me, Ronnie's attitude appeared to be, 'They're married, let them get on with it.' I don't believe he was in any way instrumental in breaking up the marriage.

In the dark days after Frances died Reggie seemed capable of doing anything. One night he said to me, 'You got a car with you, Tony? Drive me round to the Vic.' The Victory was a pub in Murray Grove, Hoxton. We got in the car and when we got to Old Street, it suddenly dawned on me: he knew Frankie Shea drank in the Vic with a fella called Twiggy Llewellyn.

Despite the fact that Frances and her family were from Hoxton, and the twins themselves had been born there, they generally didn't like the area or anyone from it. Now Reggie was going to see the very people that he wanted to take it out on. He had a gun on him, and I realised that he was thinking about shooting Frankie Shea. By now, the animosity between them had intensified. Frankie had taken Reggie to court over a debt of £1,000, which I thought was a wrong thing to do. The reason why Reggie hadn't paid him was purely and simply to get back at him over Frances.

Now, driving towards Hoxton, I found myself in a difficult position, knowing both parties. We're talking about a Reggie Kray who was not the Reggie Kray that I knew – a man who was bitter about his wife dying, tending to blame the other side. In his shoes I would have felt the same – anybody would – and I understood his feelings, especially since other people were putting a lot of poison in, sticking up Frances' name while knowing it was a sore point. At the same time I saw the other side of it all and I could never have harmed Frankie Shea; could never have seen him shot.

I parked the car opposite the Victory and sat there for half an hour talking to Reggie as a pal. In my heart of hearts, I was almost certain that Reggie could not have hurt Frankie. If he'd come face to face with him, he'd have been more likely to break down, because every time he saw him he saw Frances; or maybe he might even have given him a few quid rather than do anything to him. But when Reggie was in a funny mood, you could never be completely sure.

I said to him, 'Look, Reggie, you don't mean it. Come on, you don't mean it.' And as we talked, I knew that the moment of danger had passed. Reggie calmed down; he was rational again.

I remember one night at the height of the bad feeling I went into a club called Oscars in Albemarle Street, Mayfair. A lot of the chaps used to drink there at the time. I was talking to the co-owner, Peter Hogg, at the door while my Nicky went on inside. Frankie Shea, who was in there, must have seen my brother, because he came walking out immediately and bumped straight into me.

He said, 'Am I all right? I know you and Chris are very strong with the twins now.'

I answered, 'Frank, we go back a long way, we were boyhood friends, and I'd never do anything to harm you. I'd be insulted if you thought I would.'

One day in the Carpenters Arms I said to Reggie, 'Don't ask me to go against Frank.' 'I wouldn't,' he replied.

The police campaign against us was now gathering momentum. We were aware of the pressure increasing gradually, even though we still had no inkling of the lengths the gangbusters were going to, or the amount of information they were gathering. It was now more than a year since Ronnie's murder of George Cornell in the Blind Beggar, which happened while I was in prison in March 1966.

On the face of it, things couldn't have looked better for the Kray firm. The twins were at the height of their power and there was no opposition: the law had done them a favour by nicking the Richardson brothers, Charlie and Eddie, and the rest of their gang.

There had been a big rivalry with the Richardsons, dating back to when I first started working and drinking in the West End, with certain incidents causing a build-up of ill feeling. Looking back, there was no need for it. It was all to do with personality clashes and bravado, with everybody doing well and congregating in the same places. We all used clubs like the Astor and the Starlight, for instance, and if a member of one firm walked in and saw five members of another, words weren't necessary. It wasn't what was said, it was the whole feel of it. A clash had to come.

Up to then everybody had tended to keep to their own side of things, their own territory, not treading on each other's toes within the circles. The Richardsons were powerful in south London, we were powerful on our side of the water, and we had other firms connected and allied to each of us throughout London. But then the so-called Swinging Sixties took off.

It was a boom time, and the West End was where it all happened. Everybody wanted a slice of that. The opportunities were there for all of us to get a good living, but people are greedy. Each firm wanted a bit more than the other, so of course it caused conflicts and developed into a power struggle. Several firms were getting their whack out of the West End, but the twins organised it and wound up with a larger slice. In time, though, too many people started trying to jump over each other, especially the south London lot. The Richardsons, who were well known and feared, were expanding fast.

The twins called a meet in a club just south of the river, with the intention of sorting it out. All of the firms in London were expected to attend. The Richardsons, obviously, were invited, but did not send any representatives, which was a direct challenge. So it was decided, rightly or wrongly, that something should be done about them. But unfortunately they were all nicked, barring George Cornell, before anything could happen.

There was a shoot-out in a club called Mr Smith's in Catford, when the Richardsons and another south London gang had a confrontation. It was alleged that Eddie Richardson was one of the leaders and that he jumped up and challenged the other firm by saying, 'No more drinks unless you ask me.' I don't know the truth of that, because I wasn't there.

Eddie Richardson was more of a fighter, more of a villain, than his brother Charlie. He was the sort of man who, when he put his mind to something, would do it, and he wouldn't take shit from anyone.

Charlie, on the other hand, never struck me as a bloodthirsty man. He was first and foremost a businessman, a car dealer, and although he knew his roots, he never suffered fools gladly; he could be hard when he had to be. Allegations were later made that he held kangaroo courts, sat with a wig and gown on, sentenced his victims to torture and generally did outlandish things. I think this was an exaggeration. Charlie never came across to me in that way, although they did have business to do, the Richardsons, and they ran a formidable empire.

They were faced with an equally heavy gang on the night of the Mr Smith's affair, and all hell broke loose. Frankie Fraser, who was with the Richardsons, was hit by gunfire, and Dickie Hart, a good friend of the twins who happened to be there at the time, was shot dead. Although the twins were not involved in the Mr Smith's row, their allegiance to other people, namely Dickie Hart, brought them directly into conflict. Ronnie was all for an out-and-out war, and there could only be one winner: Ronnie Kray. With the rest of the Richardsons under lock and key, Ronnie shot George Cornell through the head a day or two later as a come-back, and also as a response to Cornell's public denouncement of him as a 'poof'.

The words 'underworld' and 'gangsters' started coming into play more and more, and the papers were talking about 'leading underworld characters'. What does that mean? A number of men who drank together in a pub in the East End?

These days such a thing as an underworld exists even less than it did then. Very few successful professional criminals associate with each other. They are very paranoid. They try to live a middle-class life where everything looks legal even though it isn't. I won't deny there are people who rob security vans and banks, using members of different firms. But I prefer to call them 'circles'. And 'gangster' is a word I find very embarrassing. I hate to be called that – it's a movie name.

The things we did, we referred to as business. We didn't do them for fun. We didn't see any point in gaining a reputation only to get nothing out of it. Our game didn't involve pleasure; we did it professionally. It was a business thing, and a business thing only. It was never personal, unless the challenge to the authority of the firm was issued on a personal level. If violence had to be done in a professional way to someone else, it was always referred to as business.

Nothing was ever done without good reason. Reputations were there to be pulled down, and it was the twins' job to make sure that nobody could do that. They succeeded brilliantly. They were a one-off: if anybody had the right to be called 'gangsters', they did. In a way they belonged in the Chicago days, and that's how they were viewed at the time.

They did almost all of their own villainy, even though they didn't have to. Granted, they had to be seen to be able to do it, where violence was concerned, but they had established that long ago. I think they were the type of people who wanted to be able to say, 'Look, don't worry about that, we don't need anyone.'

When the Mafia men came over the twins looked after them well, but they let it be known that they were not going to hand over any of their business interests in London. They were the guv'nors. I think the Mafia were a bit wary of them, especially Ronnie, but they did respect them.

And so, for a while, life carried on profitably and without competition; and even though the twins, unknowingly, had one or two bad apples in the firm, they still had some good men around them. Ian Barrie, Ronnie's personal minder and an ex-military man, had had an accident in a tank. It had caught fire, leaving him badly scarred from his ear right the way down one side of his neck. It didn't spoil his looks, though, and I thought it gave him a better character. Ian was thoroughly trustworthy. He never spoke about what he got involved in – not even Ronnie's shooting of Cornell, which he witnessed – and he never complained, before or after the convictions. He was genuine and gentlemanly, a very deep thinker who never showed his feelings or put anyone down. Everything he said was constructive. He did what he thought he had to do, and that was it. He gave us help and back-up no matter what, and I never heard anyone say a bad word about him. He was very well thought of by the twins and the rest of us. Ronnie could never have picked a better man: he was a credit to Scotland.

The twins were also very lucky to have someone like Ronnie Bender around them. He was another ex-Army man, a big, jovial, good-looking fella and an accomplished all-round sportsman, hence his nickname of the Captain. He was very good-humoured by nature – until someone upset him, and then he could be a handful, as tough as they come. He wasn't someone to rub up the wrong way: he would stand up to anybody. Ronnie was a man's man, a bloke who proved himself at the end of the day and who always showed concern for people, regardless of his own problems. He was a diamond.

Big Pat Connolly was another very likeable character. Huge in both height and weight, Big Pat came in and out of the firm from time to time as a front-line soldier. He was a minder in various clubs, and if there was an immediate problem anywhere the twins would put him on the door. Just after the murder of George Cornell, Pat was stationed in Vallance Road with a pump action shotgun and told to stay there and mind the door of the Krays' house. Cornell's widow went round there, threw a brick through the window and caused a scene. Pat didn't know what she was on about, and simply told her to go away.

Chris and I attracted more than our share of attention from the police throughout 1967: we were being investigated on suspicion of two murders. One was the killing of a man called Tony Mafia, who was a very good friend of another villain, Buller Ward.

Ward lived at Haggerston, same as us, and he knew our parents. He had close ties with leading figures in the London circles, and he looked the part. Chris and I had had our own connections with the family from an early age. One day at the beginning of the fifties, we were walking along the Regents Canal between Hoxton and Queensbridge Road when a kid fell in the water. Unbeknown to us it was Buller Ward's son, Bonner, and he always respected us for saving him from drowning.

Buller always seemed pretty sociable to us, but in the middle to late sixties he had fallen foul of the twins and was keeping away from their company. Tony Mafia, his friend, had also upset certain people in the circles. He was getting around the West End clubs where he was known as the Magpie, because he would get hold of gems and lumps of gold and bullion, which he then stored in vaults.

One day Nicky and I went to the Regency with the twins, Albert Donaghue, Scotch Jack Dickson and a few others. Buller Ward was with Tony Mafia at the bar. Reggie Kray said to Buller: 'Tell Tony Mafia I want to see him downstairs.' Next thing, Buller warned Mafia to get out of the club. The minute that happened, Reggie got the hump and gave Buller Ward a right-hander.

Ward said to him, 'You'll have to do better than that, Reggie.' Without further ado, Reggie pulled out a knife and slashed him across the face. A bit of blood spattered on to a fella who was passing by. He said to Reggie, 'Be careful what you're doing.'

Ronnie stabbed him in the shoulder and replied: 'You'd better be fucking careful yourself.'

One night, Tony Mafia was found behind the wheel of a car, shot in the back of the head, on the Southend arterial road in Essex. The police believed Chris, Nicky and I had something to do with it, and they pulled us in and questioned us. I didn't deny that I knew Mafia, and I didn't deny that I knew violence had been used on him by various people he had had skirmishes with in the past. But I certainly denied any involvement in his death: it was nothing to do with us. The point was that the twins and those around them were being suspected of every violent incident that occurred: 'It's the firm.' And people were beginning to connect my brothers and me with murders: they knew we would use violence, had access to guns and were more than capable of pulling the trigger.

Meanwhile, another villain called Scotch Jack Buggy was found dead. The story goes that a police officer just happened to be fishing off a pier in Brighton and pulled up Buggy's body, wrapped in chicken wire. It must have been a very lucky catch because Buggy had been weighted down with lumps of rock and iron.

The police inquiries led to an investigation into a small yacht which happened to turn up in Birmingham, near Tony Hart's garage long firm. They believed the yacht had been used to dispose of Buggy's body. Because of that, the police decided we should be questioned. They wanted to know how this boat came to be in Birmingham, near a garage that Chris and I were involved in. It was put to me that I'd known Buggy through prison and that I was a murder suspect. The police were convinced, for a while, that Chris and I had something to do with it, and we started thinking someone was trying to fit us up. I'm not saying I knew nothing about the killing, because that would be lying, but I wasn't involved in it. One of the culprits went to America, and the other to Switzerland.

Some years later, the subject of Buggy arose again. By this time I was in Gartree prison serving the Kray sentence, and I was approached by one of the Great Train Robbers, a small, chirpy fella called Roy The Weasel James. It was rumoured that, before he died, Buggy had been looking after the Weasel's money. And the Weasel was asking me why Buggy had to go.

He said, 'The money doesn't matter to me. I just wouldn't like to think Buggy died for it.'

I was happy to be able to tell Roy that we genuinely hadn't had anything to do with the murder.

CHAPTER TEN

WHEELS OF JUSTICE

I'd spoken to Jack The Hat McVitie on and off for years, but I never got to know him closely until 1967. It all began in a pub called the Mildmay Tavern in Balls Pond Road, Dalston. I often went there to see Pa Flanaghan, whose wife ran the pub; they had a family of sons whom I was also friendly with. I went in there one night early in the New Year, not long after my release from Bristol prison, with Jack The Hat and two other men called Jimmy Briggs and Patsy Murphy. I had bumped into them in another pub, the Greyhound, further along the road.

Patsy was later to become involved in the well-known seventies' Luton Post Office robbery. He was given life and a twenty rec., on the word of a grass, and walked out of the sentence twelve years later after three different Home Secretaries had referred it back to the Court of Appeal. It was the first time fresh evidence had ever been allowed into that court. Patsy's father, Stevie, had a club, the Senate Rooms, in the Angel, which was burned down after a fall-out with a firm in north London.

Jimmy Briggs was another one who would end up in a well-known trial: he was done with George Davis for a robbery at the

Bank of Cyprus. Davis had just been freed on appeal from a fifteen-year sentence for an Electricity Board job, following the famous 'George Davis Is Innocent' graffiti campaign of the early seventies. He was released over a technicality. When he got nicked for the Bank of Cyprus job, he got another fifteen years. It was like a tit-for-tat victory for the police.

Anyway, Jimmy, Patsy, Jack The Hat and I were sitting having a drink in the Mildmay this night when Patsy said to Jack The Hat, 'Tony's just come out of the boob [prison].'

Jack said; 'Anything I can do for you?' He'd done time himself, Jack, and he told me he'd been responsible for the Great Train Robber Charlie Wilson's escape from Winson Green prison the year before. Charlie, who had been serving thirty years, hit the headlines many years later when he was shot dead by an unknown assailant in Spain in 1990.

At eleven o'clock, closing time, we went off to a club called the Tempo which had recently opened in Holloway Road at Highbury Corner. It was being run by an East End lad called Freddie Bird, an ex-docker who was only about five feet ten in height but very, very broad. He had recruited a few Geordies and Jocks with broken noses, the typical thing, from out-of-town firms, dressed them up in dickie bows and stuck them on the door, which made them a target for us lot and the rest of the London firms.

When I walked into the club with Jack The Hat, Jimmy and Patsy, I knew something wasn't right. Freddie Bird was a bit apprehensive about letting Jack in, because he'd had a drink: he was a very unpredictable character who could be highly dangerous. Anyway, we sat down at a table and Jack, who was a Londoner, was going on about these bouncers. We had a meal, and after that a few drinks started going down. The entertainment, a female singer, began her act, and Jack started. He got up on the floor and began heckling the singer.

The Geordie blokes had a few words with him, and Freddie Bird came over saying, 'Turn it in, Jack, she's trying to do her act.'

Jack said to Freddie, 'Who do you think you fucking are bringing this lot down here, Geordies and that?'

And Freddie replied, 'That's enough of that.'

We were in the middle of it all because we'd gone in there with Jack, and East Enders are like that: you stay with the person you walk in with. I didn't know what Jack had on him. I always liked to know if people were tooled up, because at the time a lot were, and it was easy to walk into something.

A few more words were said and another big Geordie fella came over. Jack pushed him away. And then before it could go any further, it stopped. Freddie said, 'That's it, you're barred.'

Jack apparently came back the next night and burst in with a gun, but was thrown out without any shots being fired. He then went on to the Regency where he muttered a few threats and ranted on about these northerners coming down here doing what they wanted.

Freddie later readmitted Jack to the club, but it was to lead to a lot more trouble, memorably when the singer Dorothy Squires arrived for a residency. She was then married to Roger Moore, who was starring in the TV series *The Saint* at the time, and everybody used to yell, 'Where's the Saint?' He would sit over by the dressing room. On the night in question, Dorothy was doing her turn rotten drunk, staggering about and swigging from a bottle of what looked like water but was obviously spirits. But I'll give her this: she could sing.

Jack The Hat shouted over to her, 'What's he like in bed, the old Saint?'

She yelled back, 'You mind your own business, he's a lot better than you.' This led to a stand-up argument between Dorothy Squires and Jack The Hat. She was screaming, 'I'll have a fight with you,' and everybody else was yelling, 'Get the Saint up, he'll get you out of this.'

Roger Moore ran out of the club, and Dorothy Squires staggered off swearing and cursing. The bouncers came in and there was a bit of an argument.

When the next act of the night, a dancer, came on, Jack got up and dropped his trousers. He was wearing a pair of swimming trunks underneath. Freddie Bird came over and blows were thrown. Freddie had no alternative now but to go to the twins.

The firm was called in for a meeting one Monday night at the Regency. About a dozen of us went from there to Freddie's club. Within two minutes of us walking in, everyone in it had walked out. The bouncers were told to leave, and from that minute on, the twins were in charge. They just took it.

Jack carried on making trouble with lots of different people. On one occasion I was in the Mildmay Tavern when he came in drunk, about eleven o'clock, and was refused a drink. His reaction was to pull out a Colt .45 and blow out the bar. Another night, I was about to walk into the Regency when I heard two bangs. Jack The Hat and Tommy Flanaghan, a well-known Scottish face, were standing there with guns firing at one another. A bullet missed me by about six inches.

Things like this were to be bad for Jack, because they would always be reported back to the twins. He was getting into a state where he didn't know what he was doing, challenging people and causing trouble. One night he walked into the Regency with his hand cut to bits, blood dripping everywhere he went. We put a towel round it and sent him to hospital. Another time he came into the place with an axe, made threats and started slamming the axe into the door. John Barry, who ran the club, calmed him down.

Yet another incident involving Jack occurred one night at Charlie Brown's, a restaurant/drinker in Stamford Hill. An argument started between Jack The Hat, Ronnie Hart and his girlfriend Blonde Vicky. She was a well-known girl around the scene, a 'gangster groupie', and she used to go around with a girl called Bubbles, who was with Ronnie Bender up to the time of his arrest. Jack had gone into this club drunk, asking Vicky what she was doing with Hart, and he ended up calling her a slag. Again, this was reported back to the twins, and all these little facts were building up – vital elements in any explanation of why Jack was murdered.

He was damaging the respect that people had for the firm in general and the twins in particular. Not only was he becoming an embarrassment, not only was he undermining the twins' guarantee of peace and quiet in the pubs and clubs they protected, but he was also starting to threaten the twins themselves. It was central to the way they worked that they could not allow that from anybody. He was warned about his behaviour on many occasions, but he carried on doing the very things that he and all of us knew would lead him into serious trouble. Nobody in our circles would have dreamed of carrying on the way he did. Jack was asking for it.

Yet there was no smell of aggravation the night before the murder. Jack The Hat, Reggie, Albert Donaghue, Chris and I sat down together and had a Chinese meal and a few drinks in the Regency. If the twins had the hump with you, you knew it, but that night I detected nothing. I knew that Jack had been getting out of tune and that he'd been told about it, but he showed no signs of uneasiness. Albert Donaghue was a bit distant, but then he always was. Albert didn't show anyone a lot of friendliness, so everything appeared to be as good as gold.

I never dreamed in a million years that twenty-four hours later Reggie would be doing him in and that Jack The Hat McVitie would become one of the most famous murder victims in British history. In the hours leading up to his death, while I sat with the rest of the firm in the Carpenters Arms, Reggie seemed to be a happy bloke, having a drink with Violet and old man Kray. What happened between then and his arrival at the Regency a couple of hours later with murder in his eyes?

Even after the murder itself, I could not, and still cannot, portray him as a vicious killer. As I've said, he wasn't himself after Frances' death – he'd been under a lot of pressure and I don't believe he knew what he was doing until he'd done it. He wasn't a bad man, Reggie Kray. None of us were. We weren't that good either, but we lived by our own code and everybody in the circles understood the rules. There are a lot worse running about today.

I regret what happened. So do Chris and Ronnie Bender. At the time of the killing, I remember thinking, 'This is not part of my life, this is not what I'm into.' Afterwards it was continuously on my mind, but at the same time it didn't register. It seemed like a faraway thing, totally beyond my reckoning. And it kept coming back at the most unexpected times, no matter how much we'd hoped that the secret would remain amongst the few of us who were in that basement flat. One night, a bloke called Bobby Cannon approached me in the Regency. He said to me, like a bolt out of the blue, 'You didn't half do me a favour, Tony . . . the Hat.'

I asked, 'What about him?'

He went, 'I know what happened.' And he did, roughly.

I put it down to one person telling him: Connie Whitehead, who was very friendly with Cannon at the time. I felt I had to tell the twins about what was said. They saw Cannon, and it was never repeated.

At the same time people were beginning to notice that Jack was missing, and there was a lot of speculation about what had happened to him. It was me who started the rumour that Jack had been badly burnt and killed in a car crash while trying to get away from a robbery. That one floated around for months.

Stories of another kind were also circulating. It was being said that the police were looking at an organised gang in London, and that we were going to be nicked. Rumours started coming out of Brixton prison that they were clearing the landing for us. Where there was smoke, there was fire.

We always knew that, when it came, it would be no picnic: we would get a lot of time. We knew that society would not endorse the idea of thugs and villains running around organising crime. But the New Year of 1968 came and we were still at liberty, leading our usual lives, with Chris still based in Birmingham and me going backwards and forwards between there and London.

The twins had acquired their mansion, 'The Brooks', in Suffolk, and it was put about that they were thinking of turning in crime and retiring to the country, where Ronnie would lead a rural life and Reggie would concern himself with legitimate business. They were doing a book with the writer John Pearson, which was eventually published as *A Profession of Violence*.

I don't believe that the twins would have retired – I don't believe they *could* have. The order of London crime would have fallen to pieces, as it did after they were arrested on 8 May 1968, in a simultaneous dawn raid on members of the firm which Chris and I managed to escape.

We'd all been drinking in the Old Horns on the night of the 7th. We went from there to the Astor Club off Berkeley Square, where Albert Donaghue and Ronnie Bender tried to take a camera off a girl who was taking photographs. Everyone was enjoying themselves, and I remember saying goodnight to the twins when they left at about two in the morning, Ronnie with a boy and Reggie with a girl. Chris and I stayed on for a little drink, and then drove straight up to Birmingham. All the others who left were followed home, and when the police hit the addresses in the morning we weren't there.

The first I knew about what had happened was when my Nicky

phoned me at about eleven that morning at the Albany Hotel in Birmingham. He said, 'The twins have been nicked.' They were always expecting it to happen, but nothing concerned them. Like everyone else, they thought it was just a hold – that it would be a case of holding charges or, as we called them, bow and arrow charges being made against them and then they would be freed. It had happened before. In the evening, it hit all the papers. It was national news that a number of men had been arrested, although there was nothing mentioned about murders, and half of the reports didn't even refer to the twins by name but just called them businessmen.

At that time the police didn't have Ronnie Hart, Albert Donaghue or the Mills brothers, so there was no undue concern on our part. The most they could have nicked us for was a couple of GBHs – grievous bodily harm. After about three weeks in Birmingham, we considered it safe to come home. I was arrested with Nicky and June McDonald, the girlfriend of Eddie Futrell, a well-known club owner, in a pub in Haggerston. We were taken to Old Street police station, held for twenty-four hours and questioned by Superintendent Harry Mooney about the murder of Jack The Hat.

He said, 'I want to put this to you, Tony. Your brother Nicky was asked to drive a car somewhere without realising what was in it. It doesn't mean that, because he drove the car, he will be charged with any offence.'

In other words, he was trying to nick us for driving a car with a body in it. But Nicky hadn't even been with us at the murder scene. Mooney had got the information wrong, and it had to be Carol Skinner (Blonde Carol) who had given it to him. I'd never spoken to the woman, and she didn't know me, but she knew Nicky: She'd mistaken me for him.

At that time, my Chris had a Ford Corsair that had to be disposed of for some reason, and the fact that this car was missing interested the police greatly; they thought it was in the Jack The Hat affair somewhere. They gave a phone number to ring if 'Nicky was prepared to talk', and let us go.

A couple of weeks later, Chris was pulled in. He was taken from Walsall to London and questioned at Tintagel House, Scotland Yard's Kray investigation headquarters, by Detective Chief Inspector Leonard 'Nipper' Read, another of the leaders of the inquiry.

Nipper said to Chris, 'The wheels of justice grind slowly, but we're going to get to the bottom of it. We know you had something to do with the McVitie murder. If you decide to tell us what happened, that doesn't mean you'll be prosecuted. You could be witnesses against the Krays. . . .'

We're not like that. Chris was released, but told he would be seeing the police again and was to remember about the wheels of justice.

I said, 'I think they'll be back.'

They dragged us in for questioning again several weeks later when they raided the Harts Hotel in Birmingham. Chris, Nicky and I were staying there at the time they arrived – Mooney, Chief Inspector Frank Cater . . . the gangbusters. They took Nicky and me to Walsall police station on the pretext of questioning us over the Cannock Chase murder. A little girl called Christine Derby had been killed in the area, and the police used this case as an opportunity to arrest us again. I was told, 'Don't worry, Tony, it's nothing to do with Cannock Chase.'

They pulled the hotel owner in too, which was amusing, because he had absolutely no connection with us. He thought we were in the Mafia. Again, Chris was taken to London to Tintagel House; and again, we were released.

The morning of 11 September 1968 started out just like any other day. My wife Pat used to bring me in the papers and ham or cheese rolls from Pellicci's, and then I'd get my little daughter ready to take to school. Karen was now six. I had enrolled her in a Catholic school in Bollo Road, Bethnal Green, which was due to a little bit of my mother's religious influence staying with me, and she was doing well there. She was a lovely little girl, and I looked forward to taking her out every day.

On this particular morning, Pat said to me, 'There are two men sitting outside in a taxi. The milkman seems to have changed, and there are two dustmen sweeping the road.'

I looked out the window, but I took no notice. . . . The next thing I knew, the door was coming in and ten policemen were round my bed telling me not to move my arms otherwise I'd get my head blown off. I was to draw out one arm at a time very slowly and get dressed. Then I was going to be interviewed by Nipper Read.

I did what they told me. I was taken downstairs and out on to the pavement, where I saw all the policemen milling about, and all the cars. The road was sealed off.

I was taken to Tintagel House, and brought to an upper floor in a lift. In the foyer of this floor I saw huge, blown-up photographs of all of us, everywhere. Obviously we were a major inquiry.

I looked round at a side office and saw Nipper Read, Frank Cater and John du Rose, head of the Murder Squad, staring out at me. I was called into the office and told this: 'We're going to ask you five questions. If you don't come up with the right answers, you'll be taken from here and charged with the murder of Jack The Hat McVitie.'

When was the last time I saw him alive? Did I take him to a party? Did I see anything happen to him at the party? Did I see the Kray twins do anything with him at the party? Did I help to dispose of anything after the party?

I answered simply, 'I would like to see my solicitor.'

I was told I would be seeing the solicitor Ralph Hyams at West End Central police station.

Chris and Ronnie Bender were there when I arrived, and Ralph Hyams told me that when any questions were put to me I was to answer, 'I've got nothing to say at this moment in time.'

Then, with Chris and Ronnie Bender, I was charged with the murder of Jack The Hat. I was taken to Bow Street, where I was held overnight to appear in court in the morning. After a two-minute hearing, I was remanded in custody for a week.

I thought, 'Something's gone badly wrong here.' Up to this point, I couldn't see them having a case against us.

What had gone wrong was that members of the firm, and other witnesses, were talking to the police. I wouldn't see freedom again for fifteen years.

I never slagged the police off for that. They were doing a job. They never abused or tried to verbal or heavy-handle me. I never thought Nipper Read was a bad man. He saw the firm as a challenge, and his orders were: 'Your job is to nick 'em.' He was leading an investigation, and he said himself he had to go into the gutter to get a case against us. He had to go into some very dirty waters, bargain with some very slimy characters, to produce the grasses. But if the police are out to get convictions, you've got to see it from their side. If I was in the same position, perhaps I'd do exactly the same thing. Nipper was a man with a mission. I don't think he had it in for us personally. Many years later, I sent him a letter from Maidstone prison and he duly replied, saying he would back any parole application I might make.

Mooney hated the Krays, pure and simple, and he would go in any back door he could find to get something on them. It was Mooney who got to the barmaid in the Blind Beggar and persuaded her to give evidence in the George Cornell case.

Cater and du Rose were more aloof. Du Rose was called One Day Johnny because of the speed of his murder inquiries. He never said anything, never voiced an opinion, but he was obviously the guv'nor. I think his attitude towards the way they were building the case against us was, 'It's not the way I'd want to do it, but it's the way it's gotta be.' Cater was a key officer in many of the sixties' major trials, including the Richardsons', and he had very few personal dealings with us. He was up at the top, overseeing.

As much as I have disliked law and order and what it's done for me, which is virtually fuck all, I have always realised you have to have it.

People have suggested that the twins had the police in their pockets. I think our arrests and subsequent convictions put the lie to that. But the concept of the bent copper is not merely a figment of the criminal's imagination. I've seen corruption, and I've heard of it happening at every level of the police force. I'm not saying for one moment it's all bent, but there are some very corrupt elements.

For instance, in 1967 a friend of mine was arrested in the East End for tying up a lorry driver and stealing his load. Two police officers approached his brother and said that, in return for a certain sum, my friend would not be recognised on the ID parade. The police officers took the money, straightened out the lorry driver, held the ID which went as promised, and told the brother: 'That just cost you a grand, and if he so much as pisses on the street around here again, we'll fit him up. Now get him out of here.'

At the other end of the scale, I don't like the rotten core within Scotland Yard. That's a firm within a firm, a law unto itself. There's no judge and jury there: they judge and jury themselves, although they sometimes come to grief. Jimmy Humphries, in the porn trials of the seventies, brought half of Scotland Yard down with him. And at least one of the police officers who investigated the Luton Post Office robbery was himself convicted and sentenced to imprisonment on corruption charges.

Other than the cases which are publicly proven, I have heard enough to be sure that a percentage of high-ranking policemen take their cut from major crimes. There was a case involving safety deposit vaults, where the defendants were accused of stealing vast amounts of valuables. Two of the men involved in the robbery said to me: 'I honestly don't remember nicking half of that. Where did it go . . . ?' Who knows what goes missing out of these places and whose pockets it goes into? I know of one top cop who is being investigated at the moment, after being filmed taking bribes.

It would be impossible to guess at the extent of criminal conspiracy within the police, since much of it remains uncovered, but there are certainly special squads of officers who are above the law. How can the law investigate the law?

Even worse, how can criminal investigate criminal? Now we've entered the era of the supergrass, that's exactly what's happening. When they are dealing with professional criminals, some police officers resort to 'professional tactics'. It doesn't really matter how they get you as long as you're gone, off the streets. Say they think a certain firm is active but taking great care to avoid being nicked. The police will seek the help of a grass. They might pull various people in on suss – suspicion – to look for the weak link.

If the case is not there to begin with, then the police have got to drag the gutters for the evidence to produce one, and I believe that convictions based on the word of a grass are very, very unsafe. So many people recently have been sentenced to long terms of imprisonment but at a later stage have successfully remade their cases to the appeal courts because of the unreliability of the witnesses. Supergrasses have been responsible for putting large numbers of men away. What makes anybody believe for an instant that their evidence is safe? Grasses are criminals who have been involved to begin with, and can then be persuaded to say anything which will have their former colleagues put away. Their word is no more, and probably less, reliable than that of the men they have condemned, and that's regarded as enough to convict you.

In the Luton Post Office case three men were sentenced to life imprisonment on the word of a supergrass, and it took twelve years to prove that they were innocent men. A man called Jimmy Saunders walked free after being convicted as one of the Wembley Bank Robbers through the evidence of the supergrass Bertie Smalls. If society doesn't trust a gang of criminals, why trust the word of one of them? The law is treading on dangerous ground here.

The reality now is that, if four men go out on a major crime, it's not the police you have to worry about, it's the accomplice who is going to put the other three away! In our case, the very men who were happy to dish out violence, people like Albert Donaghue and Scotch Jack Dickson, were the ones who pointed the finger at us. If our cases had been heard in the correct perspective, perhaps we wouldn't have received the sentences we did. I'm not beefing about my own conviction, but everybody who gave evidence against us had something to hide. They told blatant lies and they were allowed to get away with it in the name of justice. It smacked me in the face. At the same time we were pleading not guilty and were therefore denying that a crime had ever happened, so we couldn't say anything to defend ourselves. We even had Ronnie Hart going back on complete parts of his evidence, when he later made a statement to a newspaper that 'what I told the court was a pack of lies'. But once the book was closed, there was to be no opening it. . . .

We spent the final months of 1968 sitting it out on remand in Brixton prison, and to add to my worries about the impending trial I was living with the knowledge that Pat was pregnant again. She visited me regularly, and brought dinners in for Reggie, Ronnie and me at weekends, while Violet would bring them during the week.

On 17 December I was called up into the office and told that a son had been born. I remember telling Freddie Foreman, 'Hey Fred, I've got a boy,' and he said, 'That's good news. That's a bonus right away.' He idolised children, and had three of his own.

I lay down that night and felt chuffed, although the new baby represented another worry. I was concerned about Pat – 'How can she cope with two children, and me inside? What sort of life is she going to have?' Within two days of the baby being born she was visiting me again, which takes some loyalty. I first saw my son, David, through the glass which separated the visitor from the prisoner.

The marriage was still OK at this point. Everybody liked Pat. She always had a smile, she'd always have a word for people and she was getting up to see me as much as possible. Karen would usually be with her, although she often left David with her mother or with Violet. She got on well with Violet, and the twins knew and liked Pat too.

The baby, for the time being, remained distant. I didn't really know who he was. The trial seemed distant, too: in prison you tend to live for the day and hope for the best. I busied myself with seeing my brief, Ralph Hyams, and arranging for people on the outside to collect the few quid I still had coming in from various sources.

But as the Old Bailey loomed closer, I began to think more about my problems. And suddenly I knew the size of the trouble I was in.

CHAPTER ELEVEN

JUDGEMENT DAYS

I can picture myself looking at that jury. I can still see every single one of their faces. After all, I did look at them for long enough.

The trial opened in January 1969 in a blaze of publicity and continued for the best part of six weeks. When I recall it now I think of the sirens, the volume of their relentless wailing, which accompanied our twice-daily journey between Brixton prison and the Old Bailey. Everyone complained about the noise, and some of us were on tablets for the headaches and additional pressure it brought on.

Chris and Ronnie Bender were being held in Wandsworth. The coach used to collect them, pick us up on the way to the court, and drop us off again in the evening. We used to make the distance in around twenty minutes. Every morning we used to pass the funeral parlour on Brixton Hill, and the undertaker and two or three of his workers would be standing there, waving their hats and smiling. My Chris used to shout out, 'There he is,' and we'd wave back. There would be a television camera mounted on top of a car which used to try to follow us down Brixton Hill.

In the A-wing maximum-security block in Brixton, which holds about fifteen men, I was kept next door to Freddie Foreman on the ground floor. The twins, Charlie and Ian Barrie were on the second level. For some reason the prison authorities didn't want Freddie mixing with the twins, and kept them on different exercise and association periods. It was a waste of time, because messages were easily passed through the rest of us. I think it was believed that there might have been a conspiracy of some kind going on, which was typical of the authorities: they were very suspicious of people. On one occasion we heard about a con called Billy Gentry, who was in Leicester prison's security block, wanted to send eleven daffodils to his daughter for her eleventh birthday. His order was changed behind his back in case the unusual number of flowers represented a coded message. Also in Leicester prison, the screws used to take the orange peel out of the bins because someone high up had decided the cons could make explosives out of it!

During our remand weeks in Brixton everything, in a way, ran to a routine – going to court and coming back. By contrast, the things which were being said in the course of the trial were bringing new surprises and shocks every day. With all of this going on, we didn't pay a lot of attention to what was happening in the prison itself, although we did meet the odd interesting character.

One day I became curious about this bloke walking around the exercise yard. I'd seen him before on exercise, although he never stayed long and he was kept apart from us. Now and again, I'd seen him in the wing. Later, I saw an opportunity to chat to him and I asked him what he'd done. He said, 'I shot a black man in America.'

He turned out to be James Earl Ray, the man who assassinated civil rights leader Martin Luther King in Memphis, Tennessee. The day after the shooting he'd flown straight over to England and been arrested in Bayswater. He was waiting in Brixton while the authorities went through the formalities of getting him kicked out of the country, back to Memphis.

Ray was a right Southern Yank, and he couldn't stand prison food. He kept asking, 'How do you guys handle this food here?' Because he was a high-profile case politically he was never allowed to have too many dealings with anyone else, but we always had a chat when the chance arose. Years later, when a film-maker friend of mine called Adrian Penninck was granted access to him for a documentary, he said, 'Give Tony and the boys my regards.'

The beginning of the trial was a joke. The jury had to be sworn in, and the Old Bailey had about two hundred people standing by. We objected to about fifty of them as they came up, because we didn't like the look of them. We didn't have to give grounds. We were allowed to object to about seven at a time. Added to that, a lot of the potential jurors were trying to get out of it. One said, 'You don't think I'm going to stand up and give a verdict on this lot, do you? Do you think I want to end up under a motorway?' Another bloke who said roughly the same thing was threatened with imprisonment for contempt of court. The judge, Mr Justice Melford Stevenson, was determined that the jury would be sworn in by hook or by crook. And once they were, he decided he wanted numbers put round our necks because there were so many of us in the dock.

We had a little pow-wow before we went into court. The screws came down and told us about it. They said, 'Let us put the numbers on, and what you do after that is your business.' Can you imagine us sitting in the famous Number One court in the Old Bailey with numbers on pink ribbon round our necks? Stevenson ordered the screws in the dock to put them on us. I was number five in the front row. But we weren't having it. Chris took off his number, threw it at Nipper Read and said, 'Let him wear it if he wants it that bad.' I threw mine in. And Ronnie rightly said, 'This is not a cattle market.' The judge was livid – but we won that round, our first clash; he made it up in the other rounds.

This particular judge was known to be a hard-liner, and he had it in for us from the very first moment; it was a slog. He was an overpowering type of man, and as the days went by, the jury were eating more and more out of his hand. No matter what he said to them, they were going to believe it. Any time anything went well for the prosecution, he was very quick to point it out. When it went badly for the defence, he was double quick to underline that. He would turn round to the jury and, if looks could speak, he said the lot. The jury were going to bring in guilty verdicts according to the judge's directions. They were being minded twenty-four hours a day by armed detectives. The authorities weren't doing all this for nothing, to let us go. And the publicity around the trial had already condemned us. There was no possibility of justice for men like my Chris, Charlie Kray and Freddie Foreman. They were innocent of the charges against them, but they had refused to co-operate with the police so they had no chance. They were going down.

There was a flu epidemic during the trial. The judge, the jury, all the court officials were given these jabs. When it came to our turn, Stevenson complained about the cost of it. That was the type of thing we were up against.

To begin with, the whole thing was strangely constructed. I was sitting on a double murder trial when one of the murders, that of George Cornell, had nothing to do with me in law. What happened was that they had a body on one case but not on the other, the McVitie murder. Jack The Hat on its own would not have stood up, but sticking the Cornell case alongside it made it look stronger. They put the two murders together and linked them through Ronnie's alleged words: 'I've done mine, you do yours.' Yet Ronnie, as I've explained, never said that.

It was a show trial, and they wanted the whole gang. Reggie had already offered to plead guilty to Jack The Hat, and Ronnie to Cornell, if the other charges were dropped, everybody else was released and no recommendations were stipulated on the sentences. But it was a no go deal. Two men were no good. It was the whole firm versus the Metropolitan Police.

But the worst damage of all was done by members and associates of the firm who gave evidence against us. It didn't take the brains of Einstein to see that they were out to save their own skins and blame those in the dock for the violence that they'd willingly participated in throughout their careers. That was the saddest, most sickening thing – to see people you've had a cup of tea with, shared a fag with, standing up and showing that, when the crunch came, their so-called loyalty didn't mean a thing. I think the twins were shocked and disappointed.

Let's get it right. We'd all done wrong, but some of us didn't try to worm our way out of it by blaming other people. If the grasses had got up there and told the truth we might not have liked it, but we could have lived with it. If they had admitted their part and told it as it happened, it might not have changed the course of the trial, but at least we would have gone down knowing that the truth had been told. But when we heard them telling lie after lie, there was no way we could accept that. God almighty – it was unforgivable!

Scotch Jack Dickson was one of the worst. After he was nicked he decided to become a witness for the police, and during the trial he claimed he had realised at a certain stage that 'the murders have got to stop'. He had been involved up to the hilt, and now he claimed he was saying it had to stop. . . . He drove the car to the Blind Beggar, Ronnie and Ian Barrie went into the pub, Ian fired a couple of bullets into the air, Ronnie shot Cornell stone dead, they returned to the car, went back to the pub . . . and Scotch Jack knew nothing about it?

Another thing that repulsed me about him in the Old Bailey was when he was asked to state whom he drove to the Blind Beggar. He said, 'The fat one sitting there', meaning Ronnie Kray. He would never have said that to Ronnie's face in a million years; he would never have had the guts in normal circumstances. The whole court went quiet. Ronnie Kray just looked at him and turned away.

Scotch Jack stood in the witness box for two days, and even the judge got sick of him. Stevenson said: 'You cannot believe a word that this unsavoury character has said in this court today. We will make him a hostile witness.' Which meant that he was to be perceived as someone with a vested interest in putting the twins away.

Known as Scotch Jack Jonah after Ronnie's brief, John Platts-Mills, mixed his name up, he became the laughing stock of the court. Later he wrote a book, *Murder Without Conviction,* which was published in 1986. A lot of it was untrue. This is a person who came to London to put himself on the twins' firm. Why didn't he say in his book what he did to us – that he became a grass? If I saw him today, I'd spit on him. I wouldn't hit him – he wouldn't be worth it. I wouldn't like anyone to harm him: it would be a sin. Let him live to a ripe old age, living with what he did, looking in the mirror and seeing what he is, every day. He's a disgusting piece of work.

I wish the same for Ronnie Hart. He put Ronnie Bender in the McVitie murder from top to bottom. He said Bender got down and pronounced Jack The Hat dead. Nonsense. Ronnie Bender wasn't in the room when it happened. Hart also gave evidence about the driving away of the body, naming Bender but not me and Chris. This was because Ronnie Bender had gone back to Harry Hopwood's house after the murder, and, looking for a bit of glory in the twins' eyes, said, 'I got rid of that, Ron.' He didn't mention that Chris and I had been involved, so Hart, who was listening, didn't know. What he later told the police about the disposal of the body therefore didn't include our names. That's why we were never charged with that part of it, and that's why Ronnie Bender got an extra five years – just by wanting to take the credit in front of Hart, Hopwood and other witnesses.

But Hart did more than that. He wasn't prepared to help the police unless Freddie Foreman was arrested, because he was afraid of what Fred might do. He told the police, 'You don't get me into the witness box until Foreman's inside.' So Foreman had to be put in the frame. And the way Hart did it was to bring Fred and Charlie into his story as accessories after Bender's alleged disposal of the body. This couldn't have been true, because it was me who drove the body away. Nevertheless, Hart carried on with his tale. He said that, while he was at Harry Hopwood's, Ronnie Kray asked him to get hold of Charlie. The upshot of it all, according to Hart, was that he drove Charlie to Freddie Foreman's pub to inform him that there was a body on his manor. He further claimed that Freddie said, 'Leave it down there – I'll take care of it later.' But Freddie Foreman had nothing whatsoever to do with the body of Jack The Hat.

Hart also blamed Ronnie Kray for taking part in the McVitie murder, which, as I saw myself, Ronnie had no involvement in. Ronnie Hart played a leading role in what happened that night. When I was called into the office in the Regency, who was there? Hart. And when the murder itself happened, Hart was not the innocent bystander he protested he was. Every other person in that room could verify what I say. Up until the arrests, Hart had been out to prove himself a Kray. But he was never like them, as he showed in the end. He even married Blonde Vicky, one person who could have put him fairly and squarely in the frame, a month before the trial started. Our briefs asked for access to her, and back came the message: 'She's married Ronnie Hart, and there will be no access.' Hart knew that a wife could not in law be made to give evidence against her husband, and this meant she could not be a witness for the defence.

After we went down Hart approached Fred's wife Maureen, her solicitor and a private detective. Obviously worried about the consequences of framing Foreman, he was now ready to clear

Freddie's name of any connection with the Jack The Hat business. The meeting was held on an estate somewhere in Harlow, Essex. Maureen, the solicitor and the private detective had a question-and-answer session prepared for him: Next thing, the police broke in and arrested the solicitor and the private detective for trying to pervert the course of justice. Hart said, 'I told a pack of lies. All I know is that the twins killed McVitie, and other than that, I know nothing.' The case against the solicitor and private eye was then dropped.

Next, Hart wrote a statement for a respected national newspaper, saying he had told lies at the Old Bailey. And this was the star witness against the lot of us!

He went to Australia with Blonde Vicky and tried to commit suicide by slashing his wrists a couple of times, because he couldn't sleep with the wicked thing that he did. I hope he lives to be a thousand. Since then he's tried to sell books and stories, but to little avail. Whatever he got out of his betrayal, it wasn't much. Talk about thirty pieces of silver. He certainly didn't get any gold.

We heard lies, lies and more lies from Albert Donaghue, Alan Mills, Billy Exley (in the Cornell case) and Carol Skinner – Blonde Carol – whose inconsistent testimony was actually questioned by the judge. Before she stood up in court, she made a statement to say that she saw various people in her flat that night who were disposing of evidence just after the murder. She named me, the twins and Ronnie Bender, amongst others. She also stated that she saw Chris pouring a bucket of blood down the toilet.

I never saw Blonde Carol during that part of the night. And I'm sure if she had been there, somewhere, Chris and Ronnie Bender would have let me know, given the serious situation we were in. I can honestly say that neither of them mentioned her to me. I didn't even know Blonde Carol. I'd seen her at the Regency a couple of times, but I'd never met her and I'd never been to her flat before.

After we'd driven the body away on the night of the murder we came back to Evering Road and Blonde Carol was there, helping to clear up with Connie Whitehead and a bloke she used to go out with called George Plummer. She didn't know who I was, and she didn't seem to notice I was there. In court, she was asked to identify the people she insisted she'd seen that night. She picked out Chris, the twins and Ronnie Bender, because she knew them. Then it came to me, and she couldn't put my face to my name, which she'd given. They kept giving her a cue in court – 'Who else did you see there that night?' – and she looked up and down the dock, over and over again in response to the same question, and failed to identify me. This went on for about half an hour.

The judge, realizing what was happening, called an adjournment for lunch. My brief jumped up and said, 'It's important that this woman finishes giving her evidence', but the break went ahead. Blonde Carol came back into court after lunch and 'identified' me immediately.

This is how I believe Nicky was dragged into the picture when we were first questioned about Jack The Hat. In my opinion, Blonde Carol was aware that someone had come back to the flat with Chris, after the driving away of the body. Without looking too closely, she assumed it was Nicky because she knew him and had seen him around with Chris.

Even the judge told the jury: 'I want you to think very, very carefully about this woman and ask yourselves, if she's lying, why?' None of us have ever discovered the answer to that.

Blonde Carol also claimed as part of her evidence that she'd seen me six weeks after the murder and that I'd told her to shut her mouth if she knew what was good for her. That was a bloody lie. I didn't say it. If I had, I'm sure she might have remembered my face in court. Anyway, she would have been the last person I wanted to talk to. I don't like to slag women off, but from what I'd seen of her around the Regency she certainly wasn't my cup of tea.

The twist to Albert Donaghue, who had pleaded guilty to being an accessory after the murder of Jack The Hat, was that he made himself a grass when he didn't have to. He said he tidied up and redecorated Blonde Carol's flat after the murder. Yet, if he had stood up with us and kept his mouth shut, what would he have got for cleaning up a flat? No more than what he received anyway, which was two years.

It was an education finding out whom we could and couldn't count on in the end. Frankie Fraser spoke up for us in court. He was one of the first ones to offer, regardless of what was being said at the time about animosity between the Krays and Fraser and the Richardsons. He was brought from Wandsworth prison to stand in the witness box for us, and it did him no favours in the eyes of the authorities regarding his future, but he was a man of honour.

Not so Tony Barry, one of the brothers who ran the Regency. They had always been well liked, so to hear the two of them telling blatant lies about us took a bit of stomaching. Tony brought the gun round on the night of Jack The Hat and was charged with murder, same as us. But he'd gone the police's way by admitting his part of it. He was terrified of the twins and the rest of us, and he claimed that I'd approached him in Brixton prison and told him what would happen if he gave evidence against us. It wasn't true, but he got his way. They put him on Rule 43 protection, which meant that he was kept away from us in prison for his own safety, and during the trial he stood apart from us in the dock with three prison officers around him.

I'll always remember the evening there was a mix-up when we came back from court. We were being put into cells opposite reception, waiting to be escorted over to the special wing. They always used to take Barry off first and lock him in. On this day a screw who didn't know the situation opened the door to his cell and Fred and I walked in, smiling at each other. As the screw went to shut the door, Tony Barry shouted, 'You can't do this', with a look of terror on his face. Ten screws came running up, and Fred and I had to leave. If we'd been able to stay in there . . . well, we wouldn't have been too happy with Tony Barry, would we?

He told the court he'd been living in fear of the twins. Yet, if it hadn't been for the twins, his club would never have survived. The Kray name alone carried weight, and the Regency needed that. Like a lot of people who put Reggie and Ronnie down at the end, the Barrys forgot the times they went round to the twins for a bit of help.

Tony wasn't involved in the murder; I know that. But if he hadn't called me into the office that night, maybe I wouldn't have been involved in it either. John Barry came to court to save his brother's skin by giving evidence against us. I can understand how he felt about Tony being charged with murder, but then again my brother too was standing in the dock charged with murder – yet it didn't mean that I had to get up and lie about other people.

He told one story concerning a flat called the Dungeon in Vallance Road, claiming that we held meetings of some sort of protection committee in there. Our connections with the Dungeon began when the writer John Pearson said he wanted to absorb the atmosphere of the East End. Ronnie said, 'I'll show him the fucking East End', and put him into this bare flat with a bed, a payphone and a second-hand telly. John Barry came down there one night, purely on a bit of business, when we were all having a drink together. But in court he claimed that he had walked into the Dungeon and found the twins, Ian Barrie, Ronnie Hart, Albert Donaghue, Scotch Jack Dickson, Ronnie Bender, Chris and me sitting there as a tribunal. He said he was brought there to appear before this committee which decided how protection was to be paid, and at what percentage. Rubbish. It never happened.

Johnny Barry was no angel. He was a well-known fence, and he'd had a lot of dealings with my Nicky. Anything Nicky had to sell, he'd buy. One day, shortly before we got arrested, Johnny said to me, 'It's right in your interests to come and see me in the office at the club on Saturday morning.' I had to ring the side bell because the Regency was closed during the day, and when I reached the office it was like walking into the Bank of England. I couldn't believe what I was seeing.

Johnny Barry had £1 million worth of forged £5 notes in there – cartons and boxes full of them. He said, 'These have just been printed, and none of them have gone out yet. We're going to flood the country with them, all in one hit.' He gave me £100,000 worth. They had to be sorted out – some were good, some were bad. Our idea was to take them to Birmingham, and in the end the notes did go there – but there was no return on them.

Johnny Barry did lots of things. How he could stand in the witness box, knowing what he'd done, and say the things he was saying made no sense to any of us unless he'd made a deal with the police to get himself out of a charge of forging banknotes. While Barry was giving evidence, Reggie drew a £5 note on a piece of paper and kept holding it up. And when I was in the witness box I said, 'I'll tell you what Barry's got to hide, £1 million worth of problems.'

In later years, Johnny Barry went to prison. Other cons bashed him up and one, Dave Martin, did him with boiling water. That's the life he chose for himself the minute he made himself a grass.

In the end, the trial got out of hand. We never knew what was coming next. Anyone could get up and say anything about us and it was believed. Plots in Africa, dictatorships in foreign countries, poisoned darts in briefcases. . . . It got too preposterous to be true. No wonder Ronnie Kray asked, 'Who's on trial here – Ronnie Kray or James Bond?'

Newspapers reported that we sat in the dock yawning and

treated the whole thing as a joke. We never saw it as a joke. How could we? When you're sitting in a dock and allegation after allegation is being made against you and there's nothing you can do about it, you simply tend to lose hope. 'Should we go along with this charade?' is more your feeling.

The things that were going on affected all of the people around us. Families were going to be wrecked. Throughout that trial, my father and Charlie Kray were there every day without fail. My father-in-law, Flip, took it personally, because he saw that justice wasn't being done. It hurt him greatly, and he worried for his daughter and our two kids. Pat's side of the family were decent people.

There was a three-day summing up, and then the interminable wait in a cell while the jury were out deciding on the verdicts. Reggie was trying to relax himself, Ronnie was saying nothing, Connie Whitehead was saying nothing, Charlie was trying to be chirpy, and Ronnie Bender kept saying, 'Come on, we're going to get "Not guiltys" here.' I was taking in the picture before me – nine very smartly dressed men who looked as though they could have been at a party. It was almost as though nothing had changed. . . . .

After what seemed like an eternity, I was called out for my verdict. It was like standing in a chapel. Rays of light were coming in through the big, top windows, and one fell directly on me. I'll never forget the jury foreman, a stocky man of about fifty, with greying hair, horn-rimmed glasses and a brown suit. He didn't look me in the eye when he spoke the word: 'Guilty.' No one spoke, no one smiled, in the court, but there was a sound, just like a sigh. What was going to happen now?

All of a sudden, I snapped out of it and went back down to the cells. The first thing Ronnie Kray said after he was found guilty was, 'I'm glad it's all over, I can get into my bird now.' He kept talking about going on a world cruise when he came out.

Ronnie Bender was cracking jokes. No one complained. I think we were all trying to show a brave side to ourselves. Yet it all still seemed a million miles away. The next day, the day of the sentencing, would say it all.

I woke up in the morning, put on a clean shirt and polished my shoes. I knew it was the last time I was going to wear a civilian suit, and I wanted to look my best. Everything about this day felt different, even though the routine was more or less the same. The cell doors were opened for us; and there were the usual 'Good morning's' all round. There was a very friendly atmosphere, and the screws were going out of their way to keep things low-key. I came out to get breakfast. Ronnie Kray shouted out: 'Morning all' as usual, very chirpy, and then he said, 'Well, today's the day.'

We were put out in the exercise yard to wait for the coach. As we looked round the cage, all the cons were at their windows shouting, 'Good luck, boys.' There were a hell of a lot more screws on duty. All of a sudden, this big police motorcade arrived and we got into the coach. Again, there were 'Morning's' all round. Not a word was said about what was about to happen. Sid, the driver of the wagon, came round and asked us to sign a card he'd brought with him, for posterity. We all did. I often wonder if he kept it.

The crowds were out, all along the route. We went to the Bailey cells and there was tea ready for us, the usual smiles all round. We did look smart in the dock, all suited and booted. It was said that we looked better than the jury.

Between us, we were sentenced to a total of 159 years in prison.

The twins went away with a lot of honour and a lot of dignity. They could have brought many other people down with them, but they chose not to. I took my punishment, whether I deserved it or not. I was there at the end, and hopefully I took it like a man. It wasn't a question of my killing anybody. It was a question of 'I was there', and I knew there was going to be trouble of some sort. I saw what happened. Perhaps I didn't like what I saw, but I kept my mouth shut and that's why I got the sentence I did.

That's why Chris got fifteen years too, although Chris was never aware that the party was going to be anything other than a party. I'm not saying he was an innocent man – eventually, I think, Chris and I would have gone to prison for other crimes – but on this occasion he really wasn't guilty, and there was no excuse for what happened to him at the Old Bailey. If there was any charge, it should have been as an accessory, and to keep him for five years would have been a liberty. Every one of us felt sorry for Chris. He had just been in the wrong place at the wrong time, and now he was going to spend a lot of years in prison because of that. It was unbearable, tragic. I felt guilty about him. But he didn't complain at the time, and he has never complained since. We both live with the things we've done in the past, but at the same time we can hold our heads up, knowing that we never betrayed another person.

And so we all went off to start our sentences, thinking our different thoughts, and that day brought with it the end of an era in British crime. The things we did, the power we had, could never happen to the same extent again, because the authorities wouldn't allow it. For the first time in criminal history, this country came up against organised crime.

The authorities hadn't known how to handle organised crime. It was a way of life that had to be public: the twins didn't sneakily challenge authority, they did it openly. They never, ever denied what they were into. People underestimate what they did. It was an achievement on its own – something which, in straight business, would have put them on a par with anyone. But they did it in crime, and they were very good. Their reign, in some ways, became acceptable to the public and the establishment for a while, but it was a one-off. That sort of thing can never be acceptable again.

The turning point came when the authorities decided to suppress it and learned how. Things have been a lot quieter since the day we were sentenced. One or two gangs did try to come through, but the police now knew what to do in the face of any new challenge.

But if the law learned lessons from the Kray case, so too did other criminals. They learned to work alone or very quietly, because any other way they couldn't win.

Ours was one of the three crimes of the century. The others were the Great Train Robbery and the Richardson torture case. These trials stood head and shoulders above any others, and as the years have passed the aura of glamour around them has overtaken the real and serious aspects.

People remember the sixties more vividly than any other recent decade. They remember the Beatles, the drug scene, the permissive society, the quality of life, the whole free-and-easy and exciting time of change. The Great Train Robbery, the Richardsons and the Krays were just as much a part of that era as the mini-skirts, just as much a part of the whole atmosphere, just as much a part of the continuing nostalgia.

The Great Train Robbers came out of their case in a very romantic light, and people still think and talk about them in that way. The public also remembers the torture trials and, especially, the Kray cases. The twins have passed into legend, and that legend is never going to die. There will always be books and films about them. The Krays and the Richardsons gave England, for the first time, what the Americans had: a Chicago of its own, an Al Capone, a Jesse James, a Wild West. And people still seem to relate to this in a lot of ways, even though it's history. I'm not going to say it's a very illustrious history, but we've got it and we're always going to have it. Nothing can happen now to change that.

CHAPTER TWELVE

BEHIND
CLOSED DOORS

I mmediately after our convictions, my wife brought Karen and
David to visit me in Wandsworth with her father, Flip. Karen was
very proud to have a brother. By now David was three months old,
bouncing around. I said to Pat in front of her father and the kids,
'Now look, don't even think about waiting for me on this sentence.
I'm giving you the door and I advise you to take it.' You cannot ask
a person to wait that length of time.

But I already knew her answer; I knew she was going to stick by
me. From that day onwards she never missed a visit, and she did her
best for me. I watched the kids growing up around the prison. I
never encouraged that, but I don't believe I discouraged it either.

Pat was acting with the best of intentions, but the marriage was
doomed. She and I would both change a lot over the course of the
next fifteen years. Chris finished with his wife, Carol, straightaway,
because he didn't think it fair for her to have to wait that length of
time. He said, 'That's it, I don't want to know no more.' They'd had
one kid, a daughter called Angela.

Neither Chris nor I could see any further than the sentences we'd
been given. Not in our wildest dreams could we visualise ourselves

coming out the other end. We weren't the sort of blokes to sit down and serve fifteen years like good boys, without saying a word. Some of the most dramatic and rebellious events of our lives were to take place during the prison years. . . .

We started our sentences as Category A prisoners in maximum-security blocks, away from the 'regular' cons, because we were considered to be a danger to the public and the State, and had to be heavily guarded at all times so that there wasn't the faintest possibility of escape. I was escorted everywhere. I had to take a book with my photograph in it wherever I went, and I was 'signed over' throughout the prison. For instance, if I went from the workshop to the wing where the cells were, I was signed out of the shop, handed over to the escort and taken to my destination. Out in the grounds, I was accompanied at all times by an escort and a doghandler.

There was special security in my cell. Everything was reinforced, and there were bolts on the door as well as the usual locks. It was impregnable. I was checked every hour throughout the day and night: the authorities had to know where I was at all times. Every night, I had to be seen at least once by the Assistant Governor, the Deputy Governor or the Governor. I always had a red light on in the cell, and it was searched every day. There were also frequent personal searches, which could happen at any time. My clothes were kept outside the cell during the night.

I was taken for bathing separately from everybody else, escorted out to collect my food before the rest of the cons, and locked up during mealtimes. Prison exercise was under maximum supervision. Visiting was subject to approval by the Home Office and the police. They checked out my visitors, who had to submit photographs. If, for any reason, they thought a visitor was a security risk, that person wasn't allowed to see me. And outside contact – the chance of meeting civilian people coming in and out of the prison – is kept to a minimum for Category A prisoners because of the fear of hostage-taking. The whole system is devised to stop you from escaping at all costs.

There are four types of prisoner within Cat. A, as we referred to it. These are dangerous criminals, political criminals (who are usually terrorists), sex offenders and grasses who have to be kept apart and protected from the main body of prisoners, and 'prison Cat. A' men – people who are uncontrollably disruptive within the system.

You're not considered for parole – conditional release – while you're Cat. A. The authorities went through the motions of assessing us for it – but when you think about it, you can't be considered a grave threat to society on one hand and be given parole on the other. There's no appeal against being on Cat. A, other than petitions. I regularly received the same reply: 'The Secretary of State feels that, in this case, you should remain in Category A for the foreseeable future.'

Being an A-man carried either a stigma or a certain status, depending on your point of view. It went to some people's heads. I always felt that if you had any sense, it was the last thing you should want to be. Also, a lot of non-A prisoners were impressed – 'Oh, he's in the A-book.' From the beginning of our sentences we were not only in the A-book, we were also on what was known as the E List. This meant we were considered to be an escape risk and had to wear a yellow patch on our trousers so that we could be quickly spotted at all times.

Category A prisoners can be moved to another prison at any time, without any warning: 'As you are, come with us.' You were never told where you were going. They usually came for you at four in the morning. You'd wake up and see seven uniforms standing there, and it could be a frightening thing. You'd be half asleep, and you could see the weakness in yourself. There was no other con at large to help you out if the screws got up to any villainy. Any time I was woken for a move, I would bang on the walls to let my neighbours know I was leaving the cell.

You could have breakfast in Durham, dinner in Leicester and tea in Parkhurst, and when you reached your destination you were taken straight to the wing, not through reception. They'd never move you in vans but in police cars, with other police cars in front and behind, and the police who nicked us always came along on these transfers to see that we were securely delivered to the next prison.

On one memorable occasion in August 1969, Chris, Ronnie Bender and I were being taken from Brixton prison to Leicester. We'd been in London for our Court of Appeal hearings – the token three members of the firm whose cases were being reconsidered. It was like a royal parade coming along the Mall – we had a heavy, heavy escort. We had to go through Hyde Park, and Marble Arch was sealed off.

We reached the M1 in this convoy, each of us in a separate car, cuffed to a screw on either side. Fifteen miles along the motorway, we came to an obstruction in the fast lane where workmen had been carrying out repair work. One car in front of us saw it too late and veered off to the left. All of a sudden, cars were crashing into each other. The screws and the police thought a mass escape was taking place, and before anyone knew what was happening there were armed guards standing round every car in the pile-up with their guns drawn. Chris was going mad inside his car; he'd got a bang on the head. The motorway was sealed off, and when we finally resumed the journey to Leicester we saw three police cars stationed on every bridge we went under. They had doctors waiting for us at the prison. Chris was a compulsive complainer, and this was a tailor-made meal for him: 'Get them fucking cuffs off me! You tried to fucking murder me on the motorway!'

Later we heard that the appeals had been turned down – though we only discovered this by accident, through the one o'clock news on the radio. It was stated that reasons would be given later; I still haven't heard any. It was a bit of a sad time, although none of us let our disappointment show. We were back on Category A with nothing to hope for.

The twins were still in Brixton prison, attending the Old Bailey on the Frank Mitchell murder charges, of which they were eventually acquitted. I was to have very little contact with them in the following fifteen years. I overlapped with Ronnie for a week in Durham near the beginning of my sentence and found him typically uncomplaining; everyone seemed to like him. I didn't see him again until 1974, when I was in Parkhurst. The twins were there too, in maximum security, and the Governor arranged for me to have a special visit with them in his office. It was the last time I ever saw the twins together, and I never saw either of them again until I came out of prison.

When the rest of us started our sentences, I was on one wing at Wandsworth with Ronnie Bender, who was in the hospital, and Chris was on another with Ian Barrie. After a period where I didn't see my brother for three weeks, I got a VO – the Visiting Order you send out to friends, which invites and authorises them to come and see you – and I posted it to Chris on D-wing. Next day Beast, as we called the Governor, called me up and said, 'I can assure you that your brother is doing well. He wrecked the visiting room the last time he was there, and he's in the [punishment] block.'

This was just a sign of things to come, and the Wandsworth prison authorities realised it. Not only did they have us, they had Frankie Fraser in there, one of the most notorious villains in the country, and a lot of bank robbers who went on to commit twenty of the biggest robberies of the eighties. Their whole operation was popularly referred to as the Gartree Connection, because the men had planned it all out in Gartree prison – which itself was known as the Crime Connection.

The authorities at Wandsworth could see the type of prisoners they had on their hands, and they didn't want the trouble. The idea was to get us farmed out to different prisons as quickly as possible. Within two months Chris, Ronnie Bender and I had been transferred to Durham. We remained together through our next moves, to Leicester and Hull, before splitting up for a few years in the winter of 1970.

We were hardly model prisoners. Chris and I were never going to take our sentences lying down. We were both young men, we had many years ahead of us in prison, and we weren't the type of blokes to sit there and take orders. To us, that would have been giving in. I was rebellious, out to cause as much disruption within the system as I could, just out of frustration at the sentence. My attitude was, 'If I don't get what I want, I'm gonna give you aggravation.' Chris had to find some way of getting through a sentence that he shouldn't have been doing in the first place, and his way was to cause as much trouble as possible. He was looking for it, even more than I was. Sometimes the screws sent for me to calm Chris down because they didn't dare attempt it themselves.

One morning in Durham prison, Chris went into the Chief Officer's office in his pyjamas. Ten minutes later, the CO came down to my cell. He said, 'Have a word with your brother. He should wear his uniform when he comes to the office.'

I said, 'Then you tell him.'

He said, 'Are you fucking joking?'

Chris was a very explosive man, and he was feared. If someone upset him in prison, he would never forget it. If Chris didn't like what was on the television, he'd kick it up in the air. He did that to about five TV sets in the nick.

We felt we had nothing to lose. We didn't give a damn, either of us. To get any peace, to gain any satisfaction out of our situation, we had to do things our way, do what we wanted. If we didn't feel like wearing the uniforms, we'd set fire to them and throw them out the window. It happened so many times. If we didn't want to go to work – if we didn't like the labour we'd been allocated, mailbags or whatever – we didn't do it. We'd stay in bed, or listen to the radio, or play cards with any other cons who'd decided not to work.

Apart from a direct refusal to co-operate, we had other ways of getting out of labour. We were always taken back to the wings if the temperature in the workshops fell below a certain level. So we used to put the thermometer in a bucket of cold water and repeatedly complain it was too cold to work in the shop. If that didn't work, then we'd down tools. If we didn't like the food, the lot went up in the air, and there would be a sit-out if it was the summer, or a demonstration in the television room at colder times of the year. If 150 men don't want to go back behind the doors, if they refuse to leave the exercise yard for three days, there's not a lot the authorities can do about it. If we saw anything we thought was an injustice, we'd take the side of the underdog against the authorities. Chris, in particular, was a great man for taking up causes. Say one of our pals was having problems with the screws – well, we'd make sure the screws had a problem with the lot of us too.

Anything we could do to get a blow in against authority, we'd do it. Most of the hard men were the same. Charlie Richardson had a kick against authority. He saw himself as being hard done by, getting sentenced to twenty-five years after the Richardsons' 'torture' trial, and he was a complainer just like the rest of us. He wanted his rights and he made sure he got them.

Frankie Fraser, similarly, had a fierce dislike of prison rules, and was a very hot potato within the prison system. He was quite small – a stocky bloke of about five feet two – but he was game, he was hard to handle, he was not afraid to speak out and fight for his rights, and he was more than capable of doing what he threatened. His word was his bond. People knew they should never say to Frank, 'I want to chin a screw,' unless they meant it, because he would expect them to do it, and rightly so. Yet he was a very respected man, admired by everyone, the screws included, for his principles. He had a friendly word for everyone – and, again, he would be one of the first to stick up for the underdog.

Another con, a bloke called Paul Seabourne, struck a most dramatic blow against authority. He said to Ronnie Biggs one day in Wandsworth, 'I'm going to get you out of here.' By God, did he! He didn't get paid for Biggs's escape. He organised it because he thought the authorities had taken a liberty and he wanted to kick them. He kicked them OK - right in the bollocks.

In prison, politics didn't come into it. It didn't matter that there were IRA terrorists amongst us. We were all together, and we were all anti-authority, pure and simple. We would have done anything to fuck the system – me probably more than a lot of people.

I spent more than three years of my fifteen in punishment blocks. At different times throughout the sentence I was done for assault, breaking and entering within the prison, and stealing. I was involved in riots and attempted escapes. I was generally a troublemaker, a bloke who didn't take orders, and I couldn't have cared less what punishment might result. What could they do to us? Put us down the block? We were already deprived of our liberty. The block was just a less privileged form of imprisonment. It was no deterrent. You were behind a locked door, whatever part of the prison you were in.

If anything, you came out of the block in a more belligerent frame of mind, more likely to create further trouble than you were when you went in. The screws and the governing staff knew this, and they would punish offences according to how they viewed them. If it wasn't an explosive incident, they'd find it better just to let it die a natural death.

They also had to be careful not to upset other inmates. If major trouble broke out on one wing, the news would spread across the whole prison. If one wing wasn't going to labour, the message would reach the rest of us and we would all stop work. If we were refusing food because it wasn't up to standard, everybody would end up refusing food. Within the prison fraternity, everybody was expected to take part when a widespread protest arose. Those who didn't found that life could become difficult: cells might be set on fire; people might be given righthanders or generally isolated and tormented, denounced as stags and grasses. You can't play with the fox and run with the hounds. There were exceptions, notably lifers who were coming to the end of their sentences. No one would want to endanger their chances of parole.

The screws knew that if a protest really went off, it would be bad, and for a lot of the time they pursued a policy of appeasement. I've seen prison Governors sitting in the exercise yard begging the men to come back inside, just trying to contain what they feared might happen. It could, and did get dangerous. And from what I can see, things have not changed greatly in the prison system over the years: the Strangeways riots in Manchester in 1989 would seem to prove that inmates were as discontented later on as they were in my time.

Food was one of the main problems. In some places the meals were a lot of filth. The food that came into the nick was of a pretty good quality, but it's what they turned it into at the end of the day that caused the problems. Then there were the people who dished it up, cons who weren't always 100 per cent hygienic. I watched them to see how they bathed and that, and if I wasn't impressed I wouldn't touch the grub. Then we'd have to have another of our demonstrations to get them out of the kitchen.

Sometimes, certain cons would be seen to be getting favours; they made themselves busy to go out and get that bit of extra, while others were too lazy. Straighten up the cook and you were on your way. Chris was like that: if he wanted something, he went down there and demanded it. And he got it. As a villain he was ranked alongside Frankie Fraser, and the general attitude towards Chris was, 'Don't fuck about with him or you'll get yourself in trouble.'

Visits were another common cause of complaint, on occasions when cons were refused permission for special visits with their families. Letters, too, became a source of aggravation. You'd hear some of the men saying, 'They're fucking about with the mail.' Other cons were always complaining about the quality of the outside exercise facilities. Little things could easily build up into big things.

And moods could change very quickly. You could wake up in the morning on top of the world, but if your pal had the hump and he did something, it was your duty to back him up. You got drawn into many hostilities other than your own.

Additionally, there were various campaigns going on outside the nick which involved certain prisoners. One which we all enjoyed concerned the Great Train Robber Tommy Wisbey, a very down-to-earth man, whose wife Renee wanted her conjugal rights with him while he was serving his sentence, and made an issue of it in the sixties – unfortunately, without success. She was a real personality.

Chris and I soon discovered in prison that we had more to prove than most. As members of the Kray firm we had a reputation which walked before us, and we had to live up to it at all times. It was a reputation which was open to challenge – always there for people to try to bring down, just as it had been on the streets of London. Other cons weren't interested in Joe Bloggs, but they were interested in Charlie Richardson and Frankie Fraser and Tony and

Chris Lambrianou. If we made a mistake, the rest would be on us like a bunch of vultures.

We had to make sure that people feared and respected us, and again, as we had discovered on the outside, it was the threat of violence rather than the use of it that carried the day – although obviously we had to be seen to be able to do it on the occasions when it did come to a confrontation. We always carved a tool, because we never knew what we were dealing with. Interestingly, the greatest weapon you could have in prison was a pot of piss. Not many people would take that on!

My brother once had a set-to with a Londoner called John in Maidstone prison. One day, this John was going into the wing as Chris was leaving it to go to labour. He shouldered my brother out of the way, so Chris spun round and smacked him in the face. Later in the day, John approached my brother and pulled out a small knife he'd made up in the prison shop. Chris produced a six-inch nail and nearly dug his eyes out with it. They both got put down the block, and John was then transferred to another prison. His behaviour had been a challenge, and no challenge could be shrugged off. A slight on us, or the twins – or indeed the name of the Kray firm – would be quickly pounced upon.

In the early days of our sentence in Wandsworth, Chris gave a bloke called Tony Laing a right-hander for hitting Connie Whitehead on the chin. Laing said, 'I thought Whitehead did some harm at your trial.' Whether Whitehead had or hadn't done that, he still stood in the dock with us at the end of the day, he was still widely regarded as one of ours, and no attack on him could go unremarked because it would reflect on the rest of us.

The twins themselves could count on dozens of people throughout the prison system to stand up for their name – even people they didn't know and people who would act anonymously on their behalf. One con called Trevor Rogers, who was at

Parkhurst, mistook the twins for soft touches and was overheard describing them as 'a pair of mugs'. One day after his release, he was walking along the road in north London somewhere when he was suddenly shot in the leg. A stranger said to him, 'The pair of mugs send their regards,' and disappeared. The twins had nothing to do with it, but there were a lot of people in and out of prisons who wouldn't hear a wrong word said about them.

Several times, I talked to men in the nick who ended up murdering other cons in there. There was no way to survive that sort of environment without being a bit naughty. We had to think in a wicked way, to be aware that someone was always likely to take a pop at us.

Cons are the greatest hypocrites there are. They'd put the knife in the minute you turned your back. But it was rare for anyone to issue a direct challenge to Chris or me. Occasionally, we would sense from someone's attitude or little remarks that they were trying us out, and we'd have to stamp on that as quickly as possible. If violence was necessary, then, as Chris showed in Maidstone, we'd use it.

For the most part everybody knew their place, we didn't feel we had to exert our authority, and we got along with the other cons on equal terms. We were all in the same boat together, after all. And the way we lived reflected that. As long-term prisoners we had no time for tobacco baroning, for example. We had dealings in the gambling in prison, but tobacco baroning – selling tobacco to other cons at an inflated price – we looked upon as a very petty thing. If a man didn't have a smoke, you'd help him out. If you borrowed an ounce of tobacco, you returned an ounce. You wouldn't be expected to give back an ounce and a half, which was the racket in short-term prisons. We had a certain consideration for fellow-lifers. In turn, the long-term prisoners' predicament was treated with respect by cons in more fortunate circumstances.

No one ever talked about his own parole in front of a lifer who had no release date. Even the screws avoided mentioning your time. I remember one day in the mid-seventies in Gartree prison when Chris, Ronnie Bender and I were talking to Bobby Welch, one of the Great Train Robbers. Bobby was very well liked, and we were all concerned about the problems he was having with his knees: he suffered from very bad cartilage trouble. On this day, we were asking how he was when the Chief Officer and the Governor came along to tell him that they had good news. He knew what it would be: that his parole had come through. But instead of asking about it straightaway, he said to the Chief: 'Don't say anything in front of these boys here. They're all doing life.' I'll never forget that, and I'll always wish Bobby well.

Surprising as it may seem, we had to stamp on the screws more than we ever did on the other cons. Violence was rarely used, although when it did break out, it was heavy. What confrontations we had were more to do with attitude. The screws could make your life very awkward if they wanted to. We had to let them know, 'Don't fuck about with us, 'cause we'll fuck about with you.' I've seen fire bombs left in the workshops. I've seen tools disappear. We had to make life just as difficult for them as they did for us.

Sometimes they could be sneaky, seeking out information from those prisoners who were likely to give it. At the same time, they often couldn't help using that information to stir up trouble.

They'd go to cons and say, 'Let us know about anything going on, any little plots,' and it was an easy matter for the grasses to slip notes into the prison postbox. There was one of these boxes on each wing. All of the outgoing mail had to be censored, so any internal note was immediately discovered. Certain cons used this deal with the screws to try for a transfer. In the guise of posting a letter, some prisoner might put in a note saying, 'I'm being threatened by the Lambrianous. If I don't get a move from the wing, I'm sure something's going to happen.' They knew that, by dropping our name, their cases would seem extremely serious. But the screws were the first people to let us know who was saying what, and we'd then have to give the offending con a smack in the mouth.

Mostly, though, the screws' attempts to infuriate us were simply wind-ups, which we ignored. We often arrived at new prisons to be told that this person or that person, who was thought to be an enemy of ours, was an inmate. We never showed the authorities we had any bad feeling towards anyone – even if we had.

The first person to greet me at Leicester prison in 1969 was Charlie Richardson. He came over and shook hands to show the screws there was no ill feeling. Half an hour later, I was warned to 'be careful about the sugar because someone might have put grated glass in it' – another ridiculous reference to Charlie. In the years to follow, we served a lot of time together, Charlie and I.

The same sort of thing happened again at Gartree prison in the seventies when Chris and I were called up by the Governor and told that George Ince was coming. He was a villain who became a household name over his affair with Charlie Kray's wife Dolly. It was a little test to see what Chris and I would do. Of course, we showed no reaction.

I never encouraged screws to talk to me. It wouldn't have been right, given my attitude to the prison system throughout most of my sentence. If things weren't running the way we liked them, then we'd make sure the screws didn't go home of a night. We'd make something happen to keep them there. We'd refuse to bang up until it was sorted out. They had to adapt to our way of thinking. If we wanted a certain person off the wing, or if a particular screw was giving the cons a lot of pressure, a deputation would be made to the Assistant Governor or the Principal Officer. The officers didn't want the aggro. They knew they were dealing with very unpredictable people, and they usually transferred the person we were complaining about to another part of the prison.

If a major problem was going to arise in the nick, there would sometimes be an undercurrent, a series of little incidents leading up to the big one. You might get a screw being assaulted, or the men refusing to go to work. Day-to-day problems we dealt with as they arose. For example, during my second stay at Gartree prison, around 1974, they redid the whole place but failed to put bookshelves in the cells. We wanted the shelves put in, and the authorities refused. We took everything out of our cells, all the units, and stuck them out on the landings. They soon gave in, and we got our bookshelves.

By now, Chris and I and various other 'top' cons had realised that our natural aggression could be channelled into useful, rather than indiscriminate troublemaking. The whole idea was to make life as cushy as possible. For the first time in history the cons were beginning to run the nicks, and not the screws or the authorities.

Eventually, the screws grew to respect us just as much as the other cons did. They had to come to terms with us and worked around us. The screws couldn't run a prison, they could only try to implement the rules; and we found different ways to bend and break those rules. It became a game of cat and mouse with the screws in some ways, but we learned to understand them, even if we were understanding things they'd never tell us in so many words.

Prisons were going through a change in the early seventies. They were now housing a different type of criminal, the 'supercriminal' if you like, and the sentences which the courts were starting to hand out reflected that. Eighteens, fifteens, fourteens were becoming common, and they were producing prisoners who were not going to settle down quietly to do their time. They were men without hope, who saw no reason why they shouldn't take the law into their own hands in prison.

So, suddenly, the authorities were sitting on a potential bomb in our long-term prisons. And it stood to reason that if the cons were kept happy, then there would be fewer problems. If a Governor came along and said, 'They're getting it too cushy,' and had a crack-down, that would definitely lead to trouble. Everybody was aware of that.

Gartree prison in the early seventies was run like a three-star hotel, a holiday camp. It was a joke. We did what we liked. The screws never interfered, unless we did something to rock the boat. The authorities liked to be able to announce that their prison was well behaved, even though 'we're dealing with some of the most dangerous criminals in England'.

The prison cook would bake cakes for our friends' birthdays. The friend would come on a visit and the cook would come out to the table with his white chef's jacket and hat on, wish the person a happy birthday, and give them a beautiful cake with lit candles for the visitor to blow out.

Whatever my Chris wanted to do, the authorities let him do. They never bothered him. He had other contacts in the kitchen who sent him down tins of corned beef and fruit.

Many of the country's most notorious criminals were turning up in Gartree, and the more there were, the more potentially explosive the situation became. Accordingly, the authorities grew very cautious and the system very lax: 'Just leave them alone and let them get on with it.' A blind eye would be turned to a lot of the goings-on. It was so cushy, it got boring. And of course it had to go up in the end – but in the meantime our lives ran very happily.

We managed to get VIP treatment a lot of the time in a lot of the prisons. Rarely in my prison career did the screws give me any hassle; it was me who gave them the hassle. If they tried to nick something off you, like privileges, you'd nick something back off them.

Generally, wherever we went – and by 'we', I mean the Richardsons, the Great Train Robbers, the Wembley Bank Robbers and us – we were guaranteed an easy ride. The Governors and screws knew which men to look after, and if we were happy then we'd be keeping the rest of the prison in line, because of our standing amongst the other cons. This was confirmed by a prison Governor called Lakes, who was in charge of Gartree in the mid-seventies; Lakes had a Greek relative who knew my Dad.

One day, when Chris and I were on a visit with our Dad, Lakes came over to be introduced to him. By this time we'd been in Gartree for three years, a long time, and Chris wanted to know why.

Lakes said, 'We don't want our prison falling into the wrong hands.' He had the IRA in there, and a lot of dangerous men doing big sentences. He wanted to have a London gang in control, keeping a bit of peace.

But even when things were running smoothly, something could suddenly come along to upset the apple cart. How *do* you keep a con happy? You don't. I've heard it said by everyone from the Governors to the lowest screws – you could put the cons in a hotel, give them a steak every night of the week, and if you locked the door they'd still find something to complain about. Lock a man up and he's going to start rebelling; he's going to start looking for a weakness in the system. But there's going to be much less trouble if life is made as easy as possible.

The prison authorities' priority was to contain us. Controlling us was a lesser consideration. As long as we weren't escaping, they were prepared to put up with anything. You could smash a prison up, and they could rebuild it. You could tear up all the prisons you wanted. They could afford to lose a prison now and again, but they couldn't afford to lose the people in it.

However, it was an attitude that started to go badly wrong for the authorities at Gartree. I don't think they realised the amount of boredom and unrest that was brewing under their softly-softly regime, or anticipated the extent of the trouble and violence that it would have to endure.

The situation was simmering just below boiling point. There were increasing numbers of demonstrations, sit-outs and escape attempts, incidents which were building towards a bloody climax in the Gartree riots of 1972.

A great many people fell by the wayside during this period. There was no one you could open up to in there, and even if you just wanted to give a view, there was no guarantee that anybody would listen to it. You'd see broody blokes sitting around the prison on their own, with no one taking any notice of them.

Things were either up or down in there. There was no in-between. There were laughs and there were characters, the comedians of the prison, and for most of us they were enough to keep the days ticking over. But some people got to the stage where they felt they just couldn't go on. They'd smash up their cells in sudden fits of anger. They'd cut their wrists to get attention. They'd try to commit suicide for real.

And it wasn't just inmates who sometimes found the whole thing impossible to cope with; it was the screws as well. Just as much as there was good and bad amongst the screws, there was strength and weakness as well. During my two stretches at Gartree alone, from 1970 to 1972 and from 1974 to 1977, I saw at least fifteen screws crack up. I remember one cook smashing the kitchen to pieces and leaving the prison on a stretcher. Another screw got seven years for interfering with children, and a Principal Officer's son was nicked for housebreaking.

The screws did take a lot of stick in that place. Gartree prison was built specially for the secure detention of dangerous criminals, and it was designed to resist every possible means of escape. It's situated in the middle of a flat wasteland near Market Harborough in Leicestershire, and the feeling of isolation is overwhelming. No screw wanted to be there.

Those who were there tried to liven up their evenings by inviting some of the women prison visitors they met to the officers' club. A mate of mine called Danny Leishman, knowing this, set them up beautifully. He arranged for two blokes, dressed in very convincing drag, to come in on a visit. They were invited to stay for a drink after the visit, and two screws took them to the club, where they spent hours trying to chat them up. This went on until closing time, at which point one of the lads went, 'Well, boys, goodnight,' and lifted his skirt. He wasn't wearing any underwear, either. . . .

There were certain screws we could wind up very easily. The one who always comes to mind was a Brummie called Ranger, a Senior Officer (SO) in charge of C-wing, where we were in Gartree. We had a laugh with him when the officers' uniform was changed from dark blue to light blue – we called the new suits Postman Pats. Ranger didn't want to give up his dark blue uniform, and the cons wound him up to stage a one-man protest. To the great delight of the men, he refused to give in until he was officially ordered by the Governor to hand the old uniform back.

He was as thick as a plank, Ranger, with great big hands and fingers like bananas. He was a nervous man with a habit of tapping on things, always tapping away, with a spoon or whatever else was in his hand. Ronnie Bender used to take the piss out of him for that, and he would get very embarrassed.

He used to supervise the serving of the dinners, and he was so determined to catch someone nicking an extra bit of chicken or whatever that he watched too closely. We used to take things from right under his nose. But he could only stand so much. One day he yelled, 'I've had enough,' and chucked everything into the air – the pots, the pans, the dinner, the lot. And he just walked out.

When Ranger cracked up, it was the culmination of various things. Life had become unbearable within the prison system. His mind couldn't take it. He was living under constant pressure, with the perpetual fear of violence breaking out.

Some screws would say, 'Leave me out of it. It's nothing to do with me – I'm only doing my job,' but some cons would make allowances for no one: they saw a uniform, and a uniform only. These were dangerous and often paranoid men who would think nothing of sticking a knife in a screw. Screws got assaulted and battered – they were trying to contain men who had nothing to lose.

Certainly, the authorities came to learn a lot from the way they set out to deal with the 'super-criminals'. By the late seventies, they were starting to regain control of their own long-term prisons. Significantly, this was happening at a time when many of the inmates who'd been sentenced in the sixties were moving to lesser-security prisons, or, like us, had burnt up a lot of anger and frustration after years of confrontation and chaos.

CHAPTER THIRTEEN

WAR
GAMES

The dirtiest fight I ever heard of took place at Durham prison just before Chris, Ronnie Bender and I arrived there in May 1969. It involved a con, called Micky Keogh – a man who was unlucky enough to be run over by a bus and killed the day he came out of prison.

Micky was a post office and bank robber. People still talk about the time he went out with a shotgun, dressed as a Mexican bandit with two rolls of shells round his neck – while staying at Wormwood Scrubs prison hostel, the halfway house between his imprisonment and release. Needless to say, he didn't remain at liberty for very long. He went back to prison for a second long stretch, after which he met his fate.

We came across him in Durham during his first term of imprisonment. Things were very rough there in the wake of the John McVicar escape; the army was even brought in at one point to control the prison. This happened after the Assistant Chief Constable of Durham announced that professional criminals were now able to lay their hands on a lot of money and, because of their contacts, could have limited access to nuclear weapons. He added that these criminals would not hesitate to use such weapons, or get others to use them on their behalf, to break out of prison. It was a ridiculous theory, obviously, but the authorities took it seriously, and for several months we had troops with machine-guns guarding E-wing, where the most dangerous criminals were housed.

There was quite a bit of bad feeling between the cons and the screws, who were a very thick breed. Their pride and joy was hearing themselves, and knowing that everybody else could hear them, as they marched to the prison across the cobbles in their hobnailed boots. They didn't like the Londoners, especially since we all stayed together in a clique, as we did in every prison; they saw us as mouthy bastards.

We had arrived at Durham to find Micky Keogh at the height of fame over his confrontation with a certain screw. It all began the day he shouted out at this screw, 'You should be at home with your old woman,' and the screw yelled back, 'I wonder who's doing *your* old woman?'

Micky couldn't do anything about it at the time because he was locked up, but several days later another pal of ours, Joe Martin, spotted the same screw coming on duty. Micky had deliberately not gone to the toilet for a few days, and he had collected these tablets called 'yellow perils' from the doctor. They're guaranteed to make you run to the toilet like you've never been before. Take one and you're in trouble. Take two, and they'll completely do you out. Keogh immediately took six, and then he disappeared for a while. Shortly afterwards, he came back with a bag which he'd done his business in. He walked into the work room and straight up to the screw, who was leaning backwards on a chair, balancing on its two back legs.

The screw opened his mouth, startled, when he realised he was about to be attacked. At exactly the same moment Micky produced this bag from behind his back, said 'Remember me?' and went whack, straight in the screw's face. Nobody could believe what was happening. Micky's stomach must have been completely gone for a week afterwards, and what the incident did to the screw, psychologically, is anybody's guess. The cons used to wind him up rotten. Every time my brother saw him he'd say loudly, 'There's a terrible smell round here.'

Micky had to go before a VC or Visiting Committee. These were called when an offence was considered too serious for the prison authorities to deal with. A disciplinary body composed of local landowners and civic dignitaries would be brought to the prison to hear the case and impose punishment.

At Micky's VC, there was a reaction of utter shock. Someone commented, 'Only an animal would do this.'

He said, 'Never mind about that, who wants to be Richard the Third?', and tried to jump over the table at the committee members. He was famous for that. I should explain that Richard the Third is Cockney rhyming slang, and a 'Richard' is prison slang for a toilet.

Another screw – this time a Principal Officer – suffered almost as horribly in an incident I myself was involved in, one or two years later in Gartree. Simply out of boredom and for the sheer devilment of it, I decided with three other men to take two screws hostage and smash up the chokey (punishment) block. I was already in the block with a Geordie boy who looked like Genghis Khan, a little gay fella called Barry and a bloke called Ronnie Bolden.

Ronnie Bolden was in the nick for a robbery in London. The gang had got away with £30,000, but Ronnie's wife was so frightened of the amount of money he'd brought home that she put it in the washing machine and tried to wash it away. All the police took away with them when they came to search his home was one big lump of goo which the forensic people later proved had once been banknotes.

I'd been down the block for quite a long time because I'd been involved in an attempted escape, and I had a job on the hot plate, where the food was served. The PO used to come over from his office, and he'd be standing there talking to me while he was putting the tobacco into his pipe.

On the morning we decided to have the tear-up, I turned the hot plate fully on. I called the PO out of his office and stood talking to him about radios. Just as he put his tobacco down, I grabbed hold of his wrists and pulled him across the hot plate. The pipe dropped out of his hand. He ended up writhing around on the floor, refusing to let go of one of the four legs at the bottom of the hot plate.

Ronnie Bolden, meanwhile, had come up behind a screw called Saunders, whom I'd had recent disagreements with. He got his hands behind his neck, frogmarched him into a cell, took his whistle, his hat and his keys, and banged him up. Then Barry jumped on him, started to kiss him and gave him a love bite on the neck.

Next thing, the Geordie came out with a bucket which he'd urinated and done all sorts in. He poured the contents all over the PO. I'd already let go of the PO because I saw what was coming, and I didn't want it over me. We dragged him into a cell and locked him up. Then we barricaded the one gateway entrance to the block, but all of a sudden the alarms were going off. One of the security cameras had probably picked something up.

We held out for five hours, but the screws' reinforcements finally got in by cutting the doors from the outside. They were going to beat the life out of us, but I ripped the piping from the toilet and I said to the Chief, 'Anybody touches me and I'm going to kill one of you.' There must have been sixty screws there for four of us. And they knew I meant what I said. I was known and feared for being capable of carrying out my threats.

The Chief said, 'I assure you if you decide to go back, not a finger will be laid on you.' Not one of them touched us. Obviously we got nicked and charged with assault, smashing prison property, etc.

When it came to the VCs, we played up. When the screws arrived to take us to the hearings we were all standing there naked, refusing to get dressed – even the little gay bloke. They had to wrap blankets round us and carry us in. The committee comprised a male and female magistrate and another woman who was taking notes. Barry was charged with causing damage and assaulting a prison officer. He said, 'I fancied the screw. I decided to kiss him and give him a love bite.' He got twenty-eight days' punishment. I was given fifty-six days extra in the block.

When it was Bolden's turn he threw the blanket off so the two women could see him naked, and started masturbating in front of them. This, plus the fact that he'd thrown a bucket of piss and shit over a Principal Officer, went down very badly at the VC. He was given fifty-six days and shanghai'd out to another prison.

Around the same time Chris, who was then at Albany prison on the Isle of Wight, got involved in a confrontation with screws; but he came out of it a lot worse than I did. There had been some trouble about food and conditions, and Chris had been sent to the block with a few fellas called Charlie Robson, Don Barrett, Norman Parker, Taffy Thomas and Freddie Sanson, whose nephew is the England footballer Kenny Sanson. One night, they all decided that the next day they would have a disturbance. But it looked as though one of them put the word in the ear of authority. . . .

The next morning, before anything could happen, seven screws opened Chris's door and started bashing him to hell. He did his best to defend himself: he broke one screw's jaw and another's hand. Freddie was out of his cell and came to Chris's aid, but the screws battered him to the floor. Don Barrett also could have helped but he didn't lift a finger, which caused a rift between my brother and him.

Chris was left in such a bad state that they had to get him out of Albany prison. They decided to send him to Parkhurst, but when he arrived there they refused him entry because of his injuries. It was then decided to drive him halfway across the country, to Hull. They refused to accept him there too. He was sent back to Albany, and again moved out. In the end he was returned to Parkhurst, where he was finally taken in.

Just after this, Freddie Sanson was transferred to Hull prison. One day, after finishing a game of football, he went back to his cell. When Jimmy Hussey, one of the Great Train Robbers, took him in a cup of tea he found him dead. Some people suggested it was a result of the beating.

Violent scenes with screws were usually triggered by boredom, provocation or dissatisfaction with prison conditions and facilities. Fights among cons, on the other hand, could flare up for any number of reasons. Spur-of-the-moment arguments, usually over simple things, were a common cause; so were personal grudges and unresolved arguments. Charlie Richardson, for instance, held a grudge against John McVicar and Joey Martin after they blanked – ignored – him on the escape from Durham prison. Charlie was shouting, 'You rats, you stags, you left me here!' out of the window as he watched them breaking out. Charlie was there when McVicar was recaptured and brought to Leicester, and he wound up a bloke called 'Hate 'Em All' Harry Johnson to have a go at McVicar. One day McVicar was having a wash when Harry came up behind him and tried to do him. Johnny Dark, a professional boxer who had fallen foul of Securicor, ended up knocking them both out. Harry Johnson was a man you could never turn your back on. For no reason whatsoever, he once stabbed a geezer on the landing in front of all the screws at Hull prison; on another occasion he cut George Ince for humiliating Charlie Kray by having an affair with his wife Dolly. After that, Harry was sent to Gartree. I was doing my second period in Gartree at the time, and Chris, Ronnie Bender and Ian Barrie were with me. A lot of people were worried about Harry being there because he was so unpredictable. He was told by Chris and Ronnie Bender, 'Step out of line and you'll never walk in a straight line again.' It was the only language he understood.

Hostilities between prisoners could carry on for weeks, months or even years before they came to a physical conclusion, and Chris always seemed to have several feuds on his hands at once. Some he was able to settle quite promptly, like the one with Dougie Parkes, a known villain from Sheffield. He upset Chris in Gartree during that boiling hot summer of 1976. About four or five weeks went by. One night we were watching *Top of the Pops* as usual, which was a favourite thing in prisons; in the small BBC TV room. ITV had a bigger room.

Dougie Parkes was in his regular seat near the front when Chris went to get a jug of boiling water for some tea. As he returned to his seat, he 'accidentally' tripped over Parkes and spilt boiling water all down his neck, shoulders and chest. Parkes was immediately rushed to hospital with second degree burns, and was on the danger list for about two weeks.

When they brought him back to prison, he said: 'Chrissy Lambrianou did it deliberately because of previous incidents in Gartree.' He was told by us in no uncertain terms that if he didn't drop this allegation, he would never leave the hospital alive. After three or four days of kicking that idea around, he saw sense and the charge was dropped. Chris went in front of a VC and was given a caution about taking care when getting boiling water from the tea urn.

Other scores may have taken longer to settle, but they were no less satisfying for Chris. Take the instance of Don Barrett. Chris had it in for him after the fight with the screws in Albany and Freddie Sanson's subsequent death. Even though they didn't meet for another seven or eight years, Chris was gunning for him straightaway. It was 1979 when Barrett was moved to Maidstone prison. By now, rumours were widely circulating that he had been giving information to the police. Chris went up to him one day and said, 'You're a grass.'

So Barrett came to me to find out where he stood. I said, 'I don't know anything about it, but I'll give you a bit of advice, Don. Stay away from Chris.'

I was about to be decategorised and sent to a Cat. C prison. While I was waiting, I worked as the swimming pool attendant at Maidstone. One Saturday afternoon, I was sitting by the side of the swimming pool. Next to it was a little putting green, where they used to give you steel golf clubs to knock a ball about. Next thing, Chris came walking out, picked up a club and put it up to the end of Don Barren's nose. He said, 'When my Tony moves from here, I'm going to do you.'

He wouldn't risk it until I'd left the prison, because he didn't want me getting linked to any trouble. I moved the following Monday, and at the same time Chris was sent down the block for some misdemeanour or other. He escaped from there, went straight into the wing where Barrett was and broke his jaw. Barrett is now known to have put more than two hundred men away as a grass. He's the only man to have gone supergrass twice: apparently he fingered the Wembley Bank Robbers.

Grasses, obviously, we hated; and Jimmy Humphries, the porn king, was another. Our differences with him began in Maidstone. We'd been hearing all sorts of stories about him. He was said to have boasted that right from the beginning he could have cleared the names of Patsy Murphy and the others convicted of the Luton Post Office job; yet he didn't do a thing to help them. He let them rot in prison for twelve years, after which they walked out on appeal. We'd also heard whispers that he was running with the police, and Chris was starting to get the hump with him, but the thing that sealed it was something Humphries said in a cell one day in front of about seven of us. Out of the blue, he announced, 'I'm going to get a man twenty years.'

Chris asked, 'Who?'

'Ginger Dennis,' he said.

Ginger Dennis was a known villain and a friend of Freddie Foreman, but he had done nothing wrong.

Once Humphries said that, of course, Chris was going to do him. Jimmy Humphries had no friends, so he paid another con called Chester Barnes to be his minder. Chris attacked them both in the dinner queue one day. He picked up the food and let them have it. They got whacked up in the air a bit, and after that Humphries decided he needed Rule 43 protection in the block – isolation from other prisoners.

In order to get it he went to the Governor, Peter Timms, with his ally Chester Barnes, claiming he wanted to grass up Chris and me. This was enough to guarantee protection from us. He made a statement alleging that we were involved in drugs, gambling and all kinds of rackets. I won't deny that I was a bookmaker at Maidstone – I'd done a bit of that throughout my prison career. The currency for gambling was half-ounce packets of tobacco, and the odds on a horse, or whatever, were the same as outside. I had access to a lot of tobacco – I won it in card games and so on – and when I had more than my official limit of two ounces, I'd get other cons to carry it for me.

The rest of Humphries' accusations were false. Chester Barnes, it turned out, had been promised a few quid by Humphries for conspiring in the allegations against us, but after the meeting with Timmsy he immediately realised what could happen to him for being a grass – and, worse, for being a lying grass. He went to Chris, told him what had happened and said he would tell the Governor it was all a get-up. I went to see Timms myself. He said, 'Look, I know it's a pack of lies. I don't even want to read it,' and as good as threw it in the bin.

It was too late by now for us to do anything about it. Humphries and Barnes had gone straight on to protection, and Chris was being sent back to Albany, a tougher prison, for a twelve-month quietening-down period. The authorities felt he was getting out of control after the scene in the dinner queue, the incident with the six-inch nail and various other clashes. But no one had the bottle to tell Chris he was moving back to Albany.

Timms approached me the previous evening and asked, 'Would you be prepared to tell Chris?'

So I went and shouted through the door to my brother, 'You'd better get your kit packed, you're on the way tomorrow.'

He yelled back, 'Yeah, and you can fuck off as well.'

The screws and the Governor all jumped back from the door. 'He says, "I ain't going," I told them. I had to talk to Chris all night long before he would allow them to take him to Albany. They didn't know how to handle him.

Sex offenders, obviously, were the people who would incite the most hostility within any prison, but because they were kept in isolation, under Rule 43 protection, little violence ever occurred. Chris, however, is proud to be the only man who has been able to get at Ian Brady, the hated Moors Murderer.

This happened during the summer of 1969, while we were in Durham – Chris, Ronnie Bender, Ian Barrie and I. Because we were maximum-security prisoners, we were in an isolation wing with four of the most notorious sex offenders this country has ever seen: Brady, the Cannock Chase Killer, the Gravel Pit Killer and John Straffen, the longest-serving prisoner in Britain. The PO on the wing explained the position. He said, 'We have in the unit people you ain't gonna like, but you can rest assured you'll never get near them.' They were segregated from us almost as effectively as they were from the general prison population, and they exercised on their own.

Although the other three of these prisoners frequently fought and argued amongst themselves, I never saw Brady speak to anybody other than a screw. He was constantly surrounded by about ten prison officers, and he looked like a thoroughly evil bastard. He never, ever smiled. To hang him would be a crime against the children he murdered, and the families of those children. I sincerely hope that he lives to be a hundred and serves and suffers every day of that. We saw him living the life of a recluse, shunned by everybody. He was treated like trash; the screws who had to deal with him held him in contempt. My Chris happened to be on the stairs one day when Brady went past with his entourage of screws. Suddenly Chris saw an opening, and he whacked him.

As a sequel to this story, I was in the same prison as Brady three years later when I was being held in the control unit at Wormwood Scrubs. He sent a message to me, asking how my brother was. My reaction is unprintable.

Peter Morris, the Cannock Chase Killer, who'd murdered a little girl, looked like the sort of person who'd done it with pleasure. He was an arrogant character. When he was being escorted around by screws, going to exercise or being taken down for food, he'd shout out something like 'Hello, boys', trying to talk to us. We spat on him.

Burgess, the Gravel Pit Killer, had murdered two little girls. He was an inadequate, a pervert. Straffen, on the other hand, was mentally disabled. He had the mind of a child of four, and for that reason was accepted by us. A tragic case, he was sentenced to death for the murder of a child in Bristol, but was found to be insane and reprieved to life imprisonment. He escaped from either Broadmoor or Rampton maximum-security hospitals, and was alleged to have murdered another little kiddie. He was again sentenced to hang, but again reprieved because of his insanity.

He used to peel the stamps off envelopes for the *Blue Peter* appeal, and he was the first man ever to be allowed a television in his cell, early in the sixties. It was donated by Lord Cadbury, a member of the famous chocolate family, as a gift of compassion. From that day on, Straffen would buy nine bars of Cadbury's chocolate at a time from the prison canteen. He used to put them at his cell window where the sun would melt them, and he'd come down to us crying, with the chocolate melting all over his fingers.

He was allowed to come down and make our tea and generally talk to the boys. I saw a picture of him recently. His head looks like a space dome now, after all the beatings he's taken over the years from cons who have had access to him. The most humane thing that could be done for Straffen would be for someone to say, 'Here's a pill – swallow it if you want to end it one day.' Tragic as he is, he's not safe ever to release.

I have probably seen more violence in prison over homosexual quarrels than anything else. You might get one man trying to pinch another one's boyfriend, or a couple being split up by prison transfers. Events like these have led to rape and murder within prisons while I've been there.

Having lived in prison as long as I did, I can understand the homosexual attitude. It's not a thing I ever got involved in, but most of the men who did seek it out were not, by nature, homosexuals. They were known in the system as 'prison poufs', and they accounted for maybe 10 per cent of the population in the nick. They were men who were heterosexual in freedom but inside, because of sexual deprivation, would turn to homosexuality. You'd see them sitting with the wife and kids in the visiting room. They'd kiss the missus and then go back to bed with the boyfriend. They tended to stay amongst themselves, although some of the men who were doing it on the sly – not wanting the stigma or the derisive comments of other cons – would discreetly keep away from homosexual company in day-to-day association and never talk to anyone about what they were doing at nights and in the shower room.

When you've got a number of men thrown together like that, then obviously it's going to happen, especially where you've got young guys of twenty or so coming in at the peak of their sexual endeavours. It's not within the prison rules, it's not something the authorities encourage, but there's not a lot anyone can do about it. In my experience most of the screws just turned a blind eye, and the attitude of a lot of them towards new arrivals seemed to be, 'Find yourself a boyfriend, settle down and do your best.' If a screw goes to a cell door and finds someone in bed with another con, what does he do? Normally, he'd know what was going on and stay out of the way until one of the couple appeared.

It was a very touchy subject in prison, treated with either great embarrassment or jokes. At the same time, it was capable of causing tremendous trouble. Some of the inmates were out-and-out gay, so you'd come across quite a bit of poaching. They'd be after the younger boys. There would be stabbings and all sorts of violent incidents over this kind of thing. I have known the authorities try to break up a relationship by transferring one of the blokes to another prison. Then, in the interests of a peaceful life, they'd have to reunite the pair they'd just separated.

A Yorkshireman known as the Bull took a liking to a young gay boy in Parkhurst while I was there in 1974. They fell out, and the young fella went off with another bloke. The Bull kidnapped his former boyfriend, barricaded himself and the young lad inside his cell and refused to let anybody in or out for three days.

Another rape case took place in Maidstone prison, which was also the scene of a sexually-motivated murder. A man called Kessler was there during our time, serving life imprisonment. He was about six feet tall and wore dark glasses. He always tried to give the impression he was one of the boys, but he delved into the murky side of life with younger, practising homosexuals. Eventually he came clean about it and said to me one day, 'They've moved my mate.' His boyfriend had been transferred to a nut-house. He wanted to get himself sent off to the same nut-house to be with his bloke, and in order to achieve this he decided to kill a fellow-con. He befriended another guy on the wing, started sharing a cell with him and one day, after asking the chap to make him a cup of coffee, battered him to death with a bed leg wrapped up in a towel. I was unaware of this when I passed the prison hospital and saw Kessler there.

I said, 'What are you doing here?'

He replied, 'Oh, I don't feel well.'

No wonder he didn't feel well: he'd just killed someone stone dead and it was still his secret.

In the hospital they gave him some Panadol, and later on he decided to go back. Then the screw saw the bloodstains round his cuffs, and Kessler confessed: 'I've just killed my cellmate.'

All hell broke loose. He was charged and sentenced to life imprisonment to run concurrent. And he never did get the transfer to be with his boyfriend.

CHAPTER FOURTEEN

BREAD AND BUTTER

From the moment I got my sentence, the thought of escaping was never far from my mind. I was involved in three break-out attempts, all during 1972 at Gartree prison. I tried to go over it, under it and through it, but I never succeeded. I was at a stage where I couldn't see the end of my sentence, I didn't care what I did and, like every other long-timer, I was looking for opportunities. There was a certain challenge about the idea of escaping. It was all about beating security. It was exciting, too. You could always tell who was buzzing and who wasn't, and every escape bid caused a lot of rumblings within the prison. Nearly all of the plans were doomed to failure from the beginning, especially at Gartree, which was the toughest nut to crack in Britain. But it was always worth a try. It was better than sitting there doing nothing. If you do nothing, nothing happens. I never wanted to get sucked into my sentence, never wanted to settle into the humdrum routine of prison life.

By the time I arrived at Gartree in November 1970, I had been taken out of the maximum-security blocks and moved into what was called the dispersal system. This operated in certain high-security prisons, and allowed association between Cat. A and Cat. B cons – prisoners who were regarded as less dangerous than the A-men, although still a potential threat to society, should they ever escape. Their movement within the prison was less restricted, and they were granted more privileges. The idea was that if you put two or three bad apples in the barrel, some good might come out of them. The reality was probably a bit different: those two or three bad apples would rot the rest. Naturally, I was classified as a bad apple.

As an A-man in the dispersal system, I found conditions only slightly easier than they had been in the security blocks. The only improvements were that we had access to other cons, we had a few more privileges and there was not such a huge prison officer presence around us – although it was big enough. I was still being signed over from one part of prison to another, still having cell searches every day, still being checked day and night, still being filmed by security cameras everywhere I went.

A typical day would begin at seven o'clock when the cell was unlocked, and I'd wake up and turn on Radio 2. You were allowed to have quite a few things in your cell – carpet, curtains, bedspreads, towels, a record player, a two-band radio and PT stuff. You could also have small pets, within reason, if you wanted them. I personally didn't have a lot of clutter in my cell – and any photographs I had I'd never put on display. Most cons were the same. If someone got the hump, they'd immediately go and do your photos.

I used to wander down past a gauntlet of screws to collect my breakfast at about 7.30.

Porridge – a very low-grade porridge – would be left out for you to help yourself. Some prisons would provide milk too, but it wasn't usual. You didn't get sugar. There would also be a bit of bacon, or a serving of goulash, a famous prison meal which was a savoury mixture of ingredients such as bacon or beef, potato and cabbage, and a mug of tea with no sugar. The tea was made from what looked like tea-leaf dust, and a screw would come along with a scoop and go *whack* into each cup with cheap powdered milk. It was terrible stuff, that tea; if you were to fill your car up with it, it would take off. We used to buy tea bags and tins of Marvel from the canteen and make our own.

The A-men were locked up again to eat breakfast in the cell, and taken out to the workshops at around a quarter to nine – always with an escort and a dog-handler, and separately from the Cat. B cons. We were only ever allowed to work in supervised shops, never in the grounds. We had our statutory one hour's exercise every day.

We'd have a cup of tea when we got to the shop, and another pot after about an hour's work. Life in prison revolved around cups of tea, and a lot of the cons drank gallons and gallons of the stuff. I had two flasks for keeping boiling water in, and before I went to bed I'd make sure they were full up.

At around half past eleven we'd be handed back to the escort and taken out of the shop before the Cat. B boys. We'd collect our lunch and return to our cells, where we were locked in while the rest of the men were served. Lunch was the main meal of the day. There was always soup and a bread roll, a hot meal and a sweet, usually a floating duff – a pudding with about two currants in it, in custard made mostly with water. All three courses would be in separate compartments of a metal tray, and you were lucky if you got it back to your cell without the custard running into the main course. On Sundays, we'd get a 'roast dinner' with four or five potatoes which were like chips. They were small potatoes, cut in half and fried.

In the nick, we were served what were supposed to be proper meals, all worked out by Home Office dieticians. They reckoned the menus offered a perfectly healthy diet. Basically, there was nothing wrong with the food; the problem was what they did to it. Most of it was prepared the day before or overnight, so it was left lying about. Nearly everything was steamed. The cabbage was always very watery, with none of the goodness left. Even the meat was steamed, and then given a little grilling. You got one slice, although you could have as much bread as you wanted. The potatoes were full of eyes. The men in the kitchen couldn't do anything about this because they didn't have time: they were under orders to rush the food out. A lot of cons used to mash up their dinners as a way of disguising the rubbish, hiding what they didn't want to know.

Inevitably, we found ways to liven up our food. In the canteen we could buy almost anything we wanted with our prison wages of around £1.50 a week, our working pay – but not with private cash. We'd save up our canteen money and buy ingredients to make the food more tasty. In long-term prisons we had cooking facilities in a little kitchen on the wing, so if we had chicken for Sunday dinner we'd save the legs and make our own stew out of them later, or curry them up.

Also, there were a lot of fiddles going on, with tins and parcels of food coming out of the kitchen, and the authorities knew it. At one time we could buy vitamin pills to supplement our diet, but they were eventually banned because certain cons were living on them.

The lunch hour was the most focused part of the day. The newspapers and the mail would be dished out, and the B-men, who weren't locked in cells, would hear the gossip about other cons. We'd be told all about it after lunch when we were checked back into the shop. We'd have a chat with the boys and another cup of tea, do a bit of work here and there, and knock off again about half past four to go back to the wing for tea. This would be a light meal – maybe something like baked beans or a salad with bread and butter and another mug of rocket fuel. We'd eat it in our cells while we were locked up between five and six o'clock.

Then we'd be let out for association. This was the most crime-free part of the day, because most of the cons would sit and watch television. They'd stare at anything, without moving. From the authorities' point of view, television was the greatest thing they could ever put in a prison. In my circles we watched documentaries and became very interested in politics, especially law and order issues. We used to sit and slag off all the politicians talking on television, especially Maggie Thatcher. Right the way through the six o'clock news we used to moan about the things that were going on – anything from the latest government decisions to the world's disasters and tragedies. We were also keen on nature programmes because they were about life, an escape from the twilight zone we lived in; and we'd all be there for any big football or boxing matches.

Those things apart, the television never interested me. I could not stand the soaps. If you watched those, you were classed as one of the prison sheep. There was only one thing that could drag them away from *Coronation Street* and that was the bell for the 'liquid cosh'. Medical treatment would be given out at about ten to eight, and if you didn't get there within fifteen minutes you were too late. There would be a cavalry charge when the bell went. Everyone wanted to get there first for their nightcap.

The cons were on all sorts of pills, and you could get any authorised drug you wanted. The authorities held quite a bit of control this way: when the men were sedated, there would be less chance of violence. I was on Mogadon for a long time. And if you had a headache, you were given Valium: 'That'll do you good.' Is it any wonder that men come out of prison wanting whatever uppers and downers they can get?

Medical care in prisons was in my opinion generally very bad. Cons who reported sick were given pretty dismal treatment. Everybody tried to skive, but if you had a genuine complaint you were still treated with a great lack of interest by the doctors. I don't think they could handle the numbers. Even after an operation, the follow-up treatment and the food you were given were absolutely disgusting. And you would usually be dismissed from a proper medical with one word: 'Out!'

At nine o'clock, tablets taken, we were banged up in our cells until the next morning. Then it would start all over again.

Several years into my life sentence I realised that time had stopped meaning anything; the outside world seemed far away, unreal, despite what we watched on television. It gave us a very false picture anyway.

We tried to lead a bit of a civilian life. I had the moustache and the long hair in the seventies, and a lot of the boys used to wear bell-bottom jeans. We tried to keep up with the trends, but it was very difficult. As far as women were concerned, I personally forgot all about that side of life.

Visits became more and more of a strain. I never understood what my visitors were telling me about their problems outside; I couldn't imagine myself in their position. Instead of looking forward to visits, I started to dread them. On a good morning or afternoon they could make you feel very high, but most of the time I came away with terrible headaches and I'd be down for two or three days afterwards.

I lost interest in letters as well. None of the people who wrote to me told me anything I could relate to, and for my part I had nothing interesting to say in any of my replies. I was living in a completely different world. Our wages, for example, were out of touch with anything approaching reality, and the things we could buy, and chose to buy, from the canteen would have caused no great excitement outside. Who else but us would want to celebrate the news that we were going to be allowed to buy our own toiletries instead of having to use prison soap?

Cleanliness is a number one priority among cons in long-term prisons, and Gartree was spotlessly clean. So were its inmates. That was one thing all lifers had in common: you always left the washbasin and the shower clean, and you always had to have access to water. We were continually washing.

The majority of cons had a lot in common, especially the fact that we all hated the system, and for most of the time we coexisted in an atmosphere of uneasy peace. Everybody used to watch everybody else, we all paid attention to the prison grapevine – which was better than a newspaper – and we all knew each other in a roundabout way. But they were not necessarily the people you'd choose to have living next door in an ideal world, and the peace could give way to explosions within seconds.

Much of this was to do with the pressures and limitations of prison life; and brothers were not exempt. Chris and I had bust-ups in every prison we were in together. The other cons used to think we were killing each other in the cell, but they knew better than to interfere. It was a release. There came times when we were sick of the sight of each other; we'd have a massive argument over something trivial, and afterwards we wouldn't speak for months. But even during these periods Chris would be there for me if there was trouble. No one could have had a better ally.

Quite a few of my arguments with Chris were over his tendency to trust people before he knew for a fact they were trustworthy. He'd say, 'So and so's a nice fella,' and I'd say, 'Yeah, but . . .' And we'd have a blazing row. I was more selective: I tended to stick closely to my own circle of friends, and I spent most of my leisure time chatting with them over a cup of tea or having a game of cards. From time to time we'd have a game of snooker, or go to the gym and lift a few weights. Fitness and sports were greatly encouraged in prison, and the educational facilities were good, although A-men were not allowed to take courses unless the security was watertight, because civilian tutors were involved and the authorities were always worried about the prospect of hostage-taking.

Many inmates couldn't read or write, but at the same time I knew men who came out with Open University honours degrees. There were a lot of talented people in prison – cons who were skilled in carpentry, crafts, music and art – and it made me wonder half the time what they were doing in there.

However, it must be said that the dispersal prisons were more than anything else schools and universities of crime, and as such they gave an education second to none. There were young fellas in there learning their trade by association with professionals and making contacts for the future. The professionals, amongst themselves, would put their criminal brains together to plan in every detail the jobs they would do when they came out. Occasionally they would put their brains together for some more immediately rewarding projects.

When I first went to Gartree, there was a spate of hooch-brewing going on at the time. It was punch made out of fruit and a bit of yeast, and it always seemed to turn out green. It tasted like garbage and we used to call it Gut Rot. Some of the cons were experts and we knew we could rely on them for a good brew, but most of us had a go ourselves. We'd nick a bit of yeast out of the kitchen, along with potatoes or dried fruit, and buy a kilo of sugar and tinned fruit from the prison canteen. We'd get tepid water, and we'd brew the mixture in a plastic bucket. The secret was the amount of sugar you put in it. After about twenty-four hours, the smell of it would be all over the nick. We used to get that Deep Heat cream for muscle strains and rub it everywhere to try and hide the smell of the hooch. And we'd use a decoy. We'd make three buckets and we'd let them find one. The other two would be stashed.

I know a guy who used the tubing of his bed as a still! He plugged all the holes along the tubing so that nothing could escape. He then made the brew and, using a funnel, poured it into the bed frame through a hole he'd drilled himself, which was then plugged up.

He'd made a little tap which fitted into the hole, and when he wanted a drink he simply had to pour it from the bed into a plastic cup. It took us a long time to discover how he got so legless in the lock-up hour between five and six o'clock. . . .

The screws had a general idea of what was going on. Sometimes they would put you on report if they caught you, but at other times they turned a blind eye. Once or twice I left a bucket of hooch sitting blatantly in my cell with a towel over it and no one even bothered to look at it. They knew there would be a brew-up around Christmas or holiday times, and it was the only thing we had to look forward to as far as Christmas was concerned.

It was a very down time of year in prison. The cons themselves seemed to change a lot; and the prison became a much more solemn place. You could feel a little bit more atmosphere in as much as they'd have Christmas trees, and some of the men would do their best to cheer everyone up. The food improved a bit, and much as you tried not to admit it, Christmas still did mean something a bit special, even in prison. But there was no joy in it. There were no family aspects. It wasn't real. The best times of the year were, in fact, in the summer, when we could go out on evening exercise and enjoy the quiet of the night.

Despite sensational revelations in the press that Britain's prisons were overflowing with alcohol and brimming with illegal drugs, the hooch production, which is all I ever saw, was grinding to a halt towards the end of the seventies when the authorities were regaining control of the dispersal prisons. I heard some outrageous stories about Ronnie Bender. He was said at one time to be running things in Chelmsford prison so successfully that he had his own bar! There were even questions asked about him in the House of Commons, but he was very well liked and respected by screws and cons alike, and no one paid much attention to the rumours.

Drugs, I suppose, were available if wanted. I won't deny that a bit of that went on, but the stories that go round about drugs in prison are wild exaggerations. We were never involved in anything like that. Like everyone else, we stuck to the people and things we knew.

Everybody seemed to find their place in prison very quickly, forming friendships with others of their own kind. You could instantly tell how and where a new inmate was going to fit in. The men who were in for fraud, for example, tried to look educated and spent their time studying together. They seemed to be trying to tell us, 'We shouldn't be here.'

Then there were the cons who came in because of a bit of thieving or burglary. They kept themselves to themselves, never made any bids for power, and simply did their best to get on with their sentences.

The out-and-out villains – bank robbers and their ilk – wanted to be seen to be the same inside prison as they were outside it. They had to establish a high-ranking position in the pecking order – they had to gain and maintain respect; as a result, they were often seen to be living a bit better than the other cons. They would always support any protest on the side of the underdog against authority.

And then there were the murderers. I never believed that more than 20 per cent of murderers had committed real murders. There were arsonists who managed to kill people as a by-product of their obsession for starting fires (strangely enough, the arsonists I met were always red-haired). There were men who committed crimes of passion; and youngsters who went out for a night, got in a gang fight and ended up stabbing somebody who later died. Is that murder? Most criminals would avoid murder at all costs; it would be a last resort. The domestic murderer who killed his wife or his lover never really had any influence in prison. He was going to do four years in a closed nick and then get farmed out to a lesser prison. The bloke who murdered someone in a fight or in the course of theft would be doing anything up to twelve or thirteen years. He would most likely be a young guy. He wanted to run with the pack, be with the boys, but at the same time he realised it could damage his future and so he tried to steer a middle course. It could be very difficult.

Then there was the 20 per cent which we fitted into. We were people who had influence, who did our best in trying circumstances. The other cons tended to come to us with their problems, because of the respect we had within the system. That could make life very wearing.

To an extent, the screws observed the inmates' hierarchy. The power of personality was at play a lot here.

At the other end of the scale were what we called the hobbits, the bread and butter of the prison system, the inadequates of society. Some of the hobbits were sex offenders and some of them were prison fodder, the sort of people who were easily led, were consistent offenders in petty crime and were likely to spend their lives going in and out of prison. They had no say in the system. They were usually as harmless as they were tragic, and everyone abused them.

The hobbits usually worked for the screws around the hot plate and the tea rooms. They loved to wear their white jackets for serving out the food, and they always used to be scurrying about amongst the piles of washing up, wiping the trays and getting everything ready. You couldn't even begin to rehabilitate half of them – they were just not capable of surviving on their own. In prison they had their food and a bit of company, they could run around wheeling and dealing over little things, and that's about as far as they were going to go.

The major sex offenders were kept away from us under Rule 43 protection, but other nonces, as we called them, were integrated into the system. Many of them would approach known criminals, wanting to make their tea and do their running around in return for protection. We never went looking for these go-fers; they came to us. We seemed to collect them. I had one called Micky Fossett, who came to three different prisons with me.

He was doing life for a sex offence, a bad one. He committed it as a kid, and he never stopped regretting it from the moment it happened. He used to go and save a seat for me in the television room, and bring my pot of tea.

One night I got stopped by five Geordie boys who said, 'Look, that Mick is a nonce.'

Another bloke, a Yorkshireman called Bernie, said, 'We don't like nonces. You want to do something about it.'

I was in a bit of a funny position, because I couldn't be seen to favour Fossett, so I said, 'He does a lot of running around for me.' I also let them know what would happen to Fossett if he ever fell foul of me.

He suited my purposes. And by using him, I protected him. Without me, he wouldn't have had much of a life. He would have been under Rule 43 in the segregation unit.

Another mate of ours, Billy Gentry, used a rapist called Ted as his tea boy. Ted was a right nutter, known as the Phantom of Epping Forest. He used to run about the drainage system underneath the forest, which led out into roads and gardens. He'd force his way into houses in these different places and rape all these old dears.

He got one old lady into bed and the next thing she said was, 'Will you come back to see me again, Ted?'

During one of his raids he broke into this house and found a box full of sovereigns behind the chimney. He started giving a sovereign to each of his rape victims, and that's what led to his capture and conviction. When it came to trial in the Old Bailey thirty women gave evidence against him, and they were all calling him by his first name. But the fact that he had given each of them a sovereign turned every single one of them, in law, into a prostitute.

In contrast to the grim routine of prison life, the laughs we had seemed funnier than they would have anywhere else, and the sadnesses more tragic. There was a dreadful incident concerning Tubbsy Turner, one of my old schoolfriends. He was convicted of hijacking offences with his mate George Murray, and he had recently married George's sister Frances. She was only in her early twenties when a phone call came through to the prison to say she'd died – just suddenly dropped dead. The screws were very worried about telling Tubbsy, so Chris had to do it. He went to break the news and all of a sudden I heard this yell – this painful, anguished cry which I'll never forget. He never got over it, Tubbsy.

We came across quite a bit of tragedy during our years inside. I'll always remember a fellow con called John Duddy, who was sentenced to thirty years for his part in the Shepherds Bush cop killings with Harry Roberts and John Whitney. John Duddy had no idea what was going to happen that day, and was only involved in the murder of three policemen through his friendship with the other two.

He was a man who had a great love of children, and would cry at the slightest touch of sadness, maybe reading something in the newspaper or watching it on television. He'd often come up to me in tears about something terrible that had happened. He was quite the opposite of Harry Roberts, who was a strange man – very aloof. On Christmas Day 1970 in Leicester prison, Chris, Charlie Richardson, Fred Foreman, Ronnie Bender, Paul Seabourne, Micky Keogh and I were in a maximum-security block watching *The Inn of the Sixth Happiness* with John Duddy. Ingrid Bergman plays a missionary who leads a group of Chinese orphans over the mountains, escaping from the Japanese. Duddy couldn't help himself; he cried his eyes out. He was a very humane man. One day he said to me, 'I'll do fifteen years and then I'll turn it in. I don't want to do any more than that.' And he did. He died of a heart attack when he'd done fifteen years.

If tragedy and comedy became larger than life in the dreary surroundings of a prison, the same was the case for other dramatic events: during 1972 the idea of escaping became more and more irresistible as an adventure, the ultimate showdown with authority.

The first attempt was in July. It started as a demonstration. We'd decided to stay out for a couple of nights in the exercise yard as part of a campaign for the prisoners' rights organisation, PROP. We took our blankets out and we had access through the windows to water, coffee and tins of this and that. Some of the cons put their blankets up against the fence to make tents. Then they started digging a tunnel, under cover of the blankets, leading right from that fence to the outer one.

I went on to the roof of the gym with Ronnie Bender and another lifer called Ali Starkey, who was a second cousin of the Beatles' Ringo Starr. We were told about the tunnel by a man called Colin Beaumont, who asked us if we were interested in joining the break-out. Of course we were interested. We were told to be ready within an hour. The idea was that the cons would cause chaos in the yard to divert attention while the lifers escaped.

In the meantime, a fellow con told us he felt sick. He went back into the wing and reported the escape plan to the authorities. All of a sudden, about a hundred screws came marching out and pulled the blankets away from the fence. I thought there was going to be a bloodbath, because every man was looking forward to his bid for freedom, but the screws didn't try to manhandle us. Everyone on the demonstration was fined £1 or £2 each.

The con who reported us was put on protection and released a couple of years later to a life of misery. You can't hide from four hundred men who've got the hump with you. We were gutted.

But shortly afterwards I tried again. I was working at the time in the light engineering shop, which backed on to a fence. On the other side of that fence was a second one, about eighteen feet away, and that was the prison perimeter fence.

The shop was in a prefabricated building which had a window at the back. There was thin wire covering the window. We had access in the shop to nuts, bolts and bits of piping, and we used this to build a ladder in three sections. Along with a fellow con called Billy O'Gorman I intended to go into the back storeroom, cut through the wire at the window, get on to the building itself, get the ladder and make a bridge between the building and the first fence. Having crossed over to the top of the first fence, we'd drop down and run over to the second and final fence with the ladder.

Almost everything was against this plan succeeding. There were 'tremblers' on each fence which would set off an alarm if any pressure was felt. There were dogs patrolling the no-man's-land between the two fences. Every inch of the prison grounds was on camera. And the land surrounding the prison was flat, so any escapees could be seen and picked up immediately.

Still, I thought it was worth a try. We picked a time when the dog-handlers were supposed to be on their tea breaks, and the screws had dropped their guard. I had got through the window with the wire-cutters when suddenly the civilian instructor decided to walk into the store for a chat. As soon as he saw me, he hit the alarm bell. I was taken straight down the block and brought in front of the Governor the next day.

I had to come before a VC, and I was given fifty-six days' loss of privileges, loss of pay, solo confinement and non-associated labour. What was unusual was that they also decided I would lose 180 days' remission at the end of my sentence. I was only the second lifer ever to lose remission. But it didn't put me off the idea of getting my freedom early. And the next occasion was to prove quite a spectacular one.

CHAPTER FIFTEEN

A RIOTOUS ASSEMBLY

On the last Sunday in November 1972 I was looking forward to the latest mass escape, and hoping it would be third time lucky for me. Certain cons had decided on a plan whereby we would tie up whatever screws were in our way, get into the exercise yard and make our escape through the fence.

The great day came, but my wing and one other couldn't join in. Gartree prison was shaped like an H, and the passage connecting our wings to the other two was blocked by iron gates which had been locked. You could never tell when the gates would be locked or unlocked, there was no set pattern, and we had been taking pot luck that they'd be open. I was very disappointed I couldn't be involved in it, and because we were cut off from the other two wings we didn't know what was happening.

I found out when I wandered up to the wing dining room to collect my teatime meal. I was with a man called Patsy Sutton from Notting Hill Gate. Patsy glanced towards the window and suddenly yelled, 'Look!' The fence around the yard was ringed with cons carrying weapons, about twenty of them. Some of them had big wire-cutters, and they were getting through the fences.

I later found out that the men had come out of their cells and into the passageway leading to the dining rooms, ostensibly to collect their meals. Instead they found the screw who had access to the yard, took him hostage, took his keys and let themselves out, clamping security gates up behind them as they went so nobody could get in or out. The door which took them out to the yard was the only one by which cons could enter and leave the prison.

Alarms were going off everywhere. Everybody had made it to the fence, and a couple of cons got through but were later recaptured. The grounds were like a battlefield, in complete chaos. Bricks were being thrown, and the dog-handlers came out. One dog ran straight over and jumped on the Governor. We saw a screw who specialised in PT hitting a con called Georgie Bell with a claw hammer. He immediately went down. We saw another screw hit an Irish kid called Danny with a brick. Patsy said, 'I'm not having that!' And the next thing we know, we've got a full-scale riot on our hands inside the prison. Patsy started the riot by throwing tables up into the air, and I stormed over to the serving hatch and upped all the trays of food. Another thirty or so men had already come into the dining room to get their meals, and by now they were all glued to what was going on in the yard. But none of the other cons could follow us in, because as soon as the alarm went off the gate to the wing was automatically locked.

In the dining room they had great big boilers and metal spoons which were like shovels, about four feet long. Patsy and I picked up one of those spoons and started to smash up the glass office where the screws sat. Inside were a PO and an SO, who couldn't believe what was happening.

Patsy and I were the first to go back down the stairs. We broke the canteen door down and went in. We nicked all the tobacco, we took everything out . . . thousands of pounds' worth of stock. I walked back towards the wing with a bag full of tobacco, tins of fruit, sweets, sugar and coffee. The gate into the wing was still locked, of course, and I started throwing the goodies through the gate to the men on the other side. The trouble had still not gone off in the wing at that point, and none of them picked anything up – probably because an Assistant Governor, a PO and a couple of screws were watching me.

In dispersal prisons the ranks worked like this: below the Governor, in descending order, were the Deputy Governor, four Assistant Governors, eight Principal Officers and twelve Senior Officers. An Assistant Governor, a PO and an SO would be running each wing. There were also Chief Officers One, Two and Three who were in charge of the screws.

The Assistant Governor at the gate said to me, 'I'm giving you a direct order to return to your cell', which was impossible, because I couldn't go through a locked gate to get to it. On the other side of the gate, Patsy Murphy suddenly said to the other cons, 'What's the matter with you lot?' and started picking things up. Then the others started. The Assistant Governor suddenly realised the ugliness of the situation.

The cons began battering this solid steel gate off its hinges. It came open, and with that they started to turn on the Assistant Governor, the PO and the screws, who made a run for the gate leading into the yard, in fear of their lives. They were lucky; they made it. Another minute and they would have been hostages.

All of a sudden the wing was going up in the air, and we started breaking into the offices. We got into the welfare office and took out a bundle of papers and reports.

There were two punishment, units, one downstairs and one above our wing. The top unit was sealed off from the rest. It contained grasses and sex offenders who were under Rule 43 protection. They were kept behind thick, unbreakable glass. We started to batter that door. Some of the men were going to hang the nonces off the landing of the top floor. But because of the physical security of the unit, the glass and concrete and special precautions, we couldn't get into it. So we decided to set fire to it and burn them out, but the unit was indestructible. The authorities became very worried about these cons. We couldn't get to them ourselves, but we made sure nobody else did, and we held them hostage there for two days, in turns.

The authorities had about a thousand screws on duty within an hour of the riot breaking out. They completely ringed the prison. We were being hosed with jets of water, and the helicopters were up.

We went down the first landing and knocked a big hole in the end cell. This gave us access to the roof and we could then cross over from B-wing, where we were, to D-wing and back. The inmates in A- and C-wings had already started to tear the place up. Our whole idea was to wreck the prison, and we completely demolished it. We set fire to the gym, we ripped the wings apart, we smashed up the kitchens and the canteens, we knocked out every pane of glass in the place, and we tore all the doors off to use as barricades.

In the meantime we'd been having a look at the papers we'd taken out of the welfare office, and we found out that Billy O'Gorman, the con who was going to come with me on the escape from the workshop, had been giving information about all of us to the authorities. He'd been knocking about with the major criminals in the nick, and all the time his reports and opinions were going down in official documents.

Billy, who was a ringer for the tennis player Billie Jean King, was inside for a robbery and a wrap-up (tying people up), plus he'd been convicted in connection with the murder of a woman greyhound owner called the Merry Widow. He'd been having an affair with her. While he was in prison, he was also questioned about the proceeds from a jewellery robbery.

Nobody suspected he was a grass. Yet there he was giving his views on who should be paroled and who shouldn't, and the authorities were listening. What right did they have to ask another criminal for his thoughts about the rest of us?

On my record, I was described by O'Gorman as an anarchist and a troublemaker. In the file of another con, Terry Middlemas, he stated, 'In my view, if Middlemas was paroled he would commit major crime again.' I gave the file to Terry and said, 'I think you'd better read that.'

Billy O'Gorman had obviously done a lot of harm. One con called Charlie Manley was certain, up to the time of the riot, that he was about to be granted parole. On his record, O'Gorman said, 'This man should never be paroled at any time.' We showed it to Charlie, and he sat in his cell and cried his eyes out. We didn't take his cell door off, we were that sorry for him.

Of course the men were going to hurt O'Gorman. Cons were coming up, spitting on him and punching him. When the riot was over, and we were all in punishment, he was the only man to be seen sweeping up the landings. He was cleaning up the glass. He was later transferred to Wakefield prison, where he went on protection and hanged himself. In a way I suppose we were all to blame, but he did what he did, he knew the consequences if he was found out, he *was* found out, and he couldn't live with the guilt and the fear.

The rioting continued through the night of the Sunday it began and into the next day. The place was in uproar. We were all masked up, and nobody could get into the wings past the barricades.

About seven o'clock on the Monday evening we heard a voice coming through a megaphone outside the wing. Joe Witty, the Deputy Governor, was out there, surrounded by forty screws with crash helmets and shields. He was shouting out my name, asking me to come to the window.

He said, 'We're asking you, Lambrianou, to hand back the wing and get the men to give up their fight.' I couldn't do that. Snooker balls went flying out the window, and we began to light more fires.

We decided to give in early on the Tuesday morning, but there was a lot more trouble ahead. The nick was in ruins; there was nothing left. There were no windows, and few doors had been left standing, so we were held in groups of four or five in what cells were available. We'd insisted on this for our own protection. Every prison in the country had sent screws in there, and we didn't know what was going on.

The authorities had to know at all costs where the A-men were, so they were quick to get the doors back on our cells. When we went back on to the landing, Roy The Weasel James said to me, 'I'm sorry to have to tell you this, but your budgie's dead.' Roy had not been part of the riot, and we had left his door intact because he was coming up to his parole. We did the same for other lifers who were looking at an imminent release. The screws had murdered my budgie with a shoelace. The story was the same in all the other cells. They'd pissed on the floors. Photographs were torn up, the radios were wrecked, all our personal belongings were ripped to bits.

Obviously, after a riot like that, feelings were running very high. The screws were out to get their pound of flesh. They started giving us breakfast at teatime and dinner about eleven o'clock at night. The food was freezing cold and it looked as though it had been tampered with. They were making us slop out – empty the buckets which were for use as toilets in our cells – one at a time.

One morning I'd had enough. I said, 'If I don't get any food today, or clean clobber, I'm going to start performing again.' An hour later I was still waiting to slop out, so I flung my bucket down the landing. There were about forty screws along the landing who did nothing – just stood there with their big overcoats on. The prison was freezing cold because the wind was howling through the open spaces where there used to be windows.

I issued another threat. I said, 'If I don't get a hot meal by nine o'clock tonight and if I don't get my exercise today, I'm going to start making my own exercise ground through the cells.' One thing I never did in prison was make an idle threat. So when no food, no clean clothes and no exercise were forthcoming by nine o'clock that night, I took action.

I went back into my cell. When you're an A-man your bed is sealed to the floor, but I wrenched it off and wedged it against the door with the other cell furniture to form a barricade. I used the end of the bed frame to start digging through to the next cell.

I knocked out the first three bricks with the end of the frame, and then carried on making the hole bigger. I could see this kid, Jimmy, looking at me as I put my head through into his cell. The cells on the landing were alternately Cat. A and Cat. B., and Jimmy was a young lifer on Cat. B. There I was talking to him, and he was under the bed because he knew what was going to happen. He was going, 'Please, Tony; they're going to kill us.' By now the screws were desperately trying to get into my cell to stop whatever was going on in there. They couldn't get past the barricade until they got hold of this tool which was like a portable jack. It had a chisel end which they used as a lever to force the door open. The door collapsed, and suddenly I was confronted by fifteen screws who were about to do me. I broke out of the cell and made a run for the block, where some of my mates were. I was on a closed landing, so I could only go one way. Somehow I had to try and get along there and down the stairs, past groups of screws who were waiting for me all along the way. I had to run the gauntlet. In the ensuing battle I connected with some of them and missed others. All the time they were grabbing and kicking at me, and half of them were in each other's way, getting their legs and arms tangled up.

Finally they got me up against a wall and tried to tear the clothes off me. It was coming up to midnight and everybody was locked up, so I had no help. I ended up with half a vest on, and there was nothing I could do to defend myself. You're at a disadvantage when you've got no clothes on.

They kicked me into the strongbox, which is a special punishment cell. You get put in there when even the punishment block cannot control you. It had a steel shell and a very thick, indestructible glass panel, about three feet by three feet and twelve inches thick, set in concrete in the roof. There were ladders going spirally around the outside, so that you could be observed through any of the half-dozen peepholes at any time. The doors opened outwards, and as you went in, you came down two steps to the cell itself. It was like a cell within a cell. The bed was a solid lump of wood, and you got a leather blanket.

The screws had all gone in and pissed on the floor. It was a sloping floor, and any liquid drained itself off, but the stench in there was out of this world.

I remember waking up the next morning and hearing a bloke next door to me, on the other side of a big, thick grille. He was saying, 'I think they've done my legs.' I never found out who it was. The only other sound I heard for the next two days was echoes.

During this time I didn't even have a glass of water. I thought about Frankie Fraser. He must have done nearly as much time in strongboxes as the rest of us put together. I remembered an occasion when he was going down for punishment and he said to the screws, 'If you're going to punish me, punish me properly.' He wasn't going to do it in a normal punishment cell; he had to be in a strongbox. Frank said, 'Gandhi suffered, and so did God.' He didn't even want a sandwich or a radio – he wanted what he was entitled to, and that was it. He was a man of honour, Frank, and he had an acute sense of right and wrong. I was once in the punishment block at Gartree when he was brought down following a disturbance. He went into his cell, and he had to do his business in a pot. I heard the screw going, 'Frank, at least you could have put the lid on it.'

Frank said, 'One of the perks of the job, guv, one of the perks of the job.' His attitude was, 'Treat me like a human being and I'll act like a human being.'

I couldn't have felt less like a human being in that strongbox. On the third morning I was beginning to wonder if I would ever see a screw, or anybody else, again.

Finally they came in, six of them. One had a plastic spoon, one had a plastic knife, one had a plastic fork and one had a dinner on a plastic plate. The plate was scratched and all diseased-looking. God knows what they'd done to the food. Probably they'd gobbed on it; they might have drugged it. I slapped it down on the floor.

The following morning, a doctor came to see me. He said, 'A lot of good men died in China. Remember that.' Then he shut the door, and that was the last I saw of him. I still haven't fathomed what he meant by that.

The same night I was given my charge sheets. I was accused of mutiny, inciting others to mutiny, aiding and abetting escape, attempting to escape from legal custody, gross personal violence to a prison officer (two charges), assaulting a prison Governor, breaking and entering the canteen, stealing property from the canteen, damaging prison property and having an offensive weapon, which was a pole approximately four feet long.

I was in the strongbox for five days before being transferred to a normal punishment cell for two weeks on a nominal charge of assaulting a prison officer. The VC then sentenced me to fifteen months for the string of charges above. I was to serve this time in the Wormwood Scrubs control unit. This was a newly introduced form of imprisonment for cons who were impossible to control within the system. There were only two control units in the country. The other was in Wakefield.

On 23 December 1972, I was taken to the Scrubs with Johnny Crosby. He'd been given six months for attempting to escape, gross personal violence to a prison officer, assault and arson for burning down the gym. All the way there, Johnny kept saying, 'You don't half reek.' I was stinking to high heaven. I hadn't been allowed a wash for nearly three weeks, my hair was matted and I had a beard starting.

We were taken into reception at Wormwood Scrubs and immediately put into a secure room, a cell with heavy-duty glass, away from all the other inmates. Next, we were brought into the control unit through a little gate which said, 'No unauthorised movement within this wing.' I was on one side of the unit and Crosby was on the other. There was no one else there. I'd been looking forward to a shower, but all they would let me have was a jug of water.

Twenty minutes later, eight screws came back and said, 'Turnover.' That meant strip.

I said, 'You wanna play it like this, you'll see.'

The following morning, Christmas Eve, I had a visit in the cell from Honey, the Governor, a Deputy Governor called Howard Jones, the PO in charge of the wing, two SOs and about ten screws.

One of the screws said, 'The Governor for Lambrianou.'

I went, 'Fuck off.'

He said, 'I've heard about you, Lambrianou. Don't you think you're coming down here wrecking my prison. Anything you want to say, say it now.'

I said, 'I'm not gonna wash; I'm not gonna shave, and I'm going to slop out on your clean floor. If you're going to treat me like an animal, I'll act like an animal. I'm going to abuse you.' Crosby, too, was calling him everything.

On Christmas morning, Crosby and I went down to get our breakfast. It was a normal breakfast, but with a difference: on each of our trays there was tobacco, papers and matches.

They must have thought, 'It's Christmas, we'll give them a quarter of tobacco each,' because smoking in the control unit was forbidden.

I didn't believe that you should be a Christian one day of the year and not the other 364, and I declined the tobacco. So did Crosby, regretfully. He was dying for a fag.

They put us together in one exercise cage for the morning, as a Christmas privilege. Honey and the PO came to the end of the cage, and Honey called me over. He had two envelopes.

He said, 'I've thought about what you said. I don't agree with this punishment, but I have to enforce it because it's in my prison. Here's an ounce of tobacco each for you. Will you have the Christmas?' By this, he was asking us to take it in the spirit of seasonal goodwill. We finally accepted it, realising that we had won a moral victory, if nothing else.

The screws felt sorry for us. We didn't want their sympathy, but we'd often find a half ounce of tobacco left for us, or the odd bar of chocolate which was also forbidden. On Cup Final day, the PO brought in his portable television and put it in such a position we could see it through our flaps.

But for all of these occasional concessions, it was the toughest regime imaginable. You were locked in your cell twenty-three hours a day, and the bed, a hard mattress with a frame, was taken away between seven in the morning and seven at night. You didn't do labour or meet any other cons. You had a washbasin and a jug. You could have a couple of books from the little library, but nearly all of them were missing pages. That's all you had.

It was a very lonely life. Even the screws were encouraged not to talk to us. Apart from screws, the only people we saw were those who had to check on us every day – a doctor and any one of the governors.

Over the window was a plastic dome covered with a grille, which was to prevent the cons above from passing anything down. You could hardly see any daylight. If the windows were open, you could just about hear the outside world. I used to listen to the faint sound of the crowd at Queen's Park Rangers football ground on a Saturday. I could hear kids outside laughing, and I'd say, 'People are *enjoying* themselves out there.' I learned to live by my ears. I used to know when it got late because I could hear that the tubes had stopped running. You weren't allowed a watch in there.

There were two cages at the back of the unit. I walked in one, Johnny Crosby walked in the other, and that was the only exercise we got. I couldn't see Johnny, but I could shout over the wall at him.

When we slopped out we were accompanied by six screws, and a PO was always present. We were allowed to the recess room four times a day to do our slops and get our water for bathing, drinking and washing utensils, the plastic knife, fork, spoon and plate. The recess room had a tap, a slopping out bowl, a urinal and a toilet with a little half door so that your legs and head could be seen. There was a shower which you could use once a week.

You lost all privileges except a regulation visit once a month behind glass and one letter a week. I used to sit there with a sheet of paper and an envelope. What could I write? There wasn't anything to say.

I'd lost all contact with the outside world. I'd forgotten what it was like to be a civilised person. I'd learnt to sleep twenty hours a day. When they took the bed out, I'd lie on the bare floor; my pillow was the towel I washed with, which was changed once a week.

I don't know how I survived this life. I went down to ten stone in weight – from my usual thirteen and a half, and I suffered badly with constipation. The only time I came out of that wing and was able to stretch my legs was when they took me to the prison hospital for an enema.

As time dragged on I acquired two new neighbours, unusual men indeed. On my left was a bloke called Ted, otherwise known as the Beast of Jersey. Without any doubt he was mental. He used to run about Jersey in a leather mask, kicking women and raping them. When the coppers got into his house, it was like a black museum with tongs and torture equipment. He was in the control unit for his own protection.

Graham Young, on the other hand, was in the unit for the protection of other prisoners. He had poisoned six of his workmates in a photo lab, killing two of them. He had the brain of a chemist. And believe it or not, this man, the most notorious mass poisoner this country has ever known, was given a little job in the unit – making the screws' tea!

Because they were on protection, Young and the Beast of Jersey were allowed to get out of their cells a bit. I wasn't, because I was there for punishment.

The welfare officer, Mrs Pele, protested vigorously to the Home Office about the regime. She said, 'This mustn't be allowed to happen.' She came to see us every day for two months, and she cancelled her holiday to Greece because she didn't want to leave me and Crosby locked up in that unit.

Honey didn't like it, either. He turned out to be not a bad man, and he helped me quite a bit. So did the Roman Catholic chaplain, who offered to do what he could for us. However, there was nothing anybody could do at the time. Both control units were eventually closed down, but not before I'd finished my fifteen months.

When I came out, I was transferred to a 'normal' Cat. A routine in the Scrubs' D-wing. I met some interesting characters there like David Bingham, the Portland Spy. He was a strange man, who always referred to the KGB as 'the guv'nors'. He was a naval lieutenant who had gone over to the Russians, and was sentenced in the early seventies to twenty-one years. Then there was Callan, the notorious Greek Cypriot mercenary. At that time he was serving seven years. He told me about his ambitions, and invited me to join him in Angola when I was released. I put him down as a nut, but he actually did go out there and do what he said he would. He got an army, and he reputedly massacred hundreds of people. He's now buried next to my father in New Southgate Cemetery in north London.

One con who went on from the Scrubs to more admirable things was Leslie Grantham. He came to fame as an actor playing Dirty Den in *EastEnders*. When I met him, he was serving life for a murder he had committed in Germany during his army period. He was a quiet fella who was friendly with the pack, but at the same time kept himself to himself. He liked his game of cards like the rest of us, he was never involved in any trouble and he gave the impression that he wanted to finish his sentence the best way he could and get out as early as possible.

He joined the drama group, which got him out of his cell, and I saw him acting in a play in prison. Most inmates are suspicious by nature – 'He's only doing it to get parole' – and I think Leslie Grantham was viewed that way a bit, but he was the one with a difference. He took it more seriously than people thought, and he went on to make a success of it. I send him my best wishes.

While I'd been causing trouble, trying to escape and instigating riots in Gartree, Chris had been having an equally eventful time in Albany prison on the Isle of Wight. The first thing I heard about was a series of violent protests over food and conditions; Chris was heavily involved. In addition to this, he was provoked into various fights over certain cons' behaviour towards Charlie Kray.

Charlie didn't want to take any part in the troubles. He knew he shouldn't have been in prison in the first place, but since he was there he just wanted to finish his sentence peacefully and get out. However, a lot of inmates thought that Charlie wasn't doing what he should have been – joining in – and they showed a lot of disrespect, shouting out obscenities while he pushed his barrow about in the yard, picking up the bins and milk churns from around the grounds, which was his job. Charlie took no notice of the heckling; he wanted to be seen as whiter than white. But Chris Lambrianou was seen as blacker than black, and if anybody said the wrong thing about Charlie he would wallop them.

All sorts of conflicts were breaking out within the prison in addition to the demonstrations, and finally the whole thing erupted into riots. The papers started to get hold of it, and they took their coverage to extremes. There were reports that Mafia-style rackets involving gambling and villainy were being operated at Albany, and that Chris and I were behind them. I had never been to Albany prison, so I decided to sue the five newspapers who named me. I asked to see a solicitor, but after taking advice I agreed to accept a printed apology from three of them. The other two refused because of my criminal record. Chris's part in the Albany disturbances came to an end with the beating up he was given by the screws and his transference, injured, to Parkhurst prison, the incident which gave rise to his feud with Don Barrett.

It was during this early seventies' period that Chris and I were at our most explosive, although as the years went by we were still refusing to sit down and serve our sentences quietly. You couldn't have expected men of our age simply to lean back, twiddling our thumbs. But as the end of the decade approached, and I neared the ten-year mark in prison, I dared, for the first time, to look at my future. And what I saw was this: it was time to start helping, not hindering, my chances.

CHAPTER SIXTEEN

SAD STEPS
TO FREEDOM

One day in 1979, Chris and I were sitting having a cup of tea in Maidstone prison with another con called Tony Dunford. Tony had quite a history. He had killed someone with a hammer in Wakefield prison while he was serving time for another murder, and he was given the death sentence. Three days before he was due to drop, he was reprieved. He was also the man who did the negotiating after McVicar's escape from Durham prison, when a lot of other cons, including Joe Martin and the Richardsons, barricaded themselves in the offices.

Chris, Tony and I happened to be talking about lifers in general, when Tony told us something we had never known in all our years in prison, something which the authorities never made it their business to tell long-term prisoners. He said that a lifer could ask for an involvement in the procedure leading up to his release, and could have face-to-face meetings with representatives of the Home Office.

I hadn't known that these people were accessible, and I hadn't realised that a lifer could play any significant part in his own future – help to get things moving towards parole. I'd been under the impression that everything was automatically decided and done for you.

I'd already come a certain distance through the system. By the time I'd finished my second stretch at Gartree in 1977 and transferred to Maidstone, I'd been taken off the E-list and relieved of the yellow patch on my clothes. I'd also been moved on to Category B. This gave me more freedom of movement within the prison system. There was no signing-in, no identity book, no red light in the cell.

Chris had been at Maidstone for about a month by the time I got there. We'd lost Ronnie Bender and Ian Barrie to other nicks, but Charlie Richardson followed us on. He set up a prison magazine with my brother, and they sent out copies to the House of Commons and the House of Lords as well as people like Lord Longford, and Lady Sainsbury of the famous supermarket family. Lord Longford had a history of campaigning for prisoners' release, although as a champion for Myra Hindley he came to lose a lot of public support. Lady Sainsbury was another, less controversial, campaigner. Chris became very friendly with Lady Sainsbury at the time, and still is to this day.

My brother now began to mellow in certain ways, and entered into a religious phase. At first I frowned on it and had rows about it with him. It was changing him. I'd never seen any signs of religious inclinations in him in the past. Now other cons were coming up and saying, 'Is Chris all right? He's acting strange.'

Looking back, I think it was the only escape Chris had from his sentence. It gave him some peace of mind. But to his credit he genuinely took it up as a belief and it's still with him. I've never personally been one to go to church, although I have my own beliefs. I'm not a good Catholic – far from it – but I'm not a bad one. The religious influence of our mother in childhood was never very far away.

But for all my rows with Chris in Maidstone, he was helping me in other ways. He thought of the future, which not a lot of people do in prison, and he encouraged me to look for people who would support my release, write letters and follow up the things we'd been told by Tony Dunford.

One day I was at my job with the electricians in the works department when a fellow lifer called Johnny said to me, 'Major James is coming here today. He's the one who'll tell you what life holds for you in the future.' Major James was in charge of P3, the lifers' division of the Home Office. And I was now aware that prisoners were entitled to see him.

I ran to see Timmsy, the Governor, and I asked, 'Can I put down to see Major James?' I ended up third on the list.

I was filthy dirty from the work I'd been doing on the building of a new wing when I walked into the Governor's office for the meeting. Major James was a little bloke, about five feet eight, a typical civil servant. Staring out of the window away from me, he said, 'What do you want?'

I replied, 'What do you mean, what do I want? At least have the courtesy to turn round.'

He said, 'You and your brother have caused a lot of trouble, and if you've come down here looking for laurels you'll be disappointed.'

'I know I'm going to do the recommendation,' I told him.

He said, 'I can tell you that you are, but it's up to you whether or not you do over it.' He added, 'I'm not prepared to do anything for your brother at the moment, but I'll decategorize you. I'll send you up north to Acklington prison, which is four or five miles off Berwick-upon-Tweed, and I want you to give me a year's good behaviour. Then we can start talking about release. But don't think you can beat the recommendation.'

After Maidstone, I did not see Chris in captivity again.

I moved to Acklington, a semi-open prison in Northumberland, later that year as a Cat. C inmate. I was no longer considered an escape risk, and I had a lot of freedom of movement within the grounds. There was only one wire fence, no walls, no dog patrols and limited authority around us. The prison itself was an old RAF base where King Hussein of Jordan had trained to be a pilot.

To begin with, the screws didn't want me there. It was an easy-going prison, and they thought I'd be bringing trouble. But over a period of time they accepted me. I kept a lot of peace amongst the men, and they'd come to me for little bits of advice. I was the only Londoner in the place. The other cons were mostly Geordies and Yorkshiremen who kept to their divisions and didn't much like each other.

I was put to work in the gardens. We had a civilian geezer called Georgie in charge there, and I could never understand a word he said. In Northumberland they're a cross between a Geordie and a Scotsman, and I had to use one of the screws as an interpreter every time this Georgie spoke to me. He lived a life of poverty, which many people did up there in the north-east. I used to see kids in the visiting room with no shoes on, and other things there that I thought I'd seen the last of. It shook me that this could be happening in 1980.

I sat GCE exams in English and maths and passed them both. I became involved in life again, which undoubtedly helped towards my release. After the course I was given work in the prison canteen, which was a highly trusted job, selling tobacco, sweets and goods to the cons.

So, all in all, I was doing well at Acklington. But then my father fell ill. He was eighty, and he was going in and out of hospital, but he still had his independence and, no matter where we were, he had to see us. If he gave me a visit, Chris would have to have one too. That's the way he was, same as Violet Kray. He used to come and sit in the visiting room, talking in Greek as usual. Even though I didn't speak a word of it I could understand everything he was saying, as I had since I was a boy. One day my brother Jimmy came to see me and he said, 'The visiting is getting a bit much for him.' All the brothers wanted to look after the old man. Leon came on a visit and told me he was moving him into his family home at Herne Bay in Kent. Our father did actually go to Herne Bay, but he had to come back home. He missed his house in the East End.

I wrote to a man called David Atkinson at the Home Office, telling him my problems with the old man. He had taken over from Major James as the head of P3, the lifers' division.

Eventually I received a very nice letter which said, 'After considering your case we have decided to move you to Featherstone, just outside Wolverhampton, on the grounds of your father's ill health.' It was a lot nearer.

Featherstone was one of the most modern prisons in Europe. Each cell had its own toilet, and the facilities were out of this world, but because I was so used to the rough conditions I'd been in for years I found it hard at first to adapt. Also, I was in with short-termers, people who were constantly talking about the outside world. I'd always been around people who never even spoke about getting out. Ian Barrie was transferred there later, and Les Long, another old friend, turned up too. The three of us more or less kept ourselves to ourselves.

I looked for the easy option regarding work, and was given a job as a cleaner which keeps you out of the way of the other cons. I grew very bored with it, though, and went on to hotplate duty as a red-band (a prisoner wearing a red band to show that he was entitled to walk about without an escort), serving the food and keeping the dining rooms clean and tidy. To qualify for this job, you had to impress the authorities with your cleanliness, attitude and appearance. They also looked for leadership – the ability to influence without causing problems.

I made a good job of that, but I wanted to work in the open air. Eventually I was given a job with the works department, helping to build this little road around the prison grounds. I was working with a Hell's Angel called John McDonna, who was serving life for killing someone in his chapter in Brighton. He had very long hair, a beard and a moustache, and he never used to wear anything more than a tee-shirt and trousers, even in the freezing cold. I got on well with him. When we finished the road, one of its bends was named Lambrianou Way and the other one McDonna's Corner.

I stayed on in the gardens as a dumper driver. One Sunday afternoon, Jim the gardener asked if I wanted to do some overtime. It was a lovely day in April 1982, and our job was to do the football pitch – grassing it, seeding it and turfing it. All of a sudden, the dumper turned over. I thought it was going to fall on top of me, but I managed to dive out of the way and broke my wrist in three places. The medical screw took one look at me and said I had to go to a public hospital. It was the first time I'd been out in the real world for fourteen years.

I don't think I took in what was happening. I'd always been in a prison van with an armed guard when I was being moved about. Now, there I was in the back of a taxi with an escort of just a PO and one screw. In the hospital there were people running about, nurses flying everywhere. I came to realise that there were still children in this world.

I came out with a plaster on my wrist, and as we drove back to the prison I saw a bit of Wolverhampton. Back at the nick, I was telling Ian and Barrie all about my couple of hours out of prison, about what it felt like to walk in somewhere a free man, without handcuffs. In the end, they were telling me to shut up about it.

I think that was the first sign that my release was not too far away: they trusted me to go out. Nobody but the Home Office had the authority to let a lifer out of the gates, and it was greatly encouraging that some unknown person there had said yes to me.

My wrist began to get better, and five or six weeks later I was on light labour, just sweeping down landings and mopping out rooms. One Sunday afternoon after four o'clock, I was sitting watching a game of football on television when a PO came in and said to me, 'Can I see you in the office?'

He said, 'You've just had a phone call. Your father is very ill, and if you'd like to get yourself ready, we'll take you to see him tonight.'

I knew he had a hernia; I didn't know he had cancer until that day. Within an hour I was down in reception; and they lent me a jacket. We left Featherstone at 5.30 and travelled to St Leonard's Hospital in Hoxton in a taxi – me, a PO and a screw called Ted.

Suddenly, after all those years, I found myself back in the East End, standing outside the hospital. Chris hadn't been allowed out because the authorities felt he would play up. I went inside, and saw my Jimmy, Leon and his wife June, my son and daughter and a couple of neighbours. I was allowed two hours with the old man. I had a chat to him, and he knew I was there, but I think he was too ill to really comprehend it. He was on morphine. One thing you never forget is that smell.

For the second time I was in freedom with no handcuffs on, and I was allowed to have a chat with my brothers before leaving for Featherstone at 9.30 in the evening. But by the time I left, I knew it wasn't going to be long with my Dad.

The following week, on 28 June, he fell so dangerously ill that he wasn't expected to see the night through. They decided to take me to see him again that day. This time, they knew it was bad. They arranged to get Chris down there in the afternoon and me in the evening. The hospital was told, 'Any further problems, get in touch with the prison.'

Everything was happening so fast. I could see my freedom on the horizon because I was being tested, admittedly in a compassionate way, by the authorities through these hospital visits. But I was gutted about my father.

When I got to the hospital the whole family was there – my brothers, their wives and kids. They had a room at their disposal. I was told that what I was going to see was not a pretty sight. I walked into the wards, and I could see that my father had lost a lot of weight. He must have weighed no more than four and a half stone. I was told he'd been asking for me: 'I wanna see Tonys' – a Greek way of saying Tony.

I grabbed hold of him, and I saw that his eyes had gone. I wanted to say, 'Listen, give him an injection, end it.'

We all went into the side room, and the screws stayed away. They were genuinely trying to be considerate. I walked out of the hospital with Jimmy, and I stood in Kingsland Road on my own. I didn't know what to do. I could have walked away, but I went upstairs, back to the ward.

My Dad said, 'Lillie,' his pet name for my mother, and then he died.

We went back into the side room. Nobody had anything to say. I went back and kissed my Dad, and we left.

I felt numb, and for the next couple of days I spent a lot of time in the prison chapel, sitting on my own. I was totally lost. It's bad enough when one parent dies, but when two have gone, you're on your own. And you feel it even more when you're in prison. I kept asking, 'Why him? Why them? Why me?'

I blamed myself: 'If I hadn't had this sentence, I would've spent more time with him.' I felt that we let him down, because we should have been there towards the end of his life. From the day we went into prison, the old man used to say, 'I'm not going to die until my sons are out.' In our hearts we knew that he might not survive our sentence, but at least he did see us again in freedom, albeit a very limited freedom.

The biggest regret of my life is that I wasn't a free man when my parents died. Not a day goes by that I don't think of my mother and father. Had they been alive today, we could have given them back a little bit of what they gave us. My mother did her best for us; she couldn't have done any more. But she never lived to see any of the boys making something of their lives.

At least my father lived to see his other sons making some success of themselves while Chris and I were away. They put him on a pension of their own. Every week he used to go and collect it, and if one of them didn't have the money for him, he'd go and complain to the other one! He was totally honest, a good man; and he just loved his sons – he loved the boys around him. We're forever on about him today. We never talk about our mother – somehow it still hurts too much – but we're always saying things like, 'If the old man was here. . . .' His death came as a devastating blow to all of us, and Chris saw it as the end of the family. He was in a tragic state for a long time after that.

I always worried throughout my sentence that if my father died the authorities would refuse me permission to attend the funeral, as they had after my mother's death. I could never have handled that again. But in the event they were very understanding. They promised that the police and screws would keep a low profile so long as the funeral was kept within the family and there were no press involved. The same applied to Chris.

It took place at the Greek Orthodox church in Camden Town. But first the family got together at my parents' home in Belford House, Queensbridge Road. When my car pulled up at the door, the first people I noticed were Leon and Chris. I was pleased to see Chris standing there: I hadn't set eyes on him in three years. All the relatives had arrived, and everyone was putting wreaths outside the door. We went into the house, and I didn't want to believe the old man was dead.

It was the first time we'd all stood together in our old home in eighteen years. Everything was in the same place – the table in the middle of the living room with the chairs round it – but nothing looked the same as I remembered it. It seemed a lot smaller.

We five brothers went and sat in our parents' bedroom. Jimmy went out and got a bottle of vodka, and we toasted the old man. I knew, looking round the room, that it was the last time the five of us would be together in that house. It turned out to be the last time the five of us would be together at all. I'd like to think we could rectify that in the future. We had our picture taken that day; the only one there is of us together. My uncle John broke down and cried to see the five boys reunited.

There were about twenty cars in the funeral, and the prison authorities did their best for us. They allowed us our dignity and a limited freedom, and no great presence was seen around us. (This is in direct contrast to what happened when the twins attended Violet's funeral. What became of that was a shambles and a circus, with police, screws, newspaper reporters, television cameras and crowds of people milling around them.)

We went to the church in Camden Town. Lady Sainsbury was there with other members of her family, and we saw a lot of people going back many years, all assorted friends from our past. The service was all done in Greek, as the old man would have wanted it, and everyone went up and kissed his coffin. The proudest moment of my life was when the five brothers, with our eldest nephew Paul, carried our father to his grave.

Back at Featherstone I was broken up for a long time, but gradually life began to pick up. I was given what is called an F75, which was the first step towards my parole: it's an internal assessment of your circumstances in prison and your suitability to be released. Every lifer, after the first couple of years of his sentence, is given an annual F75. In dispersal prisons it is a purely routine matter, because none of the cons are likely to qualify for parole. Once, in Gartree, the landing officer who was asking me questions for my F75 had the audacity to write my answers down on the back of a cigarette packet. He said, 'Where are you going to live when you get released?' A bleeding joke. I was in Category A at the time!

In Featherstone, a Cat. C prison, they obviously took the F75 more seriously. They considered the inmate's situation very thoroughly, and I was asked to appear in front of a board to put my case for parole. I had to stand up and say, 'I'm fit to be released', and give them some very solid evidence. By this time I had acquired some support. Ian Mikardo, my MP, was very good to me, and my probation officer, Mrs Jean Heath, was a tower of strength and encouragement.

I duly appeared before the board, which comprised the Governor, a psychiatrist, a doctor, an education officer, a welfare officer, my probation officer, the works instructor and a PO. I sat in the middle while they fired questions at me, and I talked about Jack The Hat. By this time Reggie had admitted the murder, so I no longer had to protect him – there was no point in me continuing to say I had nothing to do with it.

I said, 'Yes, I felt sorry for McVitie. Yes, it was a terrible thing to happen. Yes, if I could turn the clock back I would. Of course I felt about his family, and of course I regretted that a man's life had been taken. I didn't actually commit the crime, but I was there when something happened and, yes, I do feel responsible.' I also told them, 'The sentence I'm doing, whether it carries on for a short time or a long time, will never alter what I feel inside about what happened that night. I've lived with it, and I'll go on living with it for the rest of my life, whether I'm in prison or not.'

They asked about my attitude to release, my views on the outside world, how I would take to someone shoving me in a bus queue. Would I throw violence or would I turn the other cheek?

My answer was: 'I think I would value freedom enough to want to keep it, not throw it away by having an argument with someone getting on a bus.'

I was asked about my plans. Did I have a home to go to? Would I stay in the area I went out to?

I said, 'I can't plan the future until I get a date of release. I'll take the steps one at a time.'

And that was more or less it.

It was now up to the board to decide whether or not they would recommend me to the Local Review Committee, which consisted of the same people plus a magistrate, a judge, a high-ranking police officer and a Home Office official. The Review Committee would consider my case to see if it was worthy of recommendation to the Joint Committee. And if the Joint Committee ruled in my favour the whole thing had to be assessed again by the Parole Board, which would make the final recommendation to the Home Secretary.

It would take the best part of a year for my case to go through all these channels, and the more I thought about it, the more worrying it became. It was like a tree, and to reach the top, you had to climb up every branch without falling. Would I make it?

I tried to put myself in the Home Secretary's shoes: 'If I was the Home Secretary and I had Tony Lambrianou, a member of the Kray firm, would I want the responsibility of signing that bit of paper?' And I started to have my doubts.

For the next ten months I was living on my nerves. I've seen men driven potty by this. One Thursday lunchtime, I walked into the PO's office to get an application form for batteries. There were two POs in there with the welfare officer and about five screws. No one said a word. I looked up and they were all smiling at me. I heard the welfare officer say, 'Shall we tell him?', and I instantly knew they had my answer.

I said, 'Don't tell me anything bad.'

He handed me a piece of paper and said, 'Just read that bit there.' It was my date of release: 29 September 1983.

I didn't know what to do – laugh, cry. . . . It just seemed like one hell of a weight had been lifted off my shoulders. My first reaction was to ask about Chris – if he'd been given a date too. But nobody knew. Then I went back and told the others. Ian Barrie was overjoyed for me, Les Long was smiling, everybody was coming over and shaking my hand. I couldn't believe it. I went to work that afternoon, and all the security was off me. I was allowed to wander out into the yard. No one cared any more.

I had a year to go until my full release. First, I had to serve six months in Leyhill open prison and six months in a prison hostel. Leyhill was one of only two open prisons in the country which would accept lifers. There, what restrictions they had were as flexible as possible. We were trusted not to escape, given a great deal of freedom within the prison compound and allowed out of the grounds on working parties.

Those six months flew by. So did the next six at Maidstone prison hostel. The rules gave me the freedom to go out on my own during the daytime so long as I signed in and out, returned at a certain time in the evenings and reported to the screws on a daily basis. I was allowed to spend weekends with my wife and kids. Yet, for all this privilege, I still felt very much tied to the apron strings of the prison system.

And then, suddenly, my last week arrived. The authorities had to reclothe me, and I was given a grant of about £600. A screw took me into town to do my own shopping. I had to see the doctor and the Governor. I had to draw out money from a special bank account where my hostel wages had been deposited for me, pending my release. It worked out at about £760, and I was given an extra sum of £150.

More than fifteen years had passed, and I was about to go back into society. But my head was still back in 1968. That was the difference, as I was to find out.

CHAPTER SEVENTEEN

A DOMESTIC DISASTER

The night before my release, I couldn't sleep. The whole of the past week had been sheer murder. For years, I'd had the security of the prison wall around me. Now I was in a prison hostel, and although I'd been able to go out into the world at large, I was still under supervision; I still had that security. During my weekdays at the hostel I would never, ever leave the vicinity of the prison. It was like a home to me.

Now my thoughts went, 'You're on your own, how do you feel about that?' Everything I'd looked forward to was beginning to collapse around me. How would I react to being at home for good? To my family? I knew I couldn't afford to make an error, couldn't break the rules of the life licence I was going to be living under, or I'd be inside again. The pressure was back on, every bit as much as it had been in prison. My excitement had given way to a great anxiety: I was gripped by worries about the outside.

I climbed sleeplessly out of bed at six in the morning on 29 September, and realised that my links with everything familiar were about to break. I was frightened, unsure. I was called down to the office and told to sign for my bank book and all the possessions I'd had when I was arrested – a ring, some clothes. Later that day I ripped the clothes up. They were part of history.

I didn't have any breakfast. I kept drinking tea. I must have had about nine cups in two hours.

The Assistant Governor came to see me. He said that that day, no matter what happened, I had to report to my probation officer, Mr Goode. He also passed me my life licence, and asked me to sign. I was told I had to read it carefully. A lot of people seem to think a life sentence finishes when the prisoner is released. Far from it. A life sentence is never over. You are only released on licence, and if you get arrested again for so much as a fight in a pub you can be recalled to prison to finish serving life.

The licence carried my name at the top, and it stated the conditions I was going to live under for the rest of my life: I was to be under the supervision of a nominated probation officer, report to him as often as he told me to, receive visits from him at home, live and work only in places approved by him, and get his permission before I could travel anywhere outside Great Britain. At the bottom was a sentence which summed up the absolute power this document would have over me: 'Unless revoked this licence remains in force indefinitely'. In other words, if I broke any of the conditions I would have my licence withdrawn and I'd be straight back in the nick. And it would only take one person with a grudge to pick up a phone. . . .

It was twenty past nine in the morning, and I was standing at Maidstone prison gates. I was about to walk out for the last time when PO Sneed called me back. He said, 'You forgot your rail ticket. Remember this is a one-way. No return.' My brothers had offered to pick me up, but I didn't want that. I didn't want any crowd outside the gate. I just wanted to walk away from it on my own. It was important that I did this.

I wandered down County Road to the station. It was a nice, summery day, pretty mild, and I sat down with a bag and a case at Maidstone East, waiting for the train to come in. In my mind, I was thinking about the past. Would there be any comebacks from what had happened? Did people still remember? What would be their reaction to me around where I lived? What was Chris doing? He was being released on the same day from Wormwood Scrubs hostel, and going to live in Banbury, in Oxfordshire. He wanted nothing more to do with London. I was going back to the East End because I considered it my home. It was where I had been brought up; it was what I knew and it was where my wife and kids were living.

My marriage itself had, however, died a long time back. It was just a convenient thing at the time to keep it going, however superficially, because of the terms of the licence and the condition that I had to have an approved address. I didn't know what to expect from Pat when I moved back in. I just wanted to push the problem to the back of my mind.

I arrived at Victoria Station and, for the first time in fifteen years, I was a free man in my own eyes. That's when it hit me. In Victoria. I was back in the city. I thought, 'Things haven't changed that much,' although it was certainly a hell of a lot faster.

It was about 11.30, and I was starving. In prison, you got your dinner about that time. I didn't want to booze, like I thought I might. I just walked around Victoria, and went over and had a coffee beside the theatre. All I could smell was food, and I realised I could have it. For the first time in years, I could have things. I could buy a paper without having to wait for someone to bring it in, hours late. I could actually smell women around, the femininity, without seeing them. I still couldn't help staring. Everything was a novelty, even after six months of semi-freedom at the hostel.

I took a tube to Mile End, and when I got there my son David was waiting with about eight of his mates outside the station. One of them had a book about the Krays and he was looking at it, trying to recognise me. David spotted me, and one of his friends, Raymond, took my case. Scott, his brother, took my bag. We all walked along towards where we lived, and every time I turned round, David and his pals were looking at me. I said, 'Are you going to have a drink with me?' They were only sixteen or seventeen years old, and there I was wanting to take them into a pub. By now I was on a high, and I didn't want to go back to the house.

We went into the Coburn Arms off Mile End Road. I pulled out a £20 note for a round of drinks, and the barmaid gave me about £8 back. I said, 'Have you made a mistake?'

The boys were looking at me – 'What's he on about?' When I went away, 1s 9d got you a bottle of lager, 2s 9d got you a packet of Benson and Hedges, and 4s 6d bought a gallon of petrol. The currency had gone decimal since then and the money we handled in prison was black market, worth about half of its face value, so I didn't understand the worth of money in the real world at all.

There I was sitting in the pub with all David's lot. Not one of them asked me a thing! We left there and went to the house, and Pat was there. So was Karen. We sat indoors. Pat said, 'Do you want something to eat? It's nice to see you home.' It was no great big thing to her. There were no banners out or anything.

I had a cup of tea and then I slipped out to see John Goode, the probation officer, in his office in Mile End Road. I'd met him before in the hostel. He said the police had been informed I'd been released, and he told me: 'For the foreseeable future, you'll be reporting to me once a week. You know the rules. You've got to live like I tell you. If you're going to get a job, I have to be told immediately. You've got to tell me more or less everything. Any problems, get in touch immediately.' There was something about him that I wasn't sure about, something which told me that he and I weren't going to see eye to eye. . . .

I wandered back to the house at about five, and watched the six o'clock news. And I thought to myself, 'What am I going to do now?' For years, all I'd been thinking about at this time of the evening was getting ready for bed, collecting the papers and the boiling water for the flasks, maybe getting a sandwich. Six months in a hostel was hardly what it took to break the habits of what seemed like a lifetime. It certainly didn't prepare me for what I was facing now. Here I was, a free man without limits on my first day of proper freedom, and I didn't know what to do with myself. I was bored. Lost. I didn't have any of the boys around me.

I thought, 'I'll go and have a drink,' but I didn't want to walk out of the house. It was my security. Unbeknown to me, I was making other prisons for myself. I had become institutionalised and as the weeks went by, the symptoms became apparent. I wouldn't come out of the kitchen, because it was the smallest room. It became a cell to me. I wanted to be alone for periods of time. I would get very tired around nine at night, and I was always awake by 7.30 the next day. Your day is very short in prison, and I wanted my days to be the same out here.

I had brought so many of my prison habits home with me. I'd keep a flask around me, which I didn't need. If I bought more than two ounces of tobacco, which was the regulation limit in the nick, I'd hide the extra in a cupboard: I carried on smoking roll-ups: it didn't occur to me to buy cigarettes for eighteen months. I'd go mad at the sound of a loud radio. I'd make my bed in the prison way the instant I got up, with the sheets and blankets boxed up and the pillow sitting on top. I used to watch policemen. To me, they were screws. Many a copper said to me, 'What do you think you're looking at?' I still tend to avoid uniforms.

Quite a few of these old prison habits have remained with me to this day. I still mash my food up, and I've got to have a good supply of tinned soup. I'm as fanatical as ever about cleanliness. Every last spoon has to be washed up after dinner, my bathroom is always spotless, and I cannot stand dirty ashtrays: I have to keep getting up to empty them.

My first few weeks of freedom were much the same as the first day: empty. Leon would come down, Jimmy would come down, they'd stay a few hours and then they were gone. I was with a wife who had become a total stranger to me and a son and daughter who didn't know me. I couldn't act naturally around women I met in the course of everyday life. I was frightened of them. I'd get very, very embarrassed and find nothing to say. But the strangest feeling of all was that I had nothing to hate any more.

I was confused, too. I'd come out to a different world. Going dutch? I didn't know what the bleeding hell they were on about. I didn't know what women's lib was. I'd been brought up to believe that the old man was King of the Castle. I couldn't understand why people weren't giving their seats to ladies on the bus. Men were swearing in front of women, and women were drinking as hard as the men. Women were making approaches. I couldn't believe the sort of crime that was going on, the raping and mugging and the extent of it. In my own way I was still twenty-six, the age I went away at, and I was still in the sixties. Prison suspends time. And I was finding it very difficult to adjust to life out of prison.

I started drinking. I went out to pubs with Jumbo, who was married to Pat's Aunt Gladys, and another bloke called Ronnie Lloyd. They were hard, decent, working people, rough and ready and totally honest. They loved their drink, loved their fag, loved their bet. They lived their lives to the full the way they wanted. When I came out of prison I was A1, in top condition. Within six months I had ballooned up to sixteen stone. They were professional drinkers, and I just couldn't keep up with them. But it was by being in their company that I started to feel accepted again. And I stumbled across a very interesting truth indeed: people were falling over themselves to give me money. For nothing. It all began when I started having a Sunday lunchtime drink with Jumbo and Ronnie in the East End. That's when I realised how legendary the twins and the firm had become. People really wanted to know me. Some of them thought that by giving me money they could buy my friendship, which would give them 'prestige' in the eyes of their mates. Some of them thought that by slipping me a few quid I might be able to do them a favour one day. But others genuinely did believe I had felt the rough end of British justice, and wanted to see me get on in life. They all had one thing in common: they wouldn't take no for an answer.

One Sunday dinnertime, in a pub called the Bancroft Arms in Mile End Road, I was handed a brown envelope containing £500. It was from a building contractor called Joe The Beard. I was told that an envelope would be left behind the bar for me every Sunday. People just don't give you £500 for nothing every week. I didn't even know the bloke, but when I did get to know him he told me: 'I wanted to give you this money as a sign of my respect. I couldn't have done what you did – fifteen years for keeping your mouth shut.'

I met bookmakers, club owners, business people, all asking, 'Do you need a few quid?' As it happens, I had a little bit left from before I went away, although not a lot, and I didn't ask any of these people for a penny. If I refused their money, they'd give it to someone else to give to me. I was given a car by five different people. I was offered two pubs and a business, none of which I accepted. At that time I couldn't have run a scooter, never mind a business. I would go into restaurants and clubs and I wouldn't be given a bill. I suppose the owners thought that the very fact that I was there might stop problems. I would have been a fool not to take advantage of it. If people wanted to shower me with things, who was I to refuse them? Especially when I was, and still am, what they call 'unemployable'.

By law, I had to go and 'sign on' after I was released from the hostel. I was given a letter and told to take it with me to the office. This I duly did, and I was told to sit down and wait. Ten minutes later, I was called into an upstairs room to talk to three men. Their attitude towards the idea of me finding a job was this: 'Go away, we'll send you a giro, don't worry about it.'

One of them said, 'In my experience of dealing with the unemployed, I'm at a loss with you, Mr Lambrianou. One, what have we got to offer you in your line of business? And two, who in their right mind would employ you?'

I must admit, I had to agree with him.

Things were getting very hard to handle in my home life. On paper, everything was lovely. But something was missing between me and Pat. My daughter had grown up into a woman of twenty-one with a very strong personality. David was fifteen, and he saw me as a challenge. If I sat down next to Pat, he'd get up and walk out of the room. I tried in my own way to be friendly, and I put up with weeks of being stared at by David and his friends. Every time I came into the room, it was like walking into six pairs of eyes. I expected David to do my running around. I'd say, 'Shoot round and get me a paper.' He started giving me these looks, half taking me on. If I wanted an ounce of tobacco, I wanted it there and then. I could lose my temper very quickly. What I'd done was transfer my prison into the home. Looking back on it, I can see that. At the time, I didn't.

My answer to it all was to bribe him. I'd give him a tenner to go round and get me tobacco. If he wanted to go out with his mates, I'd give him a fifty. It meant nothing to me: I still hadn't come to terms with the value of money, especially when total strangers kept coming along and giving it to me. But David resented it. I made an enemy of him by doing that. If I said anything to him, he'd go and tell Pat and it would cause a row. That caused more resentment. If I turned his music down, he didn't like it. 'Why do I have to do what he tells me?' Also, my daughter comes into the frame here a lot. She was holding a grudge against me over an argument which happened during one of my weekends on leave from the hostel.

It began on a Saturday when I refused to take Pat to Karen's shoe shop in Bethnal Green. The shop, Robert Shoes, was owned by Karen's common-law husband, a Turk called Ken. He was a nice fella, a bit older than Karen, and he gave her security and everything she wanted. But my dad was a Greek, and Turks and Greeks do not get on. In the back of my mind, my family background loomed up very close here. I wouldn't have interfered in Karen's life, but I didn't particularly like the situation and I was watching it very closely.

Throughout my prison life I always had something to take my grievances out on, and I suppose I looked for it here. Pat wanted to go to the shop, and I said no. The next Friday, when I arrived home for the weekend, Karen was waiting there with Pat. Karen said, 'Don't you think you can get away with what you did last Saturday. Any trouble out of you, and out you go.'

No one spoke to me like that, especially not in my own home where the father was the head of the household. I went mad. I grabbed hold of her and I said, 'If you ever speak to me like that again, I'll wallop you from one end of the room to the other.'

She started to scratch me, so rightly or wrongly I gave her a smack. She shouldn't have spoken to me like she did.

Karen was never the same towards me after that. So now, here I was in a house where I felt like a stranger. David was half-challenging me, and Karen was giving me a bit of a bad time, trying to run my life like a prison Governor. She was causing me a lot of grief.

I didn't know how to handle it. I had no idea. So I started laying down the law. I said, 'Now look, this is my home. I pay the bills, you do as you're told.' Little did I realise what was going on. They were ganging up on me, the three of them.

Then Pat did something very stupid. She went to see John Goode, the probation officer, and she told him I'd been getting a bit aggressive. She said known criminals were coming to the house. No, they weren't. She said there were mystery phone calls in the middle of the night. That was a total fabrication.

I was certainly up during the night. After breaking away from my prison sleeping habits, I'd become hyperactive. I wanted to do a thousand things an hour, and I couldn't sleep.

I went to see John Goode and he was like a different person. He said, 'You've got to get out of your house. Pat and Karen and David have been over here, and things aren't working out with you. If you don't find another place in fourteen days, you'll have to go back to the hostel.'

I could not believe it. I went straight round to Pat's aunt's, where I knew she would be, and I went absolutely potty. They must have called about sixty police round there, but they didn't want to get involved, even though they knew who I was and they knew I was on a licence. They looked upon it as a domestic dispute.

The terms of my licence were such that, if I wanted to watch BBC and Pat wanted to watch *Coronation Street,* all she had to do was pick up the phone and say I was playing up in the hope that she would get me recalled. Which is exactly what she'd done. I'd just come back from sixteen years, and I'd wound up with a family and a parole officer who had it in for me.

My freedom was on the line here, so I made Pat's life a misery. I made things as difficult as possible because I didn't want to give the flat up. I wanted *her* to leave it. It was my place anyway. I got to her guv'nor at work. He was told to sack her - I suppose you could say a bit of intimidation was involved. I made sure nobody would talk to her. She went to Charlie Kray in desperation, but he couldn't get involved. It was nothing to do with him.

So she left. She went to stay at her aunt's with David. I thought that because it was my home and in my name, nobody had any legal right to kick me out of it. But Pat got in touch with John Goode again and said she needed the flat back. He told me I was leaving, and there was nothing more I could do.

I was sent to an after-release hostel in Camberwell. I wasn't subject to any rules, but I was under observation and I had to sign in and out. They were keeping me under what they thought was a little bit of control.

I had to go back to the flat, occasionally, to get clothes – which David would pass out to me. By now, he had become a sort of middle man, the one member of the family I could communicate with without too much hostility. Next thing, I had every conceivable type of injunction slapped on me. I wasn't to go near the house, and I wasn't allowed to approach my children.

Injunctions were all very well, but there were things in the flat that I needed. One day in April 1984 I went round to get some stuff and had an argument with Pat. Again, it ended up with the law being called in. I arrived back at the hostel to be surrounded by police. There were so many of them milling around that they obviously thought I'd committed a crime. I was taken to Carter Street police station and held in a cell. Pat had gone back to John Goode and told him there'd been an incident. He'd gone right ahead, phoned the Home Office and got me recalled.

Ten minutes after I was put in the cell, the door opened and an inspector was standing there with a couple of CID men. He said; 'Do you know why you're here?'

I said, 'Tell me what it's all about.'

He replied, 'I really don't know, but I think you should have a word with your wife.'

Pat was under the impression that I'd be held for a few days until I'd calmed down, and I would then be released. But it doesn't work like that.

Twenty minutes later, the inspector came back and said, 'You're going to have to go back to prison. We've been given an order that you're to be returned to Wormwood Scrubs immediately.'

Within an hour I was back in D-wing in the Scrubs doing a life sentence. I couldn't believe what had happened. Nobody knew where I was. My brothers were looking for me. No one was told anything.

The next day I was called in front of the Assistant Governor of D-wing. He said, 'There was a complaint from your wife that you were getting aggressive.'

'What's the position now?' I asked.

He said, 'Within twenty-eight days of a lifer being recalled, there has to be an inquiry. The probation officer has to come and see me and submit a report.'

My Leon came to see me and got in touch with David Atkinson at the Home Office lifers' division. Chris was going up the wall to hear that I'd been recalled for absolutely nothing. The chaplain at the Scrubs wasn't having it. He said, 'I'm not satisfied with this.' And the number one Governor, McLeod – Honey had left – came to see me. I told him what had happened and he believed me. The Local Review Committee man arrived on the scene. He said, 'I'm recommending you be released as soon as possible.'

One day shortly afterwards, I was told by an Assistant Governor that John Goode and another probation officer would be coming to see me. Obviously, I was angry. It was Goode who had got me put away. When he turned up at the Scrubs to see me, I wanted to go wild, but I took one look at him and I just felt sick.

He said, 'Look, I don't know what to say, but in my view. . . .'

I exploded: 'Your view nearly wrecked my life.'

There was nothing he could say.

By the time the whole muddle had been sorted out I'd been in there for four months, one of the shortest terms ever served by a lifer on recall. I returned to the hostel in Camberwell and was assigned to a new probation officer called Keith Norton. There was nothing my wife could ever say to me again. But I wouldn't be satisfied until I'd got my revenge, and I was prepared to go back to prison for it.

It was New Year's Eve 1984. I'd been drinking in company in an East End pub called Batleys. At five to twelve I ordered a taxi and slipped out the door. I asked the driver to take me to the Bancroft Arms, where I knew Pat and her family would be drinking.

I arrived at exactly one minute to midnight. The pub was packed. Just as they were getting ready to chase in the New Year, who came bursting in the door but me. Everybody jumped back, and I just dived in the midst of them. The guv'nor nearly had a heart attack. All I wanted to do was upset the lot of it. And I did. People were flying in the air, tables were going over, there was drink everywhere. The police were called, and I was carted off to the station and banged up in a cell. I thought, 'That's it, I'm getting a recall', but it didn't matter to me because I was satisfied by what I'd done.

About an hour later, the door opened and a sergeant came in. He said, 'You know if we put you in court, you're in breach of your licence . . . so I want you to sign this piece of paper saying you won't drink, in the area of the pub inside the next twenty-eight days.' He said if I signed it, he would release me straightaway.

I could not believe my luck. I walked out of there feeling as if somebody had given me a million pounds.

I went back to the hostel, and I was expecting for quite some time to hear a bit about it from Pat's relatives. I never did. The only thing I did hear was the news of my divorce coming through. I haven't seen Pat since, and I haven't spoken to her or Karen. They haven't tried to contact me; they know better. They were totally disowned by my family.

David occasionally comes to see me in my regular pub, the Florist in Bethnal Green. I didn't go to him in the first place; he came to me. And I still don't know if I truly forgive him for his part in it all, and for the heartbreak he caused me. He may only have been fifteen, but he did go to my parole officer and put his two penn'orth in. On the other hand, he sometimes asks me, 'Where were you when I needed you?', and he's right. But, whatever the rights and wrongs of the past, I always do my best to make him welcome when we meet.

On 14 April 1985 I moved from the hostel to the flat at Borough in south-east London, where I still live. I had managed to get to the top of the council list through a contact at the town hall, and the flat they offered me was ideal. It was in a terrible state, though, and I had to do it all up myself. I had no money left by now, and I couldn't earn a living. But I had to start picking up the pieces of my life.

Before I could do that, however, there was one more hurdle to jump: an illness which nearly killed me. I was unwell anyway, after all the months of stress and worry, and I'd gone down to ten and a half stone.

I walked into my flat late one night and I felt ill. I wanted to be with someone, so I went round to see my friend June, who lived nearby. I had begun to make friends in the neighbourhood, and June and her husband Charlie were among the few I trusted. At the time of my illness, Charlie was away.

I was sitting having a cup of tea with June when I started getting a lot of pain in my back, as if someone was shoving a poker up my spine. I left June's and stopped for a Chinese takeaway on my walk home. I was sitting in the kitchen eating it when all of a sudden I felt sick. I went into the toilet and threw it up. I kept on vomiting, bringing up a brown liquid, without realising that I was bleeding inside. I had two ulcers I never knew about – one duodenal and one peptic.

I went back to June's and she said, 'Get yourself to hospital now.' I walked round to Guys Hospital, to the casualty department. I remember seeing a fox on the roadside. They put me in a cubicle, took my temperature and gave me a blood test. Al! of a sudden, there were five doctors around me.

They said, 'We're going to have to keep you in for tests. We think you're very ill.'

I insisted, 'I can't do that. I can't leave home without informing my probation officer.'

One doctor replied, 'You're not leaving this hospital.'

I said, 'I assure you I am.'

He made me sign a form and gave me a bottle of medicine, but within an hour I was back. They immediately put me on a drip in the surgical ward. They did some tests, put a camera down me and found the ulcers. They didn't know whether to operate or keep them under observation.

I got up to go to the toilet, taking the drip off, and as I walked down the ward everything went light. All I remember is trying to get off the floor while blood was coming from out of my ears, my nose, everywhere. The ulcers had burst. I was dying and I never knew it. I ended up lying in a bed with three machines keeping me alive. A doctor sat with me all night.

Eventually I recovered, and was sternly warned by the doctor: 'From now on no curries, no spicy foods, no fried food and not too much alcohol.' I had to change my entire diet, but that was only a small part of a greater thing: I was about to start changing my whole life.

CHAPTER EIGHTEEN

THE WAY
AHEAD

One day in 1988 I happened to be walking along a road in Milton Keynes with a friend of mine when we heard a terrible yelping sound. I looked over a fence and I saw this guy bashing an undernourished white boxer dog.

I shouted, 'How would you like me to do that to you?'

He said, 'If you feel that strongly, you can have him.' Without thinking about what I was doing, I took the dog. I called him Prince.

I got him home, and I didn't know what to do. He was a sick animal. I took him to the vet with the intention of getting him better and finding him a good home. I fed him up and spent over £600 in vet's fees putting him right.

When it came to getting rid of him I just couldn't do it, but at the same time I still didn't really want him. I gave him a hard time – I hit him for messing up the house and he never once complained.

At the time, I was fed up with everything. The ulcers and the stress I'd suffered after my release from prison were still taking their toll on me. I was gaunt, I wasn't eating properly and I had no energy or enthusiasm. The only interesting thing to have happened in my life over the previous couple of years had been the television documentary I presented on ITV in August 1987. I'd made the film with a friend of mine, the director Adrian Penninck, to talk about the problems of living with a life licence, and to guide the viewers round our old East End haunts.

But that excitement had subsided, and my life was back in the doldrums. I'd had a few brief romances, none of them even worth mentioning. There was nobody special in my life, and the only people I bothered seeing were the few friends who would put up with me in my depressed condition – people like Lenny Thomas, Joe Griffiths, and Charlie and June Olson, whom I'd met when I moved to Borough.

One afternoon, I looked at the dog and I said, 'What am I going to do?' He looked back at me, and suddenly I decided to treat him with kindness. This was a very important lesson for me. From that day onwards, he was a changed animal. And he changed me too. I enjoyed being with him, and together we developed an instinctive understanding of each other. I never had to give him an order: he knew. He never gave me any further reason even to raise my voice at him.

He gave me something to come home to. Before Prince came along, all I had had to look forward to was an empty house, and I didn't spend a lot of my time there if I didn't feel like it. But once I had the dog, I knew I had to be home at regular times to feed and exercise him. He may have been only a dog, but that was a big responsibility for me, which was something I had not known in my life for a long time. It was a challenge, and the fact that I met it gave me a real sense of achievement.

I'm grateful that Prince came into my life at a time when I was ill and had no one, really, to go to. I was never a man to share my problems with other people. But Prince I treated fairly and squarely as a companion. I'd had no response from him until I started to treat him like a human being. And I grew to love that animal just as he grew to love me. It took a dog to teach me about human beings, about treating other people with kindness.

That was the first major change in my life. The second was Wendy.

I was always wary where girls were concerned, because a lot of their interest in me was to do with my past. But Wendy Mason was different. I'd seen her in the Florist in Bethnal Green off and on with her two mates, and she didn't know anything about my background. I used to drink in there with some of the boys who worked in Smithfield Meat Market, and we were on about Wendy for a long time. I remember a bloke called Dave, who was a mate of the twins' cousin Kevin, saying to me: 'She ain't half nice, over there.' But I'd seen her, so I made it plain that I liked her, and kept the other lads at bay.

She was very pretty, I liked her long, dark hair, I liked her smile, I liked everything about her. Every time I turned round I saw her smiling at me. But we were making eyes at each other for months before we started talking properly.

One night in February 1989, round about Valentine's Day, I asked her if she would come out with me on Saturday night. She said she'd been invited to a party, and wasn't sure if she was going to go or not.

I said, 'If you don't go to the party, I'll be here.' And I was, but she didn't come in.

On the Sunday I went back to the Florist again, because I had a feeling she'd be there, and I was right. I must have gone in and out of the toilet about eighty-nine times just to get her attention, and when she finally came by me I grabbed her hand and I said, 'Are you going to have a drink with me?' We stayed together, talking, for about two hours. And I kept trying to get her to leave the pub.

I think she thought it was purely an excuse when I said I had to go home because my dog wasn't well, and asked her to come with me! She wasn't having it. But I took her phone number. When I rang and asked her out again, she couldn't go because she had made other plans, but I made a meet with her for another day later in the week.

I couldn't stop thinking about her – even though, at twenty-five, she was much younger than me. She was quite unlike all the other girls I'd come across since I left prison. She was interested in me for me, not for who I used to be, which she still didn't know about. She was honest, hard-working and came from a good family. Her mother was Italian and her father was English. Wendy was the youngest of the family, still living at home. She was working in promotions for a beauty company in Fleet Street, and still is.

I picked her up in my Renault from her Mum's house on the night of the date and took her to a pub in Gants Hill. Then I took her to meet my mate Bryn and his wife Lorenza, who also has Italian blood. They got on well, Wendy and Lorenza. I took her home to her Mum's, and from that point onwards we've seen each other every night bar one.

The next evening we went to a little pub in Borough, and I was telling her more about Prince. She came up to see the flat, and she noticed a photo of me and Ronnie Kray on the mantelpiece.

She said, 'Is that you?'

I answered, 'Oh, yeah, it was a long time ago.'

She didn't push the matter, but I wondered what she must be thinking. You don't always walk into someone's house and see a picture of that person with one of the Kray twins. I was worried that if anybody told her about my background it could frighten her off. I didn't want it to come from anybody but me, and I was leading her up to it gradually. But she found out in her own way after about two months.

She went to have her legs waxed one night by a girl called Lynn, who was also the barmaid in the Florist.

Lynn asked her, 'How are you getting on with Tony? My Mum knows him from before he went away.'

'What do you mean, "went away"?' said Wendy.

Lynn replied, 'Didn't you know he was involved with the Krays and went inside for a long while?'

Wendy told me later she was dumbfounded. We saw each other that night, and she asked me about it. I explained that I'd been afraid to tell her in case she decided not to see me again. I knew she wasn't criminally minded at all. She's never taken a penny off anyone.

So, yes, it was a bit of a shock to her; but she accepted me for what I was, and in the end it created a stronger bond. She moved in with me two or three months after our first date. She'd been staying over a lot of the time at weekends, and it just seemed silly for us to be living apart. Her mother, being Italian and traditional in her ways, didn't believe you should just set up home with someone. She said to me, 'I don't agree with it, but you make sure you look after her.'

Against all the odds, the family did accept me, even given my unusual circumstances. She's a diamond, Wendy's Mum, and she does insist on feeding me. I've put on a lot of weight since I met her! And Wendy and I are building for the future.

Before we met, I had nothing except my dog. I had no family as such. My brothers had all left London and gone their own ways. I was feeling down, just living a day-to-day life, going nowhere. It's not impossible that I might have drifted back into crime.

But Wendy brought a lot of stability into my life; she gave me a permanence again. With her around, keeping my feet on the ground, I'd never be tempted to go back to my old way of life. She doesn't like crime of any kind, and she keeps me on an even keel. Far from slipping back into bad habits, I've gone on to do things with Wendy I never dreamed I might do. With the permission of my probation officer we've been to America, Cyprus, Spain and elsewhere in the Mediterranean.

The difference in our ages can cause the odd difficulty, but I do understand Wendy. For her part, she's told me that my sixties' attitudes towards things like manners and chivalry are among the things she respects and likes best about me. I treat her like a lady, and I like to spoil her, but I can be a bit protective at times. I don't like people leering or looking the wrong way at her. I'll jump on that. For her own protection, I don't like her to wear a mini-skirt if she goes out on her own. It's asking for trouble in this day and age, much as it would be nice to be able to walk along the street without having to worry about other people.

Yet, for all of my feeling for the sixties and their values, I have very few dealings these days with any of the characters I knew back in that era. I went out to Spain for a couple of weeks in 1988 with a friend called Andy, and while we were touring the country we stopped at the Costa del Sol, or the Costa del Crime, as the newspapers like to call it. It was like stepping into the East End of London with the number of old faces we bumped into there – people like Ronnie Knight, Freddie Foreman and the train robber Gordon Goody. The last thing I expected to drive into was that situation, but having said that, it was good to see some of them again.

A lot of the men, obviously, are wanted in England – which doesn't make them guilty. They would love to come back for a plate of pie and mash, but they don't believe they would get justice if they did. Recent events, primarily the arrest of Fred Foreman, would tend to lend weight to that opinion. Most of them live peaceful, legitimate lives in Spain, from what I saw. Back in London, I still have the odd chat with Buster Edwards, the Great Train Robber, at his flower stall at Waterloo Station. He's become part of the character of London. Also, I went to Frankie Fraser's do when he came out of prison in the mid-eighties, and the fact that the party was attended by members of all the old gangs in London says a lot about the respect that people had for him.

Some of our ex-fellow cons, however, came out of long prison sentences only to return to crime. Eddie Richardson, for instance, was sent down in 1990 on a charge involving millions of pounds' worth of cocaine. The Richardsons today I would describe as friends, even though we started our careers on less than friendly terms. In prison they always made me welcome in their company, although we didn't make a particular point of keeping in touch when we came out of the nick.

One person I do still see socially, however, is Charlie Kray. Charlie wants to lead a normal life, like me, but because of his name he'll probably never be able to do that. As for the other members of the firm . . . they're scattered all over the place. Ian Barrie is living a quiet life in Scotland. From what I've heard, he's repping for a company and prefers not to be in touch with anyone from the past. Ronnie Bender, who I've seen on occasions, is also keeping a low profile, living with his wife Buddy in the Isle of Dogs in east London. Connie Whitehead I still see occasionally in pubs and restaurants in the East End. I have to admit to a sneaking liking for him, despite the suspicions over his loyalty in the trial, but I never have anything to do with him when we meet. He keeps himself to himself and says nothing, although his wife, Pat, is a very nice lady whom I'm always happy to talk to. Tommy Cowley has, sadly, died of cancer. I always got the impression he felt guilty because he didn't go down with us. The last time I saw him was in Durham prison when he came to visit Ron.

And so to the Kray twins, whose parole I would wholeheartedly support, having visited both of them since my release. At the time of writing, they have each served twenty-two years in prison. That's not justice, that's a pound of flesh. Revenge. There comes a time when the authorities have got to justify keeping you in prison. When they can't do that, they have to let you go. They cannot justify keeping Reggie Kray, at least, any longer. So you've got to put it down to politics. We all went away together and we should have come out together, too. We've all paid the price, if we deserved that price. Keeping Reggie Kray in prison for the McVitie murder is achieving nothing. What's the point? Once your sentence stretches beyond a certain time, is there really any difference between eighteen years and twenty-five? What good is it doing anyone? This is where I think the system is going wrong.

Reggie is in Lewes prison in Sussex, striving to keep his mind and his body in peak condition. It's a credit to him, after all this time, that he's still up to it. How much more can they ask a man to take? I say give him a chance, don't kick him when he's down. In my opinion, he should be given his parole while it's still possible for him to come out and fit into society. As Chris and I discovered, there's no such thing as rehabilitation, nothing which can prepare you for the realities of a society which has overtaken you by a couple of decades. Purely on humane grounds, Reggie ought to be released now.

I'd like to say the same for Ronnie. I'm not here to argue the case against his doctors at Broadmoor Hospital, but Ron deserves to be given a little bit of hope. He still thinks about life outside, and his pride in his appearance is as strong as ever. He has never complained. Ron has his dignity, and I believe that dignity should be respected by the authorities. I find it tragic to think that they would be quite happy to hold him in there for the rest of his days. It's time to consider the view that he ought to be given his chance.

The twins are still very well respected in every level of society, not just in criminal circles, and a real cross-section of the public now genuinely feels that enough is enough. People ask if they still control things outside, or if they would take up where they left off on their release. I believe the answer to both questions is no. If they came out now, every eye would be on them. They could never reach that position of power again; they wouldn't need to. The twins can make their money in other ways, particularly Reggie with his books. I also know that Reggie has a business brain which is second to none. He could do a lot of good in certain ways. He could go out, like they do in America, talking to people in institutions, putting a view across. He was always a very persuasive man, and we shouldn't lose that talent.

Certainly, if I had any advice for youngsters thinking of embarking on a career in crime, it would be this: forget it. Very few men earn a proper living by crime. You can't beat the law. If anybody could have done it, we would have. We don't deserve to be on any pedestal.

It's no big deal to go around saying, 'I've cut somebody, I've shot them.' The only future is in a prison in the middle of nowhere, limited and humiliated in every way possible, and the things you have to put your family through cost too much in the long run. I've sat in some of the toughest prisons in Britain reflecting on the fact that you can't buy time back again. It's gone. And so are the days of the Wild West. Go to work. An earned pound note is a better pound note than a bent one.

I've said the same thing to every would-be villain who's come knocking on my door. Some members of a black gang called the Yardies came to me for advice, and I said: 'I'm telling you, you're nicked. You can't get away with what you're doing.' The face of gang activity has changed a lot since our days. It's not so public as it was with us, and it tends to stay within its own ethnic community groups. There are the Chinese Triads, as well as the blacks and the whites, and they all keep themselves to themselves. The Pakistanis are beginning to firm themselves up now and, from what I hear, that's where the next bid for power will come from. Trouble will come between the Asians and the blacks. In 1989, a black gang challenged a Pakistani firm in Commercial Road and the blacks withdrew because they realised the Asians would win. The Asians are already running protection rackets within their own community, and I foresee that they will have a lot of power round about the turn of the century.

The point is that since the twins' time there has been no all-powerful firm to co-ordinate and keep the other professional criminal gangs in check. And now that there's such a diversity of outfits, that one power is needed more than ever. It will be interesting to see what confrontations happen where, and when. We may yet see a gangland situation developing along the lines of America's, if the police don't stop it first.

Wendy has now adopted my name to become Mason-Lambrianou. We lead a simple life at home most of the time. We'll sit indoors with a nice dinner, watch a bit of the box and take Prince for a walk. I can sit around, unshaven, in my tracksuit bottoms, and just enjoy a quiet life.

But I do tend to live two lives. Once I get dressed for the weekend, get myself suited and booted, I become a different person. I go out to impress people. Wherever I go, people tend to find out about my past, and they won't leave me alone until I give them what they want to see. So I tend to do that now and again, lay a little bit on for them. I dress the part, yes, and I play the part. They want to feel I'm at the height of activity and that I know everything that's going on.

I still consider my role in life is as a public relations man, and when I go to the pub, or to a restaurant or whatever, a lot of my conversation is a bit of a PR job for the twins. I've always respected them, always held them in very high regard, and anything I can do to help generate support for their release I will do. There's no excuse for murder and unnecessary violence, but by the standards of today's criminals the twins weren't such bad men – certainly not bad enough to deserve the sentences they got.

Still, their name does do some funny things to people, even today. When I'm chatting in company and any strangers suddenly hear that I was connected to the Krays, their whole attitude changes immediately. They become incredibly polite. 'Anything we can do for you?' They start looking for the scar on your face. You can see them thinking, 'We've heard so much about all this, but you don't look anything like it.'

I might be in the pub on a Friday night and some bloke will say, 'All right, Tone?' and then turns to his girlfriend and whispers, 'A pal of mine, him.'

We're always made welcome wherever we go. I could open my own brewery with the amount of booze that comes at me. People keep on telling me about what good things we did, the Robin Hood side of it. They always want to hear what I've got to say, and they always tell me I didn't deserve the sentence I got, but Wendy keeps my feet on the ground. She'll say, 'Tony, you've got red blood, same as everybody else.'

People come up and want to be photographed with me. I've had people I've never seen in my life before pretending they know me and claiming they were on the firm. Everyone insists they've had dealings with the Krays somewhere along the line. How the twins are ever going to cope with this when they come out, I don't know. The standard question from strangers is, 'How long do you think the twins will do?' If I don't get asked that ten times a day, there's something wrong.

I'm always aware that my past is going to precede me, and I'm usually at pains to relax people. I've learnt to let their chatter go in one ear and out the other, but sometimes it gets a bit too much. Sometimes it can be very embarrassing, and at other times it can make me feel quite isolated. There are times when I try to be polite, but in the end I have to get away from it. I'll listen for a while, nod my head, agree with whatever it is the person is saying, and then say, 'Excuse me a second, I'll be back.' But I won't. If Charlie Kray is in the room, I'll say, 'Look, there's Charlie over there. I'm sure he'd love to have a chat with you,' and Charlie will do the same thing to me. It's a standing joke between us.

Wendy and I might be out enjoying ourselves, and if someone comes up and wants to start talking to me about the twins or the trial or whatever, it can wreck our night. If it happens once too often I can turn on someone, and Wendy can always tell now when it's about to happen. You don't like to hurt people's feelings, but there comes a time when you think, 'I'm never going to know 'em because I don't want to know 'em. I've seen too many of 'em.' I've stopped using a lot of my old haunts. Wendy's been good there. She's a great reader of situations and she gives her view out as she sees it. She'll say, 'Look, you don't need this person or that person.' I still get the hangers-on, though. I suppose, in a way, I might have encouraged it at one point. But not any more.

I do like my brothers round me now and again. We remain very close, although we still have our arguments when we get together. For most of 1990, Chris was refusing to come out with us lot because of it. He knew he'd got no control over the rest of us. It's purely a family thing. We're very explosive and we can shout at each other so furiously it could give the wrong impression, but it would never come to blows. That's the Lambrianou brothers.

My relationship with Chris is a strange thing, in view of what happened in the past. We don't have a lot in common any more. He lives quietly in Oxford with his second wife and family, doing market gardening. He might come down to London once or twice a year, but our communications are very limited. I think the fact that we lived on top of one another for a long time drove us apart. But it's nice to know that he's settled down. He's a good family man. And he knows I'm here if he needs me.

The closest brother to me at the moment is probably Jimmy. After we were convicted, he moved out to Banbury and became a businessman with his own factory, working in sheet metal. He's become very successful. He helped design the new telephone kiosks, and he invented the air-door, the air system which keeps cold air out of buildings in the winter and hot air out in the summer. It's used in airports. He owns racing greyhounds, too. He's done well in life, and I'm proud of him.

Leon is the brother who makes the most effort to keep the family together. Where the brothers are concerned, he'd do anything. He'd be the first one there. Nothing pleases him more than having one or other of us to his house. From a working boy who had nothing, he's now got all the best pitches in the markets in Kent and the outskirts of London. He employs his son to run it all for him, and he has a staff of four or five people. He's got a lovely house in Herne Bay, Kent.

Nicky we all still treat like the baby of the family, even though he's a man in his forties. We continually argue about him, and we're always having a go. He's received spells of imprisonment in recent years for drug offences, receiving stolen property and robbery. He has a mind of his own, Nicky – a very game man. He lives in Banbury, but he still sees a lot of us. He's extremely likeable, and I do my best to keep my eye on him.

Part of me is always in prison. It will never leave me, I know that. Sometimes I can be walking along and find myself talking to the dog, and laughing over an incident that might have happened ten years ago in Parkhurst. I often think back to what I left behind. A lot of people I know are still inside. I try to visualise what they're thinking, and what they're going through.

I think about how long I did, and I try to remember the seventies, but I can't. I can remember isolated incidents like the troubles in Gartree in 1972, I can remember that very hot summer of 1976, I can remember being moved from Gartree to Maidstone in 1977. But I think about the actual length of time I was inside, and it doesn't mean anything to me.

I still remember what it's like to walk fifty yards, turn right, walk fifty yards and turn right again. I remember Leicester maximum-security block, and the fact that there wasn't a bit of green in the exercise yard. You don't know what you miss until you haven't got it. Today, if I see anyone damaging a tree, or drawing graffiti or dropping litter, I go absolutely potty.

In all sorts of small ways like this, a life sentence leaves its paw marks all over the rest of your life, shapes your thinking and your behaviour, and above all shows you the value of freedom. You don't understand that until you've been locked up.

I like to think I'm a trustworthy person now. I may have had difficult times since my release, and I may have had very bad patches when I've been short of money, but I've shunned any criminal opportunities that have come my way, tempting though they may have been. I'd sooner be without. At least I'm free.

I do have regrets about my past, I must admit, but more important than anything else, I'm not ashamed of it. It's important to me as a person that I can hold my head up, knowing that I didn't point the finger at anybody, that I was with the twins and I fell with the twins. I went into the deep end and, somehow, over the years, I've managed to make it to the shallow water. I haven't achieved a lot in my lifetime, but I came through my sentence more or less in one piece, against all the odds.

I don't see myself in trouble in the future at any time. I'm just getting on with my life and enjoying what I've got left of it. If I can help anybody, I will do it. I ask people not to involve me in crime, and they don't. They accept me as I am today. All the money I have ever gained from crime couldn't buy me what I've got going for me now. For once in my life, I've got no problems or pressures, I've got a stable home and hopefully, in the future, I'll have a baby son or daughter to complete the family.

In the meantime, though, I've got the only two things I want. I've got Wendy, a woman I respect and love. And I've got Prince. My commitment to them is absolute. In my limited freedom I'm a content and happy man, for the first time in many, many years. I don't think I could ask for anything more.